OXFORD HISTORICAL MONOGRAPHS

SOVEREIGNTY AND THE SWORD

Harrington, Hobbes, and Mixed Government in the English Civil Wars

ARIHIRO FUKUDA

CLARENDON PRESS · OXFORD

1997

Oxford University Press, Great Clarendon Street, Oxford OX2 6DP

Oxford New York
Athens Auckland Bangkok Bogota Bombay
Buenos Aires Calcutta Cape Town Dar es Salaam
Delhi Florence Hong Kong Istanbul Karachi
Kuala Lumpur Madras Madrid Melbourne
Mexico City Nairobi Paris Singapore
Taipei Tokyo Toronto Warsaw
and associated companies in
Berlin Ibadan

Oxford is a trade mark of Oxford University Press

Published in the United States
by Oxford University Press Inc., New York

British Library Cataloguing in Publication Data
Data available

Library of Congress Cataloging in Publication Data
Data applied for

ISBN 0-19-820683-6

1 3 5 7 9 10 8 6 4 2

Typeset by Joshua Associates Ltd., Oxford
Printed in Great Britain on acid-free paper by
Biddles Ltd., Guildford & King's Lynn

To Y. F.

It is true I have opposed the politics of Mr Hobbes, to show him what he taught me, with as much disdain as he opposed those of the greatest authors, . . . Nevertheless in most other things I firmly believe that Mr Hobbes is, and will in future ages be accounted, the best writer at this day in the world.

A sword; but that rusts, or must have a scabbard, and the scabbard of this kind of sword is a good frame of government.

James Harrington

PREFACE

THOMAS HOBBES stands as one of the leading writers of the seventeenth century. That reputation would have seemed fitting to James Harrington, who wrote against Hobbes but respected him. Harrington's own reputation stands less high. That would have seemed to him less fitting. He thought that his own best-known work, *Oceana*, had outreached Hobbes's master-piece, *Leviathan*.

This book has two aims. The first is to claim a place for Harrington alongside Hobbes at the summit of seventeenth-century English political thought. Harrington maintained that Niccolò Machiavelli had been 'neglected' in the seventeenth century until he himself had rescued him. Harrington was largely neglected in the twentieth century until John Pocock rescued him. I believe Harrington's stature to be still higher than that which Pocock has established for him. I present Harrington as a theor-ist of absolute sovereignty who merged that principle with the classical idea of mixed government. Hobbes thought the ideas of mixed government and sovereignty to be antithetical. Harrington showed them to be compati-ble. Hobbes endorsed the Rump Parliament, which ruled England after the execution of King Charles I in 1649, as an absolute sovereign power. Harrington condemned the Rump because it was not a mixed one. Writing after its collapse in 1653 he tried to lay the foundations of a government that would be both absolute and mixed.

The second aim of this book is to offer a new perspective upon the political thought of the English civil wars (a term I use loosely to cover the period 1640–60, for the fact of civil war was at the centre of the poli-tical thought I examine). Within that new perspective, which I developed from Harrington's own, I place him alongside not only Hobbes but other writers of mixed government in the period. My initial concern was not with Harrington's stature. It was when I read his writings in that perspective that I began to see how he has been underestimated. I hope that our understanding of Harrington, Hobbes, and the other wri-ters of mixed government—of Henry Ferne, of Philip Hunton, of the authors of the *Answer to the Nineteen Propositions*—gains by the perspec-tive I offer.

This book has grown out of an Oxford M.Litt. thesis of 1992. Among those who have aided my research, I wish to thank Blair Worden above all. He supervised both the writing of the thesis and its revision into a book. I have been indebted to his inspiration and great patience ever since I introduced myself to him from a telephone kiosk at Paddington Station.

I am also grateful to John Robertson and Richard Tuck, the examiners of my thesis, who commented helpfully on it and encouraged me to publish it. The editorial board of the Oxford Historical Monographs kindly accepted it for their series. I am deeply indebted to John Pocock, from whom, and particularly from whose publications, I learnt a great deal, obviously about Harrington but also about Hobbes and about the period to which the two men belonged. In this book I sometimes depart from his views, but his readers will realize that I do so 'to show him what he taught me'. I am also grateful to J. C. Davis, who offered valuable comments on my interpretation of Harrington.

Yet my academic background was formed not in England but in the Faculty of Law at the University of Tokyo, where I studied as an undergraduate first, and as a research associate afterwards. That Faculty, which has been a close witness of Japanese political upheavals since the end of the nineteenth century—three wars under the three emperors, and the postwar democratization under the new constitution—has produced a distinguished tradition in the study of political thought. Among scholars in that tradition my greatest debt is to Takeshi Sasaki, my supervisor at Tokyo, who vigorously encouraged me to study abroad. I have learnt from him immensely through his teaching and Japanese publications, which include studies of Plato, Machiavelli, Bodin, Lipsius, Hume, and others. It was another Takeshi Sasaki, now at Tokyo Medical and Dental University, at whose suggestion I asked Blair Worden to supervise me. Harrington divided political thought into ancient and modern prudence. For me, this book has been a happy marriage of the prudence of Oxford and the prudence of Tokyo. If I have conveyed something of that happiness, its secret has lain in the suggestions of the two Professor Sasakis.

My research at Oxford would have been impossible without the fellowship for 1989–90 awarded me by the British Council. I am also grateful to the governing body of my Oxford college, St Edmund Hall, which granted me a postgraduate award for 1990–1. I wish too to thank the staff of the college, who made me welcome during my two years in Oxford and on my subsequent visits, which were financially supported by the Nomura Foundation for Social Science (in 1995) and the Murata Science Foundation (in 1996). The Faculty of Law at the University of

Tokyo, which appointed me Associate Professor of History of Political Thought in 1993, has generously spared me time to write.

A. F.

St Edmund Hall, 1996

CONTENTS

A NOTE ON CITATIONS

References to the works of Harrington and Hobbes are made as follows.

Harrington

I quote and cite Harrington in the edition by J. G. A. Pocock, *The Political Works of James Harrington* (Cambridge, 1977). In the cases of the two works reproduced in Pocock's edition of *The Commonwealth of Oceana and A System of Politics* (Cambridge, 1992), I also cite that edition in square brackets. Thus '*Oceana*, 213 [p. 76]' refers to p. 213 of the 1977 edition and to p. 76 of the 1992 edition.

Hobbes

The texts I use are as follows: *The Elements of Law Natural and Politic*, ed. Ferdinand Tönnies, 2nd edn., M. M. Goldsmith (London, 1969); *De Cive: The Latin Version*, ed. Howard Warrender (Oxford, 1983); *De Cive: The English Version*, ed. Howard Warrender (Oxford, 1983); *Leviathan*, ed. Richard Tuck (Cambridge, 1991).

References to *The Elements of Law* will be made to the part, chapter, section, and page number of the 1969 edition.

As to *De Cive*, I normally give citations from *The English Version*, which reproduces the translation of 1651. When citations of *The Latin Version* are given, the English equivalents will follow in square brackets. When I take issue with that translation, I say so. References are to: chapter, section, page number of *The Latin Version*; and, in square brackets, page number of *The English Version* (i. e. *De Cive*, II. 4. 100 [E: p. 53] refers to chapter II, section 4 at p. 100 of *The Latin Version*, and p. 53 of *The English Version*).

References to *Leviathan* will be made to the chapter and page number of Tuck's edition, followed by the page number of the 1651 edition in square brackets.

I
INTRODUCTION:
A New Era in English Political Theory

1. Hobbes and Two Traditions of 'Prudence'

The two decades of the English civil wars (1640–60) were a new era of English political theory. In that time the constitution of the king-in-parliament broke down. Conventional political thinking, which centred on the prerogative of the crown and the liberties of the subject, was unequal to the task of restoring peace and order. In response to that challenge, two new types of political theory emerged: the theory of classical mixed government, and that of undivided sovereignty. Those theories were intended to re-establish peace and order upon a new basis. This book is about those theories in that new era, which was closed by the Restoration.

It may seem strange to place the two theories in a single perspective. Had not Jean Bodin's account of sovereignty and his criticism of mixed government shown them to be enemies to each other? Yet in the new era of the civil wars (and their aftermath) they were summoned to meet a common concern: peace and order. The most notable exposition of the principle of undivided sovereignty was Thomas Hobbes's *Leviathan* (1651): that of classical mixed government was James Harrington's *The Commonwealth of Oceana* (1656). Both writers saw that the English constitution had collapsed into anarchy. Both sought to establish peace and tranquillity. The two men were rivals who agreed in identifying a problem—the anarchy of the civil wars and of their aftermath—and who proposed contrasting solutions to it. The relationship of Harrington's *Oceana* to *Leviathan* will be tackled in this book. *Oceana*, much more than has been realized, is an argument with Hobbes.

It may be objected that the idea of mixed government was not new to England in the 1640s: that the traditional idea of the king-in-parliament was an expression of that idea. But the classical idea of mixed government, as Harrington argued, differed in essence from that of the king-in-parliament.

i

At the outset of *Oceana*, Harrington distinguished between two sorts of politics: 'ancient prudence', which he admired, and 'modern prudence', which he did not. Ancient prudence was the classical idea of mixed government, which had been embodied in biblical Israel, in the republics of classical antiquity, and especially in republican Rome. Harrington defines 'modern' as that which is not 'ancient'. His 'modern' history thus includes what we call the Middle Ages. According to him, modern prudence was introduced by Julius Caesar, who brought about the end of the republic, and was inherited by the Roman emperors. When the (Western) Roman Empire disintegrated, 'the transition of ancient into modern prudence' was completed.[1] '[A]ll the kingdoms [at] this day in Christendom', including the Stuart monarchy in England, belonged to modern prudence.[2] Yet ancient prudence had never been lost. Though it had been overwhelmed by modern prudence, it survived. The seat of its survival was Venice, which Harrington visited after leaving Oxford. Venice, the great exception to the European pattern of modern prudence, 'hath had her eye fixed upon ancient prudence and is attained to a perfection even beyond her copy'.[3] So, in that tiny state, the tradition of ancient prudence had been kept alive, even as modern prudence had overtaken the rest of the European world.

England, however, had experienced only one tradition. It had been ruled by modern prudence alone. Indeed, Harrington's account of modern prudence centred on English history. Modern prudence had aimed at a balance between the king's prerogative and the subject's privileges. William I and his immediate successors had striven 'to be absolute princes'. The feudal lords had fought back, asserting 'the ancient rights and liberties', until under King John the subjects 'restored the parliament'. Thereafter parliaments defended their privileges 'against the mighty' of the kings. Thanks to that achievement, the English constitution had been 'cried up to the skies as the only invention whereby at once to maintain the sovereignty of a prince and the liberty of the people'. It was 'the masterpiece of modern prudence'.[4]

---

[1] *Oceana*, 190 [p. 46].
[2] Ibid. 191 [p. 47].   [3] Ibid. 161 [p. 8].
[4] Ibid. 195–6 [pp. 52–3]. Among modern commentators, Judson and Sommerville agree with Harrington. By the early 17th century, they say, the English constitution was believed by all sides—by defenders of royal absolutism as much as by defenders of the rights of parliaments—to be properly balanced. That idea was at once uncontroversial and vague. Margaret A. Judson, *The Crisis of the Constitution* (New Brunswick, 1949), ch. ii; J. P. Sommerville, *Politics and Ideology in England, 1603–1640* (London, 1986), 134–7.

It was Harrington's aim to 'retrieve' ancient prudence, just as his hero, Niccolò Machiavelli, 'the only politician of later ages' as he called him, had done in Italy a century and a half earlier.[5] In England, 'the masterpiece of modern prudence', Harrington watched the Stuart monarchy sink in confusion. The days of modern prudence, he believed, were numbered. Having collapsed in England and Britain it would soon collapse abroad. Whereas the transition from ancient to modern prudence had occurred in Italy, the restoration of ancient prudence would begin—if only his countrymen would recognize the truths Harrington told—in England. The English civil wars, in his eyes, were a climactic moment in a long movement of history. Modern prudence had formed and operated the feudal Gothic monarchy and had persisted in the Tudor and Stuart periods. Now the tide was at last reversed, and the tradition of ancient prudence could be restored. Instead of the politics of prerogative and privilege, he called for a politics of classical mixed government and for the building of a classical republic on English soil.

ii

No such republic, however, emerged upon the fall of the Stuart monarchy in 1649. Modern prudence gave way, not to ancient prudence, but to the rule of the Rump Parliament and to the argument of Hobbes. The Rump, which consisted only of 'one single council of the people', could hardly be regarded as a classical mixed government. The Rump puzzled Harrington. As he said, it corresponded to 'neither ancient nor modern prudence'.[6] In *Leviathan* (1651), Harrington saw an apologia for the Rump and for its undivided sovereignty. Hobbes was at one with Harrington in rejecting the conventional account of English politics as a conflict between prerogative and liberties. Yet unlike Harrington he also rejected the philosophers of Graeco-Roman politics, claiming that the influence of their arguments had caused the civil wars. Harrington, having rejected modern prudence, insisted on a return to ancient prudence. Hobbes, who regarded all the traditions of political theory before him as erroneous, denounced ancient and modern prudence alike. Hobbes's principle of undivided sovereignty was intended to offer a fresh start in political theory.[7]

Yet in 1653, the Rump, and its undivided sovereignty, came to an end. It had failed to become the first English Leviathan. For Harrington, the

---

[5] *Oceana*, 161–2 [pp. 9–10].   [6] Ibid. 205 [pp. 64–5].
[7] Hobbes launched that principle as early as 1640, when the manuscripts of his *The Elements of Law* were circulated. But it was with the Hobbes of *Leviathan* that Harrington took issue.

failure of the Rump, a unicameral government, demonstrated the failure of Hobbes, whose system had been tested and found wanting. Just as modern prudence, in Harrington's judgement, sank in 1649, so the idea of undivided sovereignty sank in 1653. Now at last ancient prudence could be tested. When Harrington published *Oceana* in 1656, he set the establishment of his model republic in the moment after his imaginary legislator, Olphaus Megaletor, had dissolved a unicameral legislature.

In Harrington's view, the history of political theory is composed of three items—ancient prudence, modern prudence, and Hobbes. Harrington's championship of ancient prudence was thus conducted on two fronts: one against Hobbes, the other against modern prudence. The two 'Preliminaries' with which he began *Oceana* addressed those challenges in turn.

Yet between those two targets there is, in Harrington's mind, a significant difference. His antagonism to modern prudence is unequivocal. His antagonism to Hobbes is not. Hobbes's theory is worthy of critical analysis, in his judgement. Modern prudence is not. Thus whereas the first 'Preliminary' of *Oceana* examined Hobbes's theory strenuously, the second merely illustrated the history of the rise and the fall of modern prudence.

While Harrington criticized Hobbes's endorsement of the Rump, he joined with him in denouncing the politics of prerogative and privileges. He joined Hobbes's search for absolute sovereignty. In that respect he is Hobbes's admirer, even his disciple. By arguing for mixed government, he wanted to improve and supplement his master's argument. His objection was not to Hobbes's insistence upon sovereignty: it was to Hobbes's belief that sovereignty could only be maintained by one man or one assembly. Harrington aimed to show that mixed government, which Hobbes—and Bodin before him—had seen as the enemy of sovereignty, was capable of establishing it. He went even further in denying that one man or one assembly could ever establish it, and in claiming that only mixed government could do so. Far from setting mixed government against sovereignty, Harrington believed that he had created a happy marriage between them.

iii

This book consists of eight chapters, which are arranged chronologically. Chapter 1 treats two streams of political thought before the 1640s. Chapters 2 and 3 are principally concerned with the early 1640s, the time of the build-up to and the early part of the first civil war, although Chapter 3 is extended to 1647 so as to include the second edition of Hobbes's *De Cive*.

Chapter 4 discusses the years 1649–53, when the Rump ruled. Chapters 5, 6, and 7 belong to the period between 1653 and 1660, when the Cromwellian Protectorate (1653–9) was followed by the restoration and disintegration of the rule of the Rump and then by the Restoration. Chapter 8 deals with the restored monarchical rule after 1660.

In Chapter 1 the typical writers of ancient prudence and modern prudence will be identified. That of ancient prudence is Polybius, that of modern prudence Sir John Fortescue. While both writers are theorists of mixed government, the difference between their ideas is crucial. The Fortescuian idea of mixed government is the conventional English one, of which the main concern is to maintain a healthy balance between the royal prerogative and the liberties of the subject. The Polybian idea, which has a Graeco-Roman origin, focuses its attention upon a balance among the components of the constitution, among which the functions of government are divided. The Polybian idea, it will be shown, had not been familiar to England before the 1640s.

The early 1640s, which opened the new era in English political theory, are the subjects of Chapters 2 and 3. When the constitution of the king-in-parliament broke down, the Polybian idea of mixed government, and the idea of undivided sovereignty, emerged. Chapter 2 discusses the former, Chapter 3 the latter. The two ideas are in conflict, but belong to the same years.

Chapter 2 examines how the Polybian idea of mixed government was Anglicized when the regime of the king-in-parliament was in trouble. In 1642 *His Majesty's Answer to the Nineteen Propositions* introduced the Polybian idea to the debates preceding the outbreak of the civil war.[8] The *Answer* claimed that the authority of the king-in-parliament could be defended only by the maintenance of a 'balance' among the king, the lords, and the commons. Philip Hunton and Henry Ferne, who took over this new English theory of mixed government in the period between 1642 and 1644, agreed that when the balance was lost, anarchy would follow. They shared that view even though they took opposite sides over the issue of armed resistance to the king.

Harrington does not mention the *Answer*, Hunton, or Ferne. He seems to have seen himself as the first English writer of ancient prudence. Yet if

---

[8] John Pocock maintains that Harrington may have considered the *Answer* to belong to modern prudence since it dealt with the politics of 'king, lords, and commons'. I place the *Answer* in the category of ancient prudence because it adopted the Polybian idea. For Pocock's argument, see his 'Historical Introduction', *The Political Works of James Harrington*, 19–21, 41.

the essence of ancient prudence is to be identified as the Polybian idea of mixed government, ancient prudence can be found in an Anglicized form as early as the beginning of the 1640s by the writers discussed in Chapter 2.

Chapter 3 (1640–47) focuses upon Thomas Hobbes, who took a very different view in *The Elements of Law* of 1640. He argued that sovereignty can be established only when the subjects renounce the exercise of their private judgements on the question of obedience. Hunton and Ferne looked to 'conscience' to maintain the constitution in times of stress and to prevent its disintegration. Hobbes rejected conscience as merely another term for 'private judgement'. Instead he set 'fear' at the core of his theory of obedience. He repeated the same idea in *De Cive* (1642), the second edition of which was published in 1647.

Chapter 4 concerns the situation after 1649. Neither the argument of Hobbes nor the theories of Polybian mixed government had prevented the extension of the civil wars through the 1640s or the end of monarchy in 1649. The balance among the king, the lords, and the commons, which the *Answer*, Hunton, and Ferne were so keen to defend, no longer existed, and their theories of mixed government lost their immediate relevance. Yet Hobbes's theory of sovereignty, unlike their theories of mixed government, remained pertinent after the collapse of the monarchy. He used it to demonstrate that the English people were obliged to obey the new government. In *Leviathan* (1651), he employed the notion of a 'commonwealth by acquisition', and considered the parliament to be the new sovereign in England. Yet in doing so he adjusted his argument. The adjustment involved a redefinition of the condition of conquest.

Chapters 5, 6, and 7, which are the crux of this book, handle James Harrington, who emerged after 1653, the year when the Rump Parliament was dissolved in spite of Hobbes's clear endorsement of it. The year 1656, in which *Oceana* appeared, is placed at the division of those three chapters. The division is, admittedly, a little artificial. In Chapter 5 we see how Harrington attacked Hobbes's theory of sovereignty, and in Chapters 6 and 7, how he constructed his own theory of sovereignty.

Chapter 5 shows how he criticized Hobbes's notion of conquest. Harrington's doctrine of 'the balance of the land' implied that, in the post-feudal world, there could be no Hobbesian conqueror in a civil war. The focus of Harrington's criticism of Hobbes was not on his concept of a 'commonwealth by institution' but on that of a 'commonwealth by acquisition'. Harrington believed that fear could no longer be employed as a principle of obedience, for the conditions in which a conqueror could impose fear upon the subjects did not exist in mid-seventeenth-century England.

In Chapter 6 we see why Harrington was so concerned with constitutional arrangements, and how his 'model' of a commonwealth is constituted and designed to work for peace and order. In the place of 'fear', Harrington's argument about obedience relied upon 'interest'. Only when the private interests of the people are contained by 'the common interest' expressed by the government will the possibility of rebellion cease, and only then will the government achieve its 'absolute' sovereignty. Only through his proposed constitutional arrangements, where the 'balance' between the senate and the popular assembly is secured, will the common interest be found. He calls a commonwealth equipped with the perfect constitutional arrangements 'an equal commonwealth'.

Chapter 7 examines the basis of Harrington's belief in 'an equal commonwealth'. When Matthew Wren mocked his idea, Harrington vigorously vindicated his model, because it was derived, he believed, from the tradition of ancient prudence, which had been woven by the collaboration of 'reason and experience'. What Harrington presented was the idea of 'balanced' 'absolute' sovereignty, which adopted the principle of mixed government at its core. Hobbes had eliminated the space for 'private judgement' in relation to authority. Harrington restored it. Where Hunton and Ferne had given space to 'conscience', Harrington gave it to 'interest'. It is upon 'interest' that his balanced and absolute sovereignty is built in response to Hobbes.

The Restoration of 1660 closed this unique era in English political theory. In Chapter 8, the concluding chapter, we briefly visit the Restoration period. The chapter closes in 1683, the year when Algernon Sidney is believed to have completed his *Discourses Concerning Government*. Harrington's followers after 1660, Sidney among them, did not inherit his idea of sovereignty. As Pocock pointed out, 'the neo-Harringtonians' adopted Harrington's language with significant modifications and employed it to defend the subjects' rights in the English constitution. It was at this stage, I argue, that the Polybian idea was absorbed by the Fortescuian one.

There are four appendices which discuss issues that arise from the men's argument of the book but extend beyond it. Appendix A considers the place of religion in Hobbes's and Harrington's idea of sovereignty. While Hobbes believed toleration to be compatible with sovereignty, Harrington went further and maintained that toleration is necessary to preserve it. Appendix B visits Harrington's agrarian law, and its relationship to the notion of immortality in *Oceana*. Appendix C shows how Hobbes found a logical exit from the circularity of his argument for the sovereign-making contract. Appendix D suggests the possible influence of the Venetian writer Gasparo Contarini upon Harrington's notion of equality.

2. 'Ancient Prudence': Polybius and Mixed Government

The significance of classical political thought during the English civil wars has been acknowledged, particularly in the pioneering study of Zera Fink's *The Classical Republicans* (Evanston, 1945) and in J. G. A. Pocock's *The Machiavellian Moment* (Princeton, 1975). Pocock presented Harrington as the thinker who planted civic humanist ideas in English soil. Yet the connotations of the term 'Machiavellian moment' are not identical with those of 'ancient prudence'. They contain something more. In particular, Harrington's 'ancient prudence' does not include the notion, which concerns Pocock, of active virtue through civic participation.[9] It has more to do with mixed government. It is on the classical idea of mixed government that this book concentrates.

Harrington observed that 'the ancients' had classified forms of government into 'monarchy, aristocracy, and democracy'. Considering all three of them prone 'to degenerate, to be all evil', they had 'invented another consisting of a mixture of them all, which only is good. This is the doctrine of the ancients.'[10] We tend to associate that doctrine with Aristotle. But the doctrine described by Harrington is not Aristotle's. Certainly, Aristotle hinted that a mixture of oligarchy and democracy would be the best form of government among the many options available to most peoples.[11] But he did not propose a mixture of monarchy, aristocracy, and democracy. When Harrington rebukes Hobbes's criticism of mixed government, he turns not to Aristotle's Greece but to republican Rome. Elsewhere too he normally refers to the Roman republic in vindicating the principles of mixed government.[12]

It must have been the idea of Polybius, not that of Aristotle, that Harrington had principally in mind. It was Polybius—the Greek politician of the second century BC and the historian who wrote a history of republican Rome—who discerned the mixture of the three forms and created a formula from it. He did so in the sixth book of his *Histories* of the Roman republic. Harrington shared with Polybius not only a preoccupation with the mixed government of Rome but an alertness to the similarities between that government and the polity of Lacedaemon.

---

[9] Pocock, *The Machiavellian Moment*, 393–7.
[11] Aristotle, *The Politics*, 1293b–1297a.
[10] *Oceana*, 162 [p. 10].
[12] *Oceana*, 163 [p. 10].

Several characteristics of Polybius' argument need to be noted here. First, his doctrine of mixed government is based on another doctrine, *anakuklōsis*, the theory of cyclical change. Any of the three pure forms of government is bound to deteriorate and make way for a corrupt form. Each corrupt form will be destroyed and give way to a good form: tyranny (the corrupt form of monarchy) to aristocracy, oligarchy (the corrupt form of aristocracy) to democracy, anarchy (the corrupt form of democracy) to monarchy. Thus six forms of government appear in the successive stages of the cycle. Polybius' doctrine of *anakuklōsis* marks a clear break from the two great philosophers Plato and Aristotle, who never conceived of cyclical change.[13] Plato, discussing what for him were the five forms of government—monarchy (and aristocracy), 'timocracy', oligarchy, democracy, and tyranny—describes change only from healthy forms to corrupt ones, and not vice versa. The best (or least corrupt) form is monarchy (and aristocracy); 'timocracy' is a stage more corrupt; tyranny is the most corrupt. The process described by Plato culminates in tyranny and never returns to monarchy. That is because he sees in the various conditions of government reflections of various conditions of the human soul. Human souls are least corrupt under monarchy, and most corrupt under tyranny. Monarchy and tyranny stand at the opposite ends of the same scale. Aristotle, too, whose account of political change is more empirical, did not introduce any principle of cyclical change of government.

It is true that Polybius, like Plato and Aristotle, distinguishes between good and bad forms of government. Unlike them, however, he sees no moral hierarchy among either good or bad ones. Monarchy, aristocracy, and democracy are distinguishable not by their moral standards, only by their numbers of rulers. What Polybius seeks in government is not virtue but stability. The primary aim of human government, to his mind, is security. Men live together and form a state for the same reason that beasts form a flock. In Plato and Aristotle, by contrast, the end of government is the good life, not the mere preservation of life.[14]

Polybius sees only one exit from his cycle: a government which holds in balance the three elements of monarchy, aristocracy, and democracy, and

[13] For this, see F. W. Walbank, *Polybius* (Berkeley and Los Angeles, 1972), 140-1; Kurt von Fritz, *The Theory of the Mixed Constitution in Antiquity* (New York, 1954), 60–75.

[14] Fritz, *The Theory of the Mixed Constitution in Antiquity*, 45–62. Paul A. Rahe maintains that Polybius accepted Plato's dictum that politics should care for souls, the dictum which, in Rahe's view, was 'the rule' of classical antiquity and was to be rejected by the American Founding Fathers. Rahe seems to me to underestimate the extent to which Polybius' idea of *anakuklōsis* distinguished him from Plato. See Rahe's *Republics Ancient and Modern* (Chapel Hill, NC, 1992), 352.

which has functional divisions corresponding to them. Such a government existed, he maintains, in Sparta and Rome. In Sparta

> Lycurgus . . . did not make his constitution simple and uniform, but united in it all the good and distinctive features of the best governments, so that none of the principles should grow unduly and be perverted into its allied evil, but that, the force of each being neutralized by that of the others, neither of them should prevail and outbalance another but that the constitution should remain for long in a state of equilibrium like a well-trimmed boat.[15]

There is a difference between Sparta and Rome. The Roman constitution was established not 'by any process of reasoning, but by the discipline of many struggles and troubles', and through the continual adoption of reforms based on experience.[16] Yet the Roman constitution, too, held the three elements in equilibrium. '[I]t was impossible even for a native to pronounce with certainty whether the whole system was aristocratic, democratic, or monarchical', for

> if one fixed one's eyes on the power of the consuls, the constitution seemed completely monarchical and royal; if on that of the senate it seemed again to be aristocratic; and when one looked at the power of the masses, it seemed clearly to be a democracy.[17]

The Romans, in Polybius' account, have achieved a complicated division of power among the consuls, the senate, and the popular assembly. Although each element may appear large enough to threaten the balance, 'their union is adequate to all emergencies, so that it is impossible to find a better political system than this'.[18]

Polybius analysed the Roman constitution within his 'pragmatic history'.[19] He wrote history for the practical purpose of teaching politicians how to govern a state. He was particularly struck by Rome's achievement in conquering the whole (Mediterranean) world within a short time. The main aim of his *Histories* was to trace Roman history from 220 to 146 BC, that is, from years preceding the defeat at Cannae (216) to the year of the destruction of Carthage, and to reveal the secret of that miraculous story.[20] The secret lay in the mixed, stable Roman constitution.[21] What then had internal stability contributed to Rome's expansion? The answer is not what

---

[15] *The Histories*, tr. W. R. Paton (Loeb Classical Library, 1923), VI. 10. 6–7.
[16] Ibid. VI. 10. 13–14.   [17] Ibid. VI. 11. 11–12.   [18] Ibid. VI. 18. 1.
[19] Fritz, *The Theory of the Mixed Constitution in Antiquity*, ch. iii; Walbank, *Polybius*, ch. iii.
[20] Fritz, *The Theory of the Mixed Constitution in Antiquity*, 31, 44; Walbank, *Polybius*, 70–1.
[21] Walbank, *Polybius*, 16–19; *The Histories*, I. 1. 5–6, 2. 7; III. 1. 4, 2. 6, 3. 9, 4. 2, 118. 9; VI. 2. 3; VIII. 2. 3.

we might expect. The decisive development was the achievement of internal stability in time of peace, not of war:

When again they are freed from external menace, and reap the harvest of good fortune and affluence which is the result of their success, and in the enjoyment of this prosperity are corrupted by flattery and idleness and wax insolent and overbearing, as indeed happens often enough, it is then especially that we see the state providing itself a remedy for the evil from which it suffers. For when one part having grown out of proportion to the others aims at supremacy and tends to become too predominant, it is evident that, as for the reasons above given none of the three is absolute, but the purpose of the one can be counterworked and thwarted by the others, none of them will excessively outgrow the others or treat them with contempt.[22]

Of course, Polybius knew the Romans' excellence in war. He saw how, when faced by external dangers, they would work together and assist their country 'as all are zealously competing in devising means of meeting the need of the hour'.[23] But Rome's military greatness he attributed not to its constitution but to its military system. He knew that military greatness was not confined to states with mixed governments. Athens had been a pure democracy, and once had enjoyed 'frequent periods of success'. Like Rome it could unite against external enemies. Unlike Rome, however, it could not remain united in peacetime—just like 'a ship without a commander', when its passengers 'grow over-confident and begin to entertain contempt for their superiors and to quarrel with each other, as they are no longer all of the same way of thinking'.[24] Thebes and Crete had the same strength but the same failing.

What then of Sparta? Polybius blames Lycurgus for having made 'absolutely no provision' for 'an ambitious policy', for expansion.[25] But, as in his account of Rome, he posits no logical connection between mixed government and the capacity for military expansion. He makes no criticism of Lycurgus as far as the provision of internal stability is concerned. It is in his discussion of Lycurgus that Polybius gives us, tantalizingly, the only indication why the mixture of the three elements produces internal stability. It is there that he describes mixed government as the combination of the merits of single governments. But he does not say what those merits are.[26] He tells us, figuratively, that simple forms tend to corrupt, just as wood is apt to be eaten by worms, or just as steel rusts.[27] But he does not explain

---

[22] *The Histories*, VI. 18. 5–7.
[23] Ibid. VI. 18. 3.
[24] Ibid. VI. 44. 2–5.
[25] Ibid. VI. 48. 6.
[26] We cannot exclude the possibility that Polybius provided an explanation in the part of book VI which does not survive.
[27] Ibid. VI. 10. 3.

how the combination of wood and steel can be made to resist worms and rust alike.

Essentially, Polybius' doctrine of mixed government is the same as his doctrine of *anakuklōsis*. A simple government cannot be stable. A stable government cannot be simple. A stable government must therefore be mixed. That is almost all that Polybius' account of mixed government implies. Admittedly, he did articulate the mixture of the neat triad of monarchy, aristocracy, and democracy in abstract terms. Polybius' idea of mixed government was influential in later ages because of this beautiful articulation. Yet his theory of mixed government went no deeper than his doctrine of *anakuklōsis*, and his contention was no more than that a stable government cannot be simple. Polybian mixed government does not have to be a mixture of monarchy, aristocracy, and democracy to achieve stability. The number 'three' is not essential in terms of stability. A mixture of any two forms will avoid the evil consequences of simple government. Or there might be four parts of a mixed government. Polybius did see that in the Roman and Spartan constitutions the functions of the government were divided and allotted to different bodies—as the consuls, the senate, and the people. That differentiation secured stability. But he never said that three governmental functions correspond to the three forms of government. Rather, stability arose because the highest functions of government were so divided among the three divisions that no one part could gain supremacy over the others.

There are difficulties in Polybius' account. What happens if the divisions which have the highest functions of government cease to co-operate? May not the differentiation of functions of government lead, not to unity, but to anarchy? Who—as Bodin and Hobbes would have asked—is to arbitrate between them? Why does Polybius expect only positive, not negative, results from the division of functions? He does not address those questions. Instead of providing a theoretical explanation of mixed government, he tells the story of its success in practice.

3. Polybius and Machiavelli

Harrington's account of mixed government among 'the ancients' at the outset of *Oceana* is very similar to Polybius' account of mixed government.[28] Harrington sets no hierarchical order either among the three good forms or among the three bad ones. He does not explain why 'the ancients'

---

[28] *Oceana*, 162 [p. 10].

believed that mixed government worked. Instead he appeals to the experience of Roman history.

In book VI of his *Histories* Polybius produced the argument that mixed government is conducive to stability. He described a mixture of the neat triad, but left little theoretical justification for it. Nevertheless, his idea of mixed government was highly influential upon political writers of many generations. Perhaps that was because his account of mixed government was coupled with his narrative of Roman history. Most political writers were interested in the glory of republican Rome, and it was Polybius who tried to explain the secret by his idea of mixed government. His successors in later ages tried to supply the theoretical framework that his account had lacked. According to Momigliano, Polybius' idea was developed in seventeenth- and eighteenth-century England not because his English successors were satisfied by his argument, but because they were dissatisfied and therefore stimulated to think for themselves.[29] That was certainly true of Harrington. Having adopted the main frame of Polybian mixed government, he contrived his own political arrangements in *Oceana*.

Yet he would have been surprised to learn that his account of mixed government is the same as that of Polybius. He does mention him, first as a critic of the huge Athenian popular assembly,[30] secondly as a writer on the Roman military system, but not as an exponent of mixed government. Though it is possible that Harrington knew Polybius' discussion of mixed government at first hand, it is more likely that he absorbed that discussion not directly but indirectly.[31] He did not say that he had learnt that doctrine

---

[29] Arnaldo Momigliano, 'Polybius between the English and the Turks', *Sesto Contributo alla Storia Degli Studi Classici e del Mondo Antico* (Rome, 1980), 133.

[30] 'These also, being exceeding numerous, became burdensome unto themselves and dangerous unto the commonwealth; the more for their ill education, as is observed by Xenophon and Polybius, who compare them unto mariners, that in a calm are perpetually disputing and swaggering one with another, and never lay their hands unto the common tackling or safety till they be all endangered by some storm.' (*Oceana*, 279 [p. 164]. See also ibid. 280, 299 [pp. 165, 190].) Liljegren tentatively suggests as the sources of this passage Polybius, *The Histories*, VI. 44 and Xenophon, *Memorabilia*, III. 5. 6 (S. B. Liljegren, *James Harrington's Oceana* (Heidelberg, 1924), 327–8.). It is hard to establish whether Harrington himself had access to those passages, but the point made in them seems unremarkable. For Harrington's reference to Polybius' account of the Roman military system, see *Oceana*, 313 [pp. 208–9].

[31] If Harrington did read Polybius' *Histories*, VI. 44, as is suggested by Liljegren, he can only have done so either in the Greek and Latin edition by Isaac Casaubon (1609), or in the English translation published in 1633 (see n. 37, below) which does not seem to have been widely read. Casaubon's edition was the only printed version to contain that passage in Harrington's time. Yet that edition, which was the first (almost) complete collection of the remaining manuscripts we know now, accommodated the full accounts of mixed government in book VI, too. Casaubon's edition was apparently the source of John Milton's invocation of Polybius as an authority of mixed government in 1641. See his *Of Reformation*, in *The Complete Prose Works of John*

directly from 'the ancients'. Rather, he acknowledged that it had reached him from Machiavelli.[32]

Polybius, though referred to in the writings of Cicero, Livy, and Plutarch, had thereafter been ignored in the Western world until the fifteenth century. His *Histories* had to be rediscovered in the West before it was widely read. The story of its rediscovery was not a simple one. *The Histories* reached the Western world through separate manuscript traditions, which divorced book VI, where the account of mixed government is to be found, from the first five books, which are chronological in character.[33] When, around 1419, Leonardo Bruni introduced Polybius to modern times by translating into Latin the passages in books I and II of *The Histories* which concern the Punic wars, he had no access to book VI (or to the remaining volumes, books VII—XVII). The discovery of book VI came later. It was Machiavelli's *Discorsi* which (re)introduced Polybius' idea of mixed government to the West. In Momigliano's words, 'Polybius was rediscovered, first by Leonardo Bruni as a historian, then by Machiavelli and his contemporaries as a political thinker'.[34] This story explains why Polybius' idea reached Harrington from Machiavelli.

Mixed government is not, however, central to Machiavelli's ideas. In the rest of this section we shall see that he merely repeated Polybius' idea, without adding to it. He did not have much faith in mixed government.

In book I, chapter 2 of his *Discorsi* Machiavelli repeats Polybius' account of *anakuklōsis*, the cyclical changes of the six forms of government. Though he does not name Polybius, he follows his argument and maintains that a mixed government is the one best suited to secure stability. Machiavelli agreed with Polybius about many things. Like him, he was impressed by, and wished to explain, the expansion of the Roman republic. With him he believed that Rome and Lacedaemon had had mixed governments; that the Lacedaemonian constitution had been established by Lycurgus at one

Milton, ed. Don M. Wolfe, i (New Haven, 1953), 599. In 1529, Janus Lascaris had published a part of book VI, but this included only a section concerning the Roman military system, and no passage concerning mixed government. The manuscripts on the Roman military system (*The Histories*, VI. 19–42) and those of mixed government belonged to different traditions of manuscripts. See J. M. Moore, *The Manuscript Tradition of Polybius* (Cambridge, 1965).

[32] ' [I]t is no wonder if Machiavel have showed us that the ancients held this only to be good' (*Oceana*, 174 [p. 25]).

[33] For details, see Moore, *The Manuscript Tradition of Polybius*.

[34] The first explicit reference to book VI in Western literature is in Bernardo Rucellai's *Libre de urbe Roma*, written before 1505. From Rucellai's work it is evident that book VI was being discussed in the 'Orti Oricellari' in Florence some years before its argument appeared in Machiavelli's *Discorsi*, the composition of which began in 1513. See Arnaldo Momigliano, 'Polybius' Reappearance in Western Europe', *Sesto Contributo alla Storia Degli Studi Classici e del Mondo Antico*, 103–23.

moment, while that of Rome had been the result of many reforms; and that Rome had been better equipped than Lacedaemon to expand.[35] Even so, the idea of mixed government, which he owed to Polybius, is not at the heart of Machiavelli's thought.

First, for all his general praise of mixed government, Machiavelli does not believe that mixed government guarantees internal peace. He does not claim that Rome ever attained internal stability. Only in Lacedaemon (and Venice among the states of his own time) did the senate and the people, in his view, live in peace. Mixed government is far from being an essential qualification for the preservation of unity among citizens. In discussing the longevity of the Spartan constitution, Machiavelli does not focus on the principle of mixture. The crucial reason for the internal peace of Lacedaemon is that the population was kept within a limit which enabled the senate to govern the people comfortably.

Secondly, the internal harmony of a republic is not an aim of Machiavelli as it was of Polybius. In Machiavelli's view, durable domestic tranquillity is not a necessary condition for durable external glory; rather, the conflict between the senate and the people was the true cause of the glorious expansion achieved by the Romans.

Thirdly, Machiavelli believes such conflict to be an inevitable, even a welcome cost of military vigour, on the ground that it cannot be avoided unless the people is prevented from taking arms (as in Lacedaemon), a course which Machiavelli opposes. Machiavelli does, it is true, acknowledge that when the office of tribune of the plebs was established, the Roman government acquired the three elements and became more stable. But his emphasis is not on the merit of mixed government. Machiavelli takes it for granted that among intellectuals the Roman constitution enjoys a high reputation as a perfection of mixed government. But he is not interested in the perfection of government. Rather, what he praises is the virtue of the conflict between the people and the senate. He emphasizes that what is called the perfection of mixed government is a product of something more valuable, internal conflict. The greatest achievement of that conflict was the Roman conquest of the Mediterranean world.

Fourthly, while good laws or good constitutional arrangements have a certain role in Machiavelli's theory, those laws or arrangements do not correspond to the Polybian idea of mixed government. Polybius' idea was to suppress the people's energy by the operation of mutual checks among the components of the government. Machiavelli does not wish to suppress the people's energy, a feat he believes to be impossible. Machiavellian

---

[35] *Discorsi*, I, vi.

constitutional arrangements regulate the energy so that it imparts military vigour rather than harming the government from within.[36]

Machiavelli is, of course, an original writer, but not on the question of mixed government. There his importance is as the mediator of Polybius' idea to England, where Machiavelli's *Discorsi* was widely read in Italian in the late sixteenth century and in English in the earlier seventeenth century.[37] Harrington was among those who learnt the Polybian idea of mixed government through the *Discorsi*.

For our purpose, then, the important question is Harrington's reading of Machiavelli. He is uneasy about Machiavelli's attitude to mixed government. His unease is evident in his discussion of aristocracy within a mixed government. Harrington, who believes that an aristocratic element is indispensable to the constitution of a good government, rebukes Machiavelli's hostility to the political role of the nobility. In Harrington's eyes, he 'hath missed it [= the importance of aristocracy] very narrowly and more dangerously'.[38] As we shall see later, Harrington considers the essence of 'the doctrine of the ancients' to be the mixture of aristocracy and democracy, a subject on which Machiavelli had nothing to teach him.

Yet Harrington warmly admires Machiavelli. He calls him a 'learned disciple' of 'the ancients', 'the only politician of later ages', 'the prince of politicians', 'the great artist in the modern world'.[39] Why, differing from Machiavelli as he did on the question of mixed government, does he praise him so highly?

He does so because Machiavelli based his discussion of politics on a reading of Livy—one of 'the archives of ancient prudence'[40]—and expressed his political ideas in an interpretation of the history of Roman republic. That was the history in which Harrington was most interested. Harrington was closer to Machiavelli than to any other writer of politics in his conviction that the study of Roman history was essential to the study of politics.

---

[36] *Discorsi*, I, ii–vii.

[37] An Italian edition was published in 1584 by John Wolf, and an English translation in 1636 by Edward Dacres. See Felix Raab, *The English Face of Machiavelli* (London, 1964), 274–5. Polybius' original account of mixed government remained unavailable in English until the appearance of the translation first published in 1633. It is true that an earlier English translation of *The Histories* had appeared in 1568, but contained only the first five books. It did not contain the sixth, the section where mixed government is discussed. A valuable account of the publishing history of Polybius in the 16th and 17th centuries can be found in *The Histories of Polybius*, 2 vols., ed. and tr. Evelyn Shuckburgh (London, 1889), i, pp. xi–xii but Shuckburgh was mistaken in supposing that book VI was not translated into English until the 18th century.

[38] *Oceana*, 166 [p. 15]. See also ibid., 257–72 [pp. 135–55].

[39] Ibid. 162, 274 [pp. 10, 157–8].   [40] Ibid. 208 [p. 69].

Admittedly he felt at odds with Machiavelli when it came to the political role of the nobility, and he may even have thought that Machiavelli, who showed him 'the doctrine of the ancients', had not fully understood it. Yet he approved Machiavelli's focus on the conflict between the senate and the people in Rome. Machiavelli had raised the question whether that conflict was curable. 'There is not', commented Harrington, 'a more noble or useful question in the politics than that'.[41] Machiavelli, he thought, had raised the right question, but given the wrong answer. Harrington thought that Machiavelli had misread Livy. Offering his own reading of Livy, Harrington discussed Machiavelli's 'noble and useful question' and gave a different answer. That answer, we shall see, is the central issue of *Oceana*.[42]

4. 'Modern Prudence': Fortescue and Parker

The politics of 'modern prudence' in England was the politics of prerogative and privileges. As we have noted, the notion that the English constitution preserved a balance between the king's power and the subject's liberties was commonly held in the early seventeenth century. If Polybius is the chief expositor of ancient prudence, the chief expositor of modern prudence is Sir John Fortescue. Unlike book VI of Polybius' *Histories*, Fortescue's *De Laudibus Legum Anglie*, written between 1468 and 1471, was widely available and highly influential in the seventeenth century.[43]

According to Fortescue, the English monarchy is *dominium politicum et regale*, in which the king can neither change laws nor levy taxes without the consent of the people. The French monarchy is *dominium regale*, where the king can make laws and levy taxes as he pleases.[44] The statutes of England, made by 'the assent of the whole realm', embody prudence and wisdom, Fortescue claims, because those statutes are 'promulgated by the prudence not of one counsellor nor of a hundred only, but of more than three hundred chosen men—of such a number as once the Senate of the Romans was ruled by'.[45] Yet Fortescue ascribes no particular merit to the Roman senate. He merely praises a number of senators. As Pocock has

---

[41] Ibid. 272 [p. 155].
[42] See Sect. 7.2 below.
[43] Here I use S. B. Chrimes's edition with his English translation (Cambridge, 1942). For Fortescue's life, see Chrimes's introduction. As for how Fortescue was quoted in the 17th century see Caroline A. J. Skeel, 'The Influence of the Writings of Sir John Fortescue', *Transactions of the Royal Historical Society*, 3rd ser. 10 (1916), 91–107. Skeel does not mention Henry Parker, to whom we refer later.
[44] *De Laudibus* 25.
[45] Ibid. 41.

observed, Fortescue's point is that no matter how prudent the prince himself may be, his wisdom and experience are very limited when compared
with the accumulation of those qualities by successive generations of his
subjects.[46]

The main purpose of *De Laudibus* is to show the general superiority of
the English law to the civil law. The idea of *dominium politicum et regale* is,
according to Fortescue, one of the blessed principles of the English law.
He insists that its excellence is also to be found in the English court procedure. Thanks to the jury system, witnesses in the English court are likely
to be fair and neutral, since they are 'chosen by a respectable and impartial
officer'. By contrast with the procedure on the Continent, which often
includes torture, in English legal procedure 'nothing is cruel, nothing inhu-
man . . . Under this law, therefore, life is quiet and secure'. Even delays in
the English court are necessary and reasonable.[47] In France, on the other
hand, due to the defects of legal and political institutions, the peasants are
impoverished and their life is miserable.[48] The English people, who 'eat
every kind of flesh and fish in abundance', are 'rich in all household goods'
and lead 'a quiet and happy life. . . .These are the fruits which the political
and regal government yields.'[49]

In summary, the merit of the English law on which Fortescue focuses is
the security of the persons and property of the people. His concern is with
the balance between the prerogative of the king and the rights of the subject.
Here there lies a crucial difference between Polybius and Fortescue.[50] Polybius, in his argument for mixed government, was concerned principally
with domestic peace and unity. What he feared most was anarchy, which
was caused by internal strife. What Fortescue feared was tyranny, which
invaded liberties and privileges.[51] For Fortescue, the maintenance of inter-

[46] Pocock, *The Machiavellian Moment*, 19. For Pocock's view of the difference between
Polybius and Fortescue, see also 'Civil War and Interregnum', in his *The Ancient Constitution
and the Feudal Law: A Reissue with a Retrospect* (Cambridge, 1987), 310–11.

[47] *De Laudibus*, 63–5, 133.

[48] '[T]he people live in no little misery. . . . They do not use woollens, except of the cheap-
est sort, . . . Their women are barefooted except on feast days; the men and women eat no
flesh, except bacon lard, with which they fatten their pottage in the smallest quantity.'
(ibid. 83–5.)

[49] Ibid. 87–9.

[50] For a different view, which does not emphasize that contrast, see J. M. Blythe, *Ideal
Government and the Mixed Constitution in the Middle Ages* (Princeton, 1992).

[51] 'St Thomas, in the book he wrote for the king of Cyprus, *De Regimine Principum*, is considered to have desired that a kingdom be constituted such that the king may not be free to
govern his people tyrannically, which only comes to pass when the regal power is restrained
by political law. Rejoice, therefore, good prince, that such is the law of the kingdom to which
you are to succeed, because it will provide no small security and comfort for you and for the
people' (*De Laudibus*, 27).

nal peace was not of prime concern. He took internal peace for granted. While the strength of the Polybian mixed government lies in the preservation of internal unity and tranquillity in peacetime, the superiority of Fortescue's *dominium politicum et regale* lies in the prevention of tyranny and the defence of the liberties of the subject. Here we can distinguish two ideas of mixed government, to which Harrington's two traditions of prudence correspond. One is the Polybian idea that a functional division within the government is conducive to the securing of internal stability, and that there needs to be a proper balance among the parts into which the government is divided. The other is the Fortescuian principle that a healthy balance needs to be maintained between the prerogative and the subject's liberties. The former mainly fights against anarchy: the latter against tyranny.

The Fortescuian view of the English balanced constitution was widely cherished in early seventeenth-century England.[52] It was sometimes expressed in the phrase 'the king, the lords, and the commons'. Although the phrase implies three actors, it corresponded, in early seventeenth-century writings, not to the Polybian notion of mixed government but to Fortescue's concern with prerogative and liberties. For although early Stuart Englishmen believed this constitution to consist of three estates, they did not conceive, as Polybius did, of a functional differentiation within the three estates. In the Fortescuian account of the English constitution, the idea of the three estates is invoked to show that the king alone cannot decide everything. There are important matters which need the agreement of the three estates in parliament. The king cannot make or change laws (or impose taxes) without the consent of the other two estates.[53]

As we saw, Harrington, who called this Fortescuian view modern prudence, acknowledged that it had been praised in England:

this government, being indeed the masterpiece of modern prudence, hath been cried up to the skies as the only invention whereby at once to maintain the sovereignty of a prince and the liberty of the people.[54]

Two years later, when he explained what he had meant by modern prudence in *Oceana*, he called it 'the politicy of king, lords and commons'.[55] In Harrington's mind, the Polybian notion of mixed government was not implied by that phrase.

---

[52] Judson, *The Crisis of the Constitution*, ch. ii; Sommerville, *Politics and Ideology in England, 1603–1640*, 134–7.

[53] Judson, *The Crisis of the Constitution*, 75–8.   [54] *Oceana*, 196 [p. 53].

[55] Harrington, *The Prerogative of Popular Government* (London, 1658), 397. See also *Politicaster* (London, 1659), 711.

He did not name any exponents of modern prudence. But there was one writer among his contemporaries who answered well to his description. In his pamphlet *The Case of Shipmony briefly discoursed* (1640), Henry Parker writes:

to come to the Prerogative of England, . . . by the true fundamentall constitutions of England, the beame hangs even between the King and the Subject: the Kings power doth not tread under foot the peoples liberty, nor the peoples liberty the King power.[56]

In that pamphlet, dated the opening day (3 November) of the Long Parliament, Parker eloquently employed the Fortescuian dualism of prerogative and privileges in defence of the subjects' liberties. When Parker refers to an 'even beame', his point is that liberty ought to be preferred to prerogative.[57] His argument that an excessive use of the king's prerogative impoverishes the subjects, and is even counter-productive for the king himself, merely repeats the claim of Sir John Fortescue, whose *De Laudibus* Parker cites elsewhere.[58]

Within the Fortescuian framework, Parker refers to three estates. His aim was not to claim the existence of any functional division within the three, but to limit the king's power effectively through parliaments.

It ought to be noted also, that as the English have ever beene the most devoted servants of equall, sweetly-moderate Soveraignty; so in our English Parliaments, where the Nobility is not too prevalent, as in Denmark, nor the Comminalty [*sic*], as in the Netherlands, nor the King, as in France, Justice and Policie kisse and embrace more lovingly then elsewhere. And as all the three States have alwayes more harmoniously borne their just proportionable parts in England then elsewhere, so now in these times, in these learned, knowing, religious times, we may expect more blessed counsell from Parliaments then ever wee received heretofore.[59]

[56] Henry Parker, *The Case of Shipmony briefly discoursed* (1640), 7. For Parker, see W. K. Jordan, *Men of Substance* (Chicago, 1942); M. Mendle, *Henry Parker and the English Civil War* (Cambridge, 1995).

[57] Sommerville, *Politics and Ideology in England, 1603–1640*, 136.

[58] 'The Kings [*sic*] words also since have been upon another occasion, That he ever intended his people should enjoy property of goods, and liberty of persons, holding no King so great, as he that was King of a rich and free people' (*Shipmony*, 4). 'How is the King of France happy in his great Prerogative? . . . wee see that his immoderate power makes him oppresse his poore Pesants, . . . His oppression makes him culpable before God . . . His sinne makes him poore . . . His poverty makes him impotent . . . His impotence, together with all other irregularities, and abuses is like to make his Monarchy the lesse durable. Civill wars have ever hitherto infected and macerated that goodly Country, and many times it hath been near its ruine' (*Shipmony*, 44–6). On p. 5 Parker cites a passage from Fortescue's *De Laudibus* ch. xxxvi, the title of which is: 'Good that comes from the political and regal government in the kingdom of England'.

[59] *Shipmony*, 38–9. This passage is also cited by Michael Mendle as the basis of his claim

In Harrington's view, however, the relationship between the three estates has been neither peaceful nor stable. Immediately after the passage where Harrington praises the English constitution as 'the masterpiece of modern prudence', he continues:

whereas indeed it hath been no other than a wrestling match, wherein the nobility, as they have been stronger, have thrown the king, or the king, if he have been stronger, hath thrown the nobility; or the king, where he hath had a nobility and could bring them to his party, hath thrown the people, as in France and Spain; or the people, where they have had no nobility, or could get them to be of their party, have thrown the king, as in Holland and of latter times in Oceana.[60]

Harrington thought modern prudence defective by nature. The old constitution was bound to collapse, because the balance between prerogative and liberties was intrinsically unstable. Modern prudence, the Fortescuian idea of mixed government, could not maintain peace once the king and his people were in open confrontation. When the conventional political wisdom proved to be invalid, only something new could rescue England from anarchy.

However, the challenge to the Fortescuian idea of mixed government did not begin with Harrington. Harrington proposed a new idea to suggest a new constitution. Writers in the early 1640s had proposed new ideas to interpret the old constitution. Those writers—Hobbes on the one hand, theorists of Polybian mixed government on the other—were less concerned than Fortescue had been with the prevention of tyranny. Their concern was rather to keep the country united and to avoid civil war. We shall look next at those writers of the 1640s who used the Polybian idea of mixed government to reinterpret the English constitution.

that the idea of mixed government in the *Answer to the Nineteen Propositions* had already appeared in 1640. From my perspective, however, whereas Parker's argument is still Fortescuian, the *Answer*'s position is Polybian. See Mendle, *Dangerous Positions* (Alabama, 1985), 130.

[60] *Oceana*, 196 [p. 53].

2
THE NEW ENGLISH THEORY OF MIXED GOVERNMENT, 1642–1644:
Balance, Authority, Conscience

1. Introduction

When King Charles I called the parliaments of 1640—the first in April, the second in November—England possessed a theory of mixed government which had been made widely available by Fortescue.[1] We have seen that this English theory of mixed government had little to do with that derived from Graeco-Roman antiquity. While Fortescue considered the English constitution to be a mixed one, he did not describe a mixture of different functions of government.

Around 1641–2 there emerged a new interpretation of the English constitution. This view, like that of Fortescue and his disciples, denied that England was a pure monarchy. Unlike that conventional belief, it adopted the Polybian idea of mixed government, and used that idea to redefine the English constitution. The redefinition is what we call in this chapter 'the new English theory of mixed government'. The theory was 'new', since it employed Polybius. And it was still 'English', since it referred to the king, the lords, and the commons. In other words, the new English theory of mixed government Anglicized the Polybian idea, and redefined the English constitution at the same time.

Among a number of events in the history of English political thought in the early 1640s, we shall concentrate on two which have a special bearing on our topic in the following chapters: the emergence of the theory of sovereignty and the innovative approach to theories of mixed government. Both

[1] For the development of English theories of mixed government, see Corinne Comstock Weston, *English Constitutional Theory and the House of Lords 1556–1832* (London, 1965). Weston takes a different view, which does not differentiate Polybius from Fortescue.

those developments were responses in the field of political thought to the political crisis of the time. They attempted, in two different directions, to prevent civil war and to keep the country together. Thomas Hobbes's theory of sovereignty will be examined in Chapter 3. Here, we focus upon the ascendancy of the new English theory of mixed government. It will be suggested that the word 'balance' was addressed in the new theory to the problem of authority rather than to that of liberties; and that the aim of discussion moved from limitation to stability. While others discussed the constitution in the Fortescuian framework, some writers turned to the Polybian idea.

Neither the exact date nor the writing which marked the innovation can be specified. There were writers in this period who read Polybius. The first person to have referred to Polybius in connection with the English constitution appears to have been John Milton, who may have known book VI of Polybius' *Histories*. In *Of Reformation*, which appeared in late May in 1641, he wrote:

There is no Civill *Goverment* [*sic*] that hath beene known, no not the *Spartan*, not the *Roman*, though both for this respect so much prais'd by the wise *Polybius*, more divinely and harmoniously tun'd, more equally ballanc'd as it were by the hand and scale of Justice, then is the Common-wealth of *England*: where under a free, and untutor'd *Monarch*, the noblest, worthiest, and most prudent men, with full approbation, and suffrage of the People have in their power the supreme, and finall determination of highest Affaires.[2]

Milton, however, did not develop that thought.[3] His priority was the reformation of the Church, not the diagnosis of the constitution. He did not suggest how the components of the constitution could be held to correspond to the idea of functional differentiation advanced by Polybius.

Thomas Hobbes did. We do not know whether he ever read Polybius. But we do find him, in *De Cive*, attributing to parliamentarian writers an understanding of the English constitution which corresponds to Polybius' idea.[4] We cannot tell which writer or writers he had in mind. He cannot have been referring to the authors of the *Answer to the Nineteen*

---

[2] John Milton, *Of Reformation, The Complete Prose Works of John Milton*, ed. Don M. Wolfe, i (New Haven, 1953), 599. Wolfe explains that Isaac Casaubon made available Greek and Latin texts of Polybius' *Histories* in 1609.

[3] Milton's view that England was a mixed monarchy seems to have been heavily influenced by Sir Thomas Smith's *De Republica Anglorum*. In Milton's 'Commonplace Book', Smith appears quite often, whereas no reference to Polybius can be found there. See 'Commonplace Book', *Prose Works*, i. 362–513.

[4] For details, see Sect. 4.1 below.

Propositions, for the manuscript of *De Cive* had been completed by November 1641, seven months before the publication of the *Answer*.[5]

In *De Cive* Hobbes denounced the Polybian idea of mixed government, which he believed to be conducive to civil wars. Yet when the Polybian definition appeared in the *Answer*, the aim of its exponent was identical to Hobbes's: to keep the country united and avoid a civil war.

2. The *Answer* and Authority

The first Polybian definition of the English constitution which I have found appeared during the critical months before the civil war. *His Majesty's Answer to the Nineteen Propositions of both Houses of Parliament, tending towards a Peace*, written by Viscount Falkland and Sir John Colepeper, was published in June 1642.[6] It warned the two Houses that once the Polybian balance was lost, remediless anarchy would follow.[7] Where Parker wrote against tyranny, the *Answer* fought against anarchy.

'We are resolved', the *Answer* reads, 'not . . to subvert . . . the ancient, equal, happy, well-poised, and never-enough commended Constitution of the Government of this Kingdom; nor to make our Self, of a King of

---

[5] For the composition of *De Cive*, see Warrender, 'Editor's Introduction', *De Cive: The Latin Version*, 5. John Sanderson suggests Hobbes's target is Henry Parker's *Shipmony* ('The Answer to the Nineteen Propositions Revisited', *Political Studies*, 32 (1984), 629), but Parker's position shares little with the one Hobbes attacks. As we saw in Sect. 1.4 above, Parker, unlike the authors of the *Answer*, did not describe the functional differentiations within the English constitution, and merely referred to the three estates within the Fortescuian framework. Lord Falkland, one of the co-authors of the *Answer*, was the host of the Great Tew circle, and Hobbes was in contact with that circle. The Polybian definition of the English constitution could have come up in the discussions of the circle. Edward Hyde belonged to the circle. Admittedly, Hyde claimed that he himself had disapproved of the use of the idea in the *Answer*. But that does not necessarily mean that the idea was new to him. See Edward Hyde, *The Life* (Oxford, 1759), 66–7; Weston, *English Constitutional Theory and the House of Lords*, 26–33; Richard Tuck, *Natural Rights Theories* (Cambridge, 1979), 119; David L. Smith, *Constitutional Royalism and the Search for Settlement, c.1640–1649* (Cambridge, 1994), 90–1. Hobbes could have encountered the Polybian definition among the Great Tew circle.

[6] It was one of C. C. Weston's immense contributions to highlight the importance of the *Answer*. See Weston, *English Constitutional Theory and the House of Lords*, 5, 23–34. There are several original editions of this document. Here I use a reprinted edition in *Historical Collections*, ed. John Rushworth, part III, vol. i (London, 1691), 725–35. For the *Answer*, see also Michael Mendle, *Dangerous Positions* (Alabama, 1985); Smith, *Constitutional Royalism and the Search for Settlement*. We do not know how the Polybian idea reached Falkland and Colepeper.

[7] For the notion of balance in the *Answer*, see particularly Pocock, 'Historical Introduction', *The Political Works of James Harrington*, 19–23; 'Civil War and Interregnum' in his *The Ancient Constitution and the Feudal Law: A Reissue with a Retrospect* (Cambridge, 1987), 310–15.

England, a Duke of *Venice*; and this of a Kingdom, a Republick'.[8] By themselves, those words can be understood within the traditional view of the
balanced polity, the Fortescuian idea of mixed government. Indeed, they
look similar to Parker's praise for the constitution.[9] Yet after this passage,
the Polybian idea of mixed government is introduced.

There being three kinds of Government among Men, Absolute Monarchy, Aristocracy, and Democracy: and all these having their particular Conveniences and Inconveniences. The Experience and Wisdom of your Ancestors, hath so moulded this
out of a Mixture of these, as to give to this Kingdom (as far as humane Prudence
can provide) the Conveniences of all three, without the Inconveniences of any one,
as long as the Balance hangs even between the three Estates, and they run jointly
on in their proper Chanel, (begetting Verdure and Fertility in the Meadows on
both sides) and the overflowing of either on either side, raise no Deluge or Inunda-
tion. The Ill of Absolute Monarchy is Tyranny, the Ill of Aristocracy, is Faction
and Division; the Ills of Democracy, are Tumults, Violence, and Licentiousness.
The Good of Monarchy, is the uniting a Nation under one Head, to resist Invasion
from Abroad, and Insurrection at Home; the Good of Aristocracy, is the conjunction
of Council in the ablest Persons of a State for the publick Benefit; the Good of
Democracy, is Liberty, and the Courage and Industry which Liberty begets.

The *Answer* goes even further. The famous passage above repeats the Polybian idea at an abstract level. More remarkable is the next passage, where
the writers distribute the functions of government among the king, the
lords, and the commons, the three estates of the English constitution.

In this Kingdom the Laws are jointly made by a King, by a House of Peers, and by a
House of Commons chosen by the People, all having free Votes and particular
Priviledges. The Government according to these Laws, is trusted to the King;
Power of Treaties of War and Peace, of making Peers, of chusing Officers and
Counsellors for State, Judges for Law, Commanders for Forts and Castles; giving
Commissions for raising Men; to make War Abroad, or to prevent or provide against
Invasions or Insurrections at Home; benefit of Confiscations, power of Pardoning,
and some more of the like kind are placed in the King. . . . the House of Commons,
(an excellent Conserver of Liberty, but never intended for any share in Govern-
ment, or the chusing of them that should Govern) is solely intrusted with the first
Propositions concerning the Levies of Monies, (which is the Sinews as well of

---

[8] *Answer*, 731.
[9] The reference to Venice was not innovative in the discussion of the English constitution.
For instance, Sir Thomas Smith writes: 'So that heerein the kingdome of Englande is farre
more absolute than either the dukedome of Venice is, or the kingdome of the Lacedemonians
was' (Sir Thomas Smith, *De Republica Anglorum*, ed. Mary Dewar (Cambridge, 1982), 85).
Although the Venetian constitution was a subject of much interest in England in the late 16th
and early 17th century, I can find no sign that the ideas of mixed government discussed in
England in the 1640s owed anything to the Venetian model.

Peace as of War); and the impeaching of those, who for their own Ends, though countenanced by any surreptitiously gotten Command of the King, have violated that Law, which he is bound (when he knows it) to protect: . . . And the Lords being trusted with a Judicatory Power, are an excellent Skreen and Bank between the Prince and People, to assist each against any Incroachments of the other; and by just Judgments to preserve that Law, which ought to be the Rule of every one of the Three.[10]

The significance of the passage lies in its identification of a functional division among the three estates, and in the allocation of functions to each of the three. Distinctive functions are allotted to the House of Commons and to the House of Lords, as well as to the king himself. Here lies the crucial cleavage between the *Answer* and Parker. The meaning of the words 'the ancient, equal, happy, well-poised, and never-enough commended Constitution' departs from tradition. The crux of the argument has moved, from 'balance' between the prerogative and the liberties, to that among functional divisions within the king-in-parliament. The Fortescuian idea of mixed government has been replaced by the Polybian one.

Why did the writers of the *Answer* bring the Polybian theory into the heart of the constitution?

First, they needed a theory to justify, from King Charles's point of view, the substantial concessions he had made since the meeting of the Long Parliament in November 1640. The king had consented to the impeachment and the execution of Strafford, the abolition of the prerogative courts, the Triennial Bill, and the Bill forbidding the dissolution of the Long Parliament without its own consent. Charles needed to deny that those were unprincipled concessions forced on him by the Houses. The *Answer* explained that the concessions had been made so as to let the constitution work more efficiently. In a bid to resume the political initiative from the parliamentarians, the king, rather than the Houses, was portrayed as the real defender of the constitution. The king, explained the *Answer*, knew how the English constitution worked, and what the essence of it was. Since he understood the essence to be the Polybian balance within the government, he could appreciate the importance of the proper functions allotted to the two Houses. When he saw that the constitution was in trouble, he was 'willingly contented to oblige' himself to call a parliament every three years, and to give up his right of dissolving the Long Parliament 'for the better enabling' the functions of the Lords and Commons to be carried out. Thus the king's concern was to keep the balance workable. He expected

[10] *Answer*, 731.

'an extraordinary Moderation' from parliament in return. By contrast, claimed the *Answer*, the parliament wanted to shatter the balance, as *The Nineteen Propositions* showed.[11]

Secondly, the writers were anxious to preserve the king's several powers within the constitution. Disaster would follow, they warned, if the parliamentarians encroached further on the prerogative. The intention of the *Answer* is clear in their description of the three pure forms of government. The defect of monarchy, we learn, is tyranny; that of aristocracy is faction and division; that of democracy is tumults, violence, and licentiousness. Why is the defect of aristocracy not—as the previous tradition of political thought would lead us to expect—oligarchy, but faction and division? The authors were arguing that the 'inconveniences' of aristocracy and those of democracy are the same: in essence, anarchy. The proper balance could be, and ought to be, maintained between the two extremes, tyranny and anarchy. In the *Answer* the focus of the argument moves to the prevention of the latter, for, claimed the authors, the concessions made by the king had made tyranny impossible: 'the Power, legally placed in both Houses, is more than sufficient to prevent and restrain the Power of Tyranny'. The logical conclusion of the argument was simple: if the Houses challenged the balance, the result would be anarchy. The Houses were claiming 'a pure Arbitrary Power' and demanding 'at once to confirm what was so taken, and to give up almost all the rest'. Their ambition would 'destroy all Rights and Proprieties, all Distinctions of Families and Merit', and 'this splendid and excellently distinguished Form of Government' would 'end in a dark equal Chaos of Confusion, and the long Line of Our many Noble Ancestors in a *Jack Cade*, or a *Wat Tylor*'.[12]

In this redefinition of the constitution, the prerogative defended by the *Answer* was mainly the power to appoint governmental officers. The writers credited that power with an important role in the balance. After the issue of the Militia Ordinance (March 1642) and of the Commissions of Array (June 1642), what was at stake was the nomination and appointment of military commanders, namely, lieutenants and deputy lieutenants.[13] The king's rejection of the Ordinance was repeated in the *Answer*. The ground on which he opposed the idea of the Ordinance was that it would lead to social disorder.

But the *Answer* did not say that the use of force by the Houses would cause disorder. Instead, it warned that the very usurpation of the power of

[11] Ibid. 731–2.
[12] Ibid. 732, 725, 732.
[13] J. P. Kenyon (ed.), *The Stuart Constitution: 1603–1688* (Cambridge, 1986), 219–20.

appointment by parliament would destroy the finetuning of the constitution and endanger peace. That power was the basis of the king's authority, the authority which bound the government together. The new definition of the constitution enabled the king to claim that the prerogative of appointing officers and ministers was indispensable to the preservation of the king's authority, without which the balance would be lost and anarchy follow.

The authority of the king is the heart of the balance. It withstands the defects of the lords and the commons, namely, 'the Ills of Division and Faction', and 'Tumults, Violence, and Licentiousness'. The king's authority will give the laws binding force, and will keep the nation united as long as the king draws 'due Esteem', 'Respect', and 'Fear and Reverence' from the subjects. But if the exclusive power of appointing officers is taken from him, he will lose his authority: nothing will be left for him 'but to look on'; and the nation will disintegrate. If the Houses interfere in the process of nomination and appointment, and confront the king's nomination with 'the scorn of refusall', the King of England will be made 'despicable both at home and abroad', and his loss of authority will 'beget eternal Factions and Dissentions (as destructive to publick Happiness as War)'.[14] If the authors of the *Answer* had merely claimed that the king was entitled to the 'esteem' and 'fear' of the subjects, they would have said nothing new or contentious. Instead the *Answer* asserted that only the exclusive power of nominating officers, which is allotted to the king within the government, could keep alive the respect for the king without which the nation would fall apart.

The *Answer* was published when the deep antagonism between the two sides was spreading from Westminster across the country, and when military conflict seemed increasingly likely. Its tenor of moderation reflected the king's anxiety to gain wider support. Unhappily for him, as Weston and Greenberg show, some presbyterian pamphleteers exploited the *Answer* by developing arguments for the legitimacy of resistance and for parliamentary sovereignty.[15] In the *Answer*, Charles officially recognized that the English constitution consisted of three estates, the king, the lords, and the commons. The pamphleteers claimed that Charles had recognized in the *Answer* that the crown was no more than one of the three estates.[16]

---

[14] *Answer*, 728, 731–2.

[15] C. C. Weston and J. R. Greenberg, *Subjects and Sovereigns* (Cambridge, 1981), ch. iii. However, as I suggest later, I cannot agree with them about the point at which they place Philip Hunton in this group of pamphleteers.

[16] Weston, *English Constitutional Theory and the House of Lords*, 28; Sanderson, 'The *Answer to the Nineteen Propositions* Revisited', 636. In *Subjects and Sovereigns*, ch. iii, Weston and Greenberg go further, and maintain that the *Answer* is an essential document in the devel-

Yet they did not acknowledge or accept the new idea of mixed government advanced by the *Answer*. Instead they turned the *Answer* to the development of their own ideas, which derived from the concept of government by consent. Although their concept of the balance leant decisively towards the subjects' side, they worked comfortably within the Fortescuian framework. What makes the *Answer* distinctive, in the perspective of this book, is its new idea of mixed government, not the old idea to which the pamphleteers adapted it.

The *Answer* introduced the Polybian idea of balance to English constitutional theory. Adjusting the Polybian idea of functional division to the English constitution, that is, to the powers of the king, the lords, and the commons, the *Answer* at the same time inherited the main concern of Polybius, internal stability in peacetime. Like Polybius, the writers of the *Answer* asked how to prevent the disintegration of the government. As Polybius found his model in the balance of the Roman constitution, so Falkland and Colepeper discovered their own answer in that of the English constitution. The very essence of the English balance is to defend the authority of the king, and the king's authority alone can restrain the divisive and anarchic tendency of the two Houses. In seventeenth-century England, the Polybian idea of mixed government served to warn against anarchy. The *Answer*, in adopting the Polybian idea, opened a new chapter in political thought.

3. Philip Hunton and Henry Ferne

After the publication of the *Answer*, while some writers—particularly Henry Parker and Charles Herle—developed their ideas within the traditional political thinking, a new debate about the right to revolt began within the new framework of the Polybian idea of mixed government.[17]

opment of the idea of parliamentary sovereignty because the theoretical origin of the arguments of those pamphleteers is to be found in the *Answer*. I disagree. First, the view which appears in the *Answer*, that the English constitution consists of the three estates, had been widely available before the appearance of that document, particularly since the calling of the Short Parliament. Secondly, and more importantly, that view of the English constitution was held by all sides since it was uncontroversial, as Sommerville has pointed out. Rather, the theoretical basis of those pamphleteers who endorsed the idea of parliamentary sovereignty is to be found in the concept of government by consent, which had been far from uncommon long before 1640. See Sanderson, 'The *Answer* Revisited'; Mendle, *Dangerous Positions*; J. P. Sommerville, *Politics and Ideology in England, 1604–1640* (London, 1986), 74–80.

[17] For the debates among Parker, Herle, Hunton, Ferne, and others in the period of 1642–4, see also Margaret A. Judson, *The Crisis of the Constitution* (New Brunswick, 1949), ch. x; Weston, *English Constitutional Theory and the House of Lords*, 34–43; John Sanderson, 'But

Philip Hunton and Henry Ferne were the main theorists in this debate. Hunton was an ordained priest, who was later appointed master or provost of Cromwell's University at Durham. Ferne was another divine, who became one of Charles I's chaplains in 1643. Although the two men had the same starting-point, that is the innovation to be found in the *Answer*, they reached quite different conclusions. Hunton allowed people to fight for the parliamentarian cause, while Ferne forbade them to do so. Yet for all their conflicting conclusions they had much in common. They agreed that neither king nor parliament had the final say if conflict arose between them, and that the judgement whether resistance is right or wrong ought to be left to an individual's 'conscience'.[18] They hoped to end the civil war by restoring the accord between king and parliament. They used the Polybian theory of mixed government to re-establish the authority of the king-in-parliament. The Polybian idea of 'balance', which was newly introduced by the *Answer*, was not used by Hunton and Ferne to defend the prerogative or the subjects' rights. It was used to secure internal peace.

Philip Hunton proposes three ways of classifying governments.[19] They are absolute/limited, elective/successive, and simple/mixed. The first and the last are important in his argument. In absolute monarchy, writes Hunton, the exercise of the king's power may or may not be limited by checks. If the limitation derives not from his own will but from an imposition upon it, the monarchy is a limited one. If the king can govern by his own will, it is absolute. The word 'will' is crucial to Hunton's theory, for he considers all sovereignty, whether limited or absolute, to be based upon the consent of the people. In his view, a man is 'a voluntary agent', and subjection 'essentially depend[s] upon consent'. A conqueror is not necessarily an absolute monarch, for the condition of subjection is specified by the subjects' agreement to it rather than by the conquest itself. In the case of a 'successive' or hereditary monarchy, the initial act of giving consent is supposed to have committed subsequent generations to it.[20]

It was only when he discussed the third distinction, between simple and mixed governments, that Hunton took up the argument of the *Answer*. A simple government, to him, is a government where the supreme authority lies exclusively with either monarchy or aristocracy or democracy. Each of these has an innate bad tendency which leads, respectively, to tyranny,

the People's Creatures' (Manchester, 1989), chs. i, ii; Richard Tuck, *Philosophy and Government* (Cambridge, 1993), 226–35; Smith, *Constitutional Royalism and the Search for Settlement*, ch. vii; M. Mendle, *Henry Parker and the English Civil War* (Cambridge, 1995), 97–101.

[18] Cf. Pocock, 'Historical Introduction', *The Political Works of James Harrington*, 22.
[19] Philip Hunton, *A Treatise of Monarchie* (London, 1643).
[20] Ibid. 19–20, 23, 34.

destructive factions, and confusion and tumult. 'Experience' and 'wisdom' have taught us another form of government, a mixture of the three.

Unity and strength in a Monarchy, Counsell and Wisedome in an Aristocracy; Liberty and respect of Common good in a Democracy. Hence the wisedome of men deeply seen in State matters guided them to frame a mixture of all three, uniting them into one Forme, that so the good of all might be enjoyed, and the evill of them avoyded.[21]

Hunton places an emphasis, which is not present in the *Answer*, on the principle that 'the supreme power' must be shared in a mixed government. Hunton calls that principle 'a mixed principle'. Whereas the *Answer* was published before the civil war broke out, Hunton's *A Treatise of Monarchie* appeared in the midst of the military confrontation between the two sides. The location of 'the supreme power' was a vital question, since it directly led to the question of the command of the army. Hunton refers to the *Answer*, which adopted the Polybian idea of mixture and distributed the powers of the government to the three components of the constitution, but still considered the legislative power to belong to all three components. According to Hunton, the *Answer* had acknowledged 'the supreme power' to be shared by the three.

At this stage of discussion, Hunton articulates the theoretical relationship between the notion of 'limited monarchy' and that of 'mixed monarchy'. Whereas not all limited monarchy is necessarily mixed monarchy, all mixed monarchy is limited.[22] What does it mean to say that the power of a monarch is 'limited' by the 'mixed principle'? In the case of the English constitution, argues Hunton, it means that none of the three can exercise its power alone. That is because the powers in the English constitution are not '*complete* independent powers' but '*incomplete* independent powers'.[23]

Hunton, when he discussed the legitimacy of armed resistance to the king, had to deal with the question of the relationship between the king's prerogative and the subjects' liberties. As we saw in Chapter 1 above, that relationship had been conventionally discussed within the framework of the Fortescuian idea. Hunton did not invoke the traditional approach. Instead he articulated the question in a different manner. He discussed, not how to limit the governing powers, but how to construct a 'complete' power out of 'incomplete' ones. In other words, his approach to the question of the relationship between the power of the government and the liberties of the people was not direct. His argument was twofold: he addressed,

---

[21] Ibid. 25.   [22] Ibid. 27.
[23] Philip Hunton, *A Vindication of the Treatise of Monarchie* (London, 1644), 15.

first, the question of the relationship among the powers within the government, and, secondly, the relationship between the government and the people. In the case of the English constitution, of course, the government in this formula means 'the king-in-parliament', and the people 'the subjects'.

The king's will, therefore, when expressed outside the parliament, has no authority over the subjects, since the law is 'the Kings publike and authoritative Will'.[24] The same principle is also applied to the parliament. Even if the two Houses work together, they are not empowered to override the king's veto. In sharp contrast both to Charles Herle and to Henry Parker, who were aggressive parliamentarians, Hunton bitterly denounced the idea of sovereignty by the two Houses:

whereas some make answere, that he is *Singulis major*, but *Vniuersis minor*, so the Answerer to Doctor *Ferne*, I wonder that the Proposition of the Observator, that the King is *Vniuersis minor*, should be so much exploded. Every member *seorsim* is a subject, but all *collection* in their houses are not: And hee sayes simply, the Houses are co-ordinate to the King, not subordinate; that the Lords stile, *Comites*, or *Peeres*, implies in Parliament a co-ordinative society with his Majesty in the Government. I conceive this Answerer to avoid one extreme falls on another; for this is a very overthrow of all Monarchy, and to reduce all Government to Democracy.[25]

Parker and Herle, who maintained that the two Houses were entitled to override the king's veto if necessary, had to explain why there was no need to worry lest parliamentary power, unchecked by the king, should become arbitrary. Parker insisted that parliament would not dare to adopt an extreme position since it was located between the king and the people. Herle stressed the diversity of self-interest among the numerous members of the parliament, and explained that this diversity would prevent the parliament from running into tyranny.[26] Hunton felt no need to deny that

[24] *A Treatise of Monarchie*, 56.

[25] Ibid. 42–3. In *Subjects and Sovereigns*, 53–61, Weston and Greenberg place Herle and Hunton in a single group as 'co-ordination' theorists who undermined the idea of the exclusive legal sovereignty of the king. According to them, it was the *Answer* which opened the way for 'co-ordination theory'. This theory was that the legal authority is shared by the three co-ordinate estates, the king, the lords, and the commons. More importantly, in Weston and Greenberg's view, the theory implied the possibility that the two Houses possessed the discretionary authority without the king. They are correct in saying that Herle felt less hesitation than Hunton in allocating the discretionary authority to the two Houses; that Hunton adopted the argument of the *Answer*; and that Hunton admitted that parliamentary control of the Militia without the king's consent was 'not formally legall' but an 'eminently legall' action. However, the *Answer* has little to do with 'co-ordination theory', and Hunton never says that the decision of the Houses has a legal binding force over the people.

[26] Henry Parker, *Observations upon some of his Majesties late Answers and Expresses* (London, 2 July 1642), 23; Charles Herle, *A Fuller Answer to A Treatise Written by Doctor*

sort of risk. Instead he praised the mixed constitution, saying 'I conceive it unparalleled for exactnesse of true policy in the whole world'.[27]

Although he denies that parliament can be sovereign without the king, Hunton defends the right of the Houses to resist. That the Houses share the law-making power with the king means, Hunton argues, that the king's most important power is fundamentally limited. No limitation without the right to resist by arms can ever be effective.[28] Once the king transcends the limit, his will has no authority; the subjects are allowed to disobey him.

Henry Ferne, a royalist, has a similar view of the English constitution. England is a mixed monarchy which maintains an 'excellent temper of the three estates'. Each of the three has a power of veto in the legislature. That is good 'for the security of the Commonwealth', since no law can be imposed on the people without their consent. The parliament consists of the king and the two Houses. Neither the king without the Houses, nor the Houses without the king, can make laws. Ferne concurs with Hunton's sharp criticism of Herle's idea of 'coordination', the idea which paves the way for the two Houses' overriding power over the king's veto. Herle and Hunton attack Ferne's *The Resolving of Conscience*; Ferne rebukes Hunton's *A Treatise of Monarchie*; and yet both Ferne and Hunton condemn Herle's *A Fuller Answer*.[29]

However, Ferne urges the people not to resist the king. Ferne's 'mixture' is slightly different from Hunton's. Ferne sees that the king's power is limited only in 'the exercise of it', and that the limitation is not 'a power of forceable constraint, but only of Legall and Moral restraint'. When the king violates the limit, the subjects may be set free from obedience to him, but do not acquire the right to resist.[30]

4. Conscience and the Constitution

Ferne has a number of further points to make. Even if the king's misconduct offers a justification for resistance, who is to judge when resistance becomes justifiable? Although the Houses may consider the king to have

---

Ferne, entitled *The Resolving of Conscience* (London, 1642), 12–14. As for the change in Parker's ideas between 1640 and 1642, see M. Mendle, 'The Ship Money Case, *The Case of Shipmony*, and the Development of Henry Parker's Parliamentary Absolutism', *Historical Journal*, 32 (1989), 513–36; *Henry Parker and the English Civil War*, 70–89.

[27] *A Treatise of Monarchie*, 44.
[28] Ibid. 53; *A Vindication*, 5, 13, 15–16.
[29] Henry Ferne, *The Resolving of Conscience* (London, 1642), 25–6; *Conscience Satisfied* (Oxford, 1643), 6, 11, 16, 19, 25.
[30] *A Reply unto Severall Treatises* (Oxford, 1643), 13, 17–18, 29–30, 37.

violated the limitation imposed by the constitution on him, they cannot force the people to fight the king, for the Houses cannot get the consent of the third part, the king.[31] At this point, Ferne and Hunton are in agreement. No more than Ferne does Hunton think that the Houses have the right to command the people to resist. The king, the lords, and the commons have the binding power over the people as long as the proper balance among the three is maintained. None of the three has the power to decide when the balance has collapsed.[32] Here, the two thinkers reach the same conclusion: the judgement ought to be left to an individual's 'conscience'. Both of them resort to that notion in order to save their notion of 'balance' from deadlock. Ferne writes,

If Conscience could be perswaded, that it is lawfull in such a case to resist, and that this rising in arms is such a resistance as they say may in such a case be pretended to, yet can it never (if it be willing to know any thing) be truly perswaded that such a case is now come.[33]

And according to Hunton,

if it be apparent, and an Appeale made *ad conscientiam generis humani*, especially of those of that Community, then the fundamentall Lawes of that Monarchy must iudge and pronounce the sentence in every mans conscience; and every man (as farre as concernes him) must follow the evidence of Truth in his owne soule, to oppose, or not oppose, according as he can in conscience acquit or condemne the act of carriage of the Governour. For I conceive, in a Case which transcends the frame and provision of the Government they are bound to, People are unbound, and in state as if they had no Government; and the superior Law of Reason and Conscience must be judge.[34]

Even so, the practical implications of the arguments of the two men are totally different. Ferne's 'conscience' urges a man to stay calm and help restore the constitution: Hunton's suggests the need to fight for the same purpose.

Ferne expects that 'Every man may be clearly perswaded in Conscience . . . that he is bound not only to forbear from resisting, but also to assist His Majesty in so just a cause.' For Ferne, an individual's conscience is, above all, what preserves allegiance to the king and tells the individual from within not to resist the king ordained by God.[35] Conscience cannot

---

[31] *A Reply unto Severall Treatises*, 37–8.
[32] *A Treatise of Monarchie*, 69.
[33] *The Resolving of Conscience*, 4–5.
[34] *A Treatise of Monarchie*, 18. Also see pp. 29, 73, and *A Vindication*, 49.
[35] *A Reply unto Severall Treatises*, 4.

be controlled by the Houses. The decisions of the Houses are no more than the results of voting, which merely satisfies 'the formality of Law' and has nothing to do with 'an unanimous, free, and generall consent'.[36] Ferne, who appeals to the individual's conscience, claims that collective decision-making is not a proper way to judge whether resistance is warrantable to restore the balance of the constitution. He denounces the two Houses for assuming the right to that judgement. His aim is to leave the matter to the individual's conscience, which works in a sphere separate from political institutions. If only conscience is left alone by the claims of the Houses, Ferne believes, it will command a man to stay with 'the Supreme Head of the Body', and 'to let Nature work it out', for conscience always values 'the safer way' and prefers suffering to revolt. Although the king himself cannot exercise the authority which gives the laws binding legal force, the king himself is still 'the Object of our subjection and obedience'. Ferne's conscience instructs the subjects to wait until the antagonism between the king and the Houses is healed, until the balance is restored, and until the king-in-parliament recovers its authority.[37]

Ferne can wait, but Hunton cannot, since Hunton's conscience does not recognize a debt of allegiance to the king once the constitution breaks down. When the balance collapses, nothing can master Hunton's conscience. While Hunton considers that the right to resist is justified *in extremis*, he claims that the parliament without the king cannot be 'a legal court' to judge the king's transgression. Even if the Houses resolve to resist, the decision, which is not 'authoritative', does not have a legal binding force. The people are not obliged to take up arms for the Houses against the king. When the constitution breaks down, the people do not have to 'receive and rest in their [= the Houses'] judgement for conscience of its authority'.[38] Conscience is now freed from the authority of parliament, and begins to work on its own. In other words, as long as the king and the Houses work together and the balance is maintained, the people should adjust their moral judgements to the judgement of the parliament. In Hunton's formula, 'conscience' is the individual's judgement by which his consent is understood to have been given to the constitution when it was established. Judgement in conscience is a 'moral' judgement, not a 'legal' one, since it cannot force others' judgements to reach the same conclusion.

---

[36] Ferne, *The Resolving of Conscience*, 35. Ferne says he prefers substance to formal procedure. See *A Reply unto Several Treatises*, 41, 69.

[37] *The Resolving of Conscience*, 4; *Conscience Satisfied*, 20; *A Reply unto Severall Treatises*, 4, 69, 91.

[38] Hunton, *A Treatise of Monarchie*, 73.

Yet this 'morall Power' of judging survives under the constitution.[39] A man is expected to exercise moral judgement as 'a voluntary agent'. If there is no government, the exercise of moral judgement is left to itself. It is the government which gives the legal judgement as a form of law or command which binds men's judgement. Only the constitution of the government retains the legal authority which guides and unites the courses of the moral judgements of every individual, since under the constitution men have given their consent. The constitution, not the king or the Houses, is the repository of authority.

That is why Hunton feels so concerned about 'the Frame' and 'the Being of the Government'.[40] Once the balance is lost, there remains nothing to control the consciences of individuals. If the balance is in danger, it must be restored before it is too late. Hunton believes, therefore, that conscience will instruct the subjects to defend the constitution. This may involve armed resistance to the king, if the purpose of that resistance is to restore the basis of obedience to the government. For Hunton, there is a clear-cut distinction between a war for peace and a mere anarchy. A short civil war might be needed to avoid a lasting civil war, for 'a temporary evill of war is to be chosen rather then a perpetuall losse of liberty, and subversion of the established frame of a Government'.[41]

Hunton and Ferne share a primary concern to stop the civil war, yet their approaches differ. Hunton's approach is to maintain, or to restore, the being of the government, which alone, in his eyes, can keep the legal authority alive. The constitution of the government and the social order are not the same thing. The former is the basis of the latter. Thus Hunton can assert, without any confusion of his vocabulary, that when the existence of the government is endangered, the frame should be restored at the expense of social order. For Ferne, that statement would be self-contradictory, for he believes that 'resistance . . . doth tend to the dissolution of that order, for which the power it self is set up of God'.[42] A body politic is an enlarged image of a natural body, and any resistance to the king involves a rebellion of the body against the head, 'which tends to the dissolution of the whole'.[43] It is better to suffer than resist, no matter how unreasonable the suffering may appear.[44] One cannot be too cautious or too prudent, for revolt leads to anarchy. A man should not act before his 'conscience' is 'truly persuaded'. In Ferne's view, the social order is not supported only by the constitutional legal authority. Even if the balance is endangered,

---

[39] Hunton, *A Treatise of Monarchie*, 18.   [40] Ibid. 63, 67.
[41] Ibid. 61.   [42] Ferne, *The Resolving of Conscience*, 12.
[43] Ibid. 8.   [44] Ibid. 31–2; *A Reply unto Several Treatises*, 91.

order can still be preserved, at least for the time being, by conscience, since conscience will tie the subjects' obedience to the king. But once armed conflicts take place between the king and the Houses, the balance will be lost and never return.

Before the civil war, as Pocock pointed out, England faced an unprecedented situation, with which conventional political thinking was not equipped to deal.[45] The regime of the king-in-parliament had broken down. Certainly, as Sommerville claims, theorists of government by consent could easily develop theories of legitimate resistance.[46] What they could not offer, in my view, was a theory to consolidate the unity of the nation. It was the *Answer* which provided England with a theory for the consolidation of the government. Adapting the Polybian idea to English soil, the *Answer* maintained the Polybian concern for domestic peace. The *Answer* offered a new formula, 'balance', to sustain the authority of the government. When the balance is lost, the authority of the government is lost, and anarchy and confusion will follow. Ferne and Hunton inherited this concept. For the *Answer*, 'esteem' for the king and 'fear' of him were the keepers of the balance: for Ferne and Hunton, 'conscience' worked to support the balance and recover it when it was in danger. Hunton conceded the necessity of resistance *in extremis*, but did so on the ground that it could save the balance within the constitution.

Hunton's distinction between a civil war, and a short civil war to prevent an all-out civil war, became irrelevant as the 1640s went on. However, another theory which was also born of the desire to prevent civil war took a different approach. It attempted to eradicate resistance in the first place. This theory, too, was unable to prevent the disaster of the 1640s. Yet it offered a novel and striking foundation for the restoration of government from anarchy. This was Thomas Hobbes's theory of sovereignty.

---

[45] J. G. A. Pocock, *The Machiavellian Moment* (Princeton, 1975), 361–71.
[46] Sommerville, *Politics and Ideology in England, 1604–1640*, 69–77.

3
THOMAS HOBBES'S THEORY OF SOVEREIGNTY, 1640–1647:
Private Judgement, Fear, Covenant

1. Introduction

Thomas Hobbes was born in 1588, the year of the Armada. He wrote in his autobiography that 'fear' and he were twins.[1] His first political treatise, written in 1640, was constructed upon an analysis of 'fear'.[2] The year 1588 was a culmination of the threat of foreign invasion: in 1640, when two parliaments were called following the wars against the Scots, the English began to dispute over the fundamental nature of the English constitution. Hobbes circulated the manuscripts of *The Elements of Law* with the intention of supporting the king's position in the debate in the Long Parliament, though it is not clear whether he thought civil war was a serious possibility in England at that time.[3]

---

[1] *Vita*, in *Opera Latina*, ed. Molesworth (1839–45), i, p. lxxxvi.

[2] *The Elements of Law*. The manuscript of this work is thought to have been written in 1640, and to have been circulated among those who supported the king's cause in the parliaments. In 1650 the first thirteen chapters of the first part were published under the title *Human Nature; or the fundamental Elements of Policy*. . . . The rest of the book was also published in the same year under the title *De Corpore Politico; or the Elements of Law*. In these versions, the contemporary editor's claim that Hobbes consented to publication is doubtful. See 'Introduction to the Second Edition' of *The Elements of Law* by Goldsmith.

[3] Later, in the preface to the second edition of *De Cive*, which he published in Amsterdam early in 1647, Hobbes wrote retrospectively that the dispute was a sign of a civil war. The following is the passage where he explains the reason he wrote *De Cive*, the manuscript of which is supposed to have been completed in the autumn of 1641, before *De Corpore* and *De Homine*. 'Hæc dum compleo, ordino, lentè moroséque conscribo (non enim dissero, sed computo) accidit interea patriam meam, ante annos aliquot quàm *bellum civile* exardesceret, quæstionibus de jure Imperii, & debitâ civium obedientiâ belli propinqui præcursoribus fervescere. Id quod partis hujus tertiæ, cæteris dilatis, maturandæ absolvendæque causa fuit. [Whilst I contrive, order, pensively and slowly compose these matters, for I only doe reason,

Hobbes's perspective was not confined to England. He had travelled on the Continent three times by 1640, and had contact with prominent Continental philosophers, Descartes and Galileo among them. In Hobbes's mind, the wars against the Scots and the disputes between the king and the parliament belonged to a broader European pattern of civil and religious war. To his subjects, King Charles appeared in the 1630s to be trying to strengthen his power. One of his claims was that the king was responsible for the safety of the nation and of his subjects, and was entitled to levy money without the consent of the subjects if necessary. In *The Elements of Law*, Hobbes claimed that the sovereign should be the sole judge of an imminent danger to the country, and implicitly defended Charles's cause in the Ship Money case. In that treatise, however, Hobbes went further; he supplied a diagnosis of and a remedy for the 'fear' of civil war. Diversity of passions among men leads them to war. Indivisible sovereignty needs to be established to prevent it.

Here, two chapters will be given to Hobbes. First, some general characteristics of his theory of sovereignty will be examined. Secondly, in the following chapter, the focus will be upon his notion of conquest in *Leviathan*. While the main frame of his political theory remained the same from *The Elements of Law* to *Leviathan*, the weight and meaning of the notion of sovereignty by 'acquisition', that is by 'conquest', was changed in *Leviathan*, where he defended the legitimacy of the new English republican government. When Harrington attacked Hobbes in *Oceana*, his target was not Hobbes's general theory but specifically the notion of conquest in *Leviathan*.

In the present chapter, Hobbes's argument in the 1640s will be examined. This investigation will confirm that his theory of sovereignty was already fully laid down in that decade, and was merely repeated in *Leviathan* in 1651—except for a small change we discuss in the following chapter. The materials treated here are *The Elements of Law* and *De Cive*.[4]

I dispute not, it so happen'd in the interim, that my Country some few years before *the civill Warres* did rage, was boyling hot with questions concerning the rights of Dominion, and the obedience due from Subjects, the true forerunners of an approaching War; And was the cause which (all those other matters deferr'd) ripen'd, and pluckt from me this third part]' (*De Cive*, 82 [E: pp. 35–6]). In the English translation, if the original Latin words were to be faithfully followed, *the civil Warres* should be 'the civil Warre'. But this discrepancy may reflect the fact that the second Latin edition, which was written before the second civil war broke out, was translated after that.

[4] The first Latin edition of *De Cive* was published in 1642 in Paris, the second edition in 1647 in Amsterdam. 'The English version' was published in London, a few weeks before *Leviathan*, in 1651. I agree with Richard Tuck that Hobbes himself is very unlikely to have been the translator of *De Cive* (Richard Tuck, 'Warrender's *De Cive*', Political Studies, 33

Passages in *Leviathan*, too, will be referred to so as to show what those three works had in common.[5] Thus the present chapter emphasizes the continuity among the three. The following chapter highlights differences between the early writings in the 1640s and *Leviathan*.

Hobbes's first political writing was *The Elements of Law*, manuscripts of which were in circulation in 1640. Admittedly, the ecclesiastical ideas present in *De Cive* would be radically transformed in *Leviathan*. But Hobbes's idea of sovereignty remained basically the same from 1640 to 1651 as far as 'civill' matters are concerned. In the autumn of 1640 Hobbes fled to Paris out of a 'fear' that he would be summoned by parliament, for he had defended the king's position in *The Elements of Law*. In Paris he published *De Cive* in 1642, a work written by November of the previous year in Latin so as to be read on the Continent.[6] In 1650–1, while the royalists were still resisting Cromwell in Scotland, he was writing another treatise, the last section of which was probably written after he had come to believe the new English government's overall victory to be clear.[7] This treatise, *Leviathan*, was written in English, and published in London in April/May 1651.

Hobbes's theory of obedience survived largely intact through the years 1640 to 1651. His argument lent support to the Rump Parliament in 1651 as it had done to Charles I in 1640. There were, of course, some who changed their arguments according to the change of government. Marchamont Nedham was a true genius in this sort of skill, and from 1650 was willing to disown his royalist writing of the late 1640s.[8] Hobbes had no need to

---

(1985), 308–15). Philip Milton ('Did Hobbes translate *De Cive*?', *History of Political Thought*, 11 (1990), 627–38) supports Tuck's claim; and more recently, so does 'Statistical Wordprint Analysis' (N. B. Reynolds and J. L. Hilton, 'Thomas Hobbes and Authorship of the *Horae Subsecivae*', *History of Political Thought*, 14 (1993), 367–8).

[5] I do not discuss those of Hobbes's works which were after 1651, of which principal political texts are *Behemoth* and the Latin version of *Leviathan*. Both of these appeared after the Restoration.

[6] Warrender, 'Editor's Introduction', *De Cive: The Latin Version*, 40.

[7] The question what finally marked the defeat of the royalists in the English civil wars is a difficult one. The execution of the king in Jan. 1649 did not finish the royalist cause, which survived in Ireland and Scotland. Its final defeat occurred only at the battle of Worcester in Sept. 1651. *Leviathan* had appeared five months earlier. However, Richard Tuck, citing the authority of Clarendon, suggests that Charles II's ministers believed his cause to have been lost after the battle of Dunbar in Sept. 1650, and that Hobbes shared this view when he wrote 'A Review and Conclusion'. See Tuck's *Leviathan*, p. xi; Edward Hyde, *The History of the Rebellion and Civil Wars in England Begun in the Year 1641* (Oxford, 1992), v. 148–9.

[8] See Blair Worden, 'Marchamont Nedham and the Beginnings of English Republicanism, 1649–1656', in David Wootton (ed.), *Republicanism, Liberty, and Commercial Society, 1649–1776* (Stanford, Calif., 1994), 60.

amend the basic tenet of his former argument. The course of events moved toward his argument and not vice versa, for he had already argued in *The Elements of Law* that sovereignty can be held by one man or one council. 'One man' can be read as Charles, and 'one council' as the Rump.[9]

Here we see a contrast between Hobbes and the writers of 'ancient prudence' whom we met in the previous chapter. For our purpose, Hobbes and those writers can be treated in parallel because their aim was the same. Yet Hobbes's argument, unlike theirs, survived from the 1640s into the new phase, the Interregnum. The English Polybian theory of mixed government lost its immediate relevance when the English constitution disappeared. While Hobbes's weakness will be revealed in the next chapter, the secret of his resilience lay in his unique view of obedience, which will be examined here.

Thus, in this chapter, first, the basic structure of Hobbes's theory of sovereignty will be briefly observed. Secondly, we shall identify the fundamental difference between Hobbes and the theorists of mixed government. The final part of the chapter will consider his view of obedience, which is different from theirs.

2. Equality and Sovereignty

Hobbes's argument about sovereignty is familiar and may be briefly summarized. Two points need emphasis: that the basic structure of his theory of sovereignty in *Leviathan* had already been established in *The Elements of Law*; and that Hobbes believed that the exercise of 'private judgement' was incompatible with peace. Those points are crucial to an understanding of the similarities and dissimilarities between Hobbes's theory of sovereignty and the English Polybian theories of mixed government. The two theories were articulated in the same period, the early 1640s. They had the same end, peace and unity. Even so, Hobbes's treatment of private judgement was opposite to that to be found in the theories of mixed government.

Hobbes's well-known phrase '*bellum omnium in omnes* [a War of all men, against all men]' appeared first in *De Cive*, in 1642,[10] but the notion was not new in his writing. In *The Elements of Law*, 'the estate of men in this natural liberty is the estate of war'.[11] There are two causes which work together and produce a war of all: diversity of passion, and equality of men.

[9] *The Elements of Law*, I. 19. 6. 103.
[10] *De Cive*, I. 12. 96 [E: p. 49].
[11] *The Elements of Law*, I. 14. 11. 73.

...eth that which pleaseth, and is delightful to himself, ...spleaseth him: insomuch that while every man differ- ...ion, they differ also one from another concerning the ...ood and evil. Nor is there any such thing as ἀγαθὸν ...ply good.   (*The Elements of Law*, I. 7. 3. 29.)

...conventional standards of morality which have been ...eek antiquity, and denies the existence of any common ...al judgement. What Greek moral philosophers teach us is, ...Hobbes, nothing more than to express our passions under the plausible name of moral judgements.[12] Hobbes claims that different men will take things differently since they have different passions. There is no reason to expect men to agree about what is right and what is wrong. To make things worse, men's desire is interminable.[13] Moreover, everybody is free to do anything they want because men are equal in terms of the capacity to kill others; 'there needeth but little force to the taking away of a man's life'.[14] But, argues Hobbes, men would not easily concede that they are equal. Among men, there is 'envy and hatred of one towards another', and men tend to think 'themselves wiser than the rest',[15] because

GLORY, or internal gloriation or triumph of the mind, is that passion which procee-deth from the imagination or conception of our own power, above the power of him that contendeth with us.   (*The Elements of Law*, I. 9. 1. 36–7)

We have to acknowledge

that it must necessarily follow, that those men who are moderate, and look for no more but equality of nature, shall be obnoxious to the force of others, that will attempt to subdue them. And from hence shall proceed a general diffidence in man-kind, and mutual fear one of another. . . . the greatest part of men, upon no assur-ance of odds, do nevertheless, through vanity, or comparison, or appetite, provoke the rest, that otherwise would be contented with equality.   (*The Elements of Law*, I. 14. 3–5. 71)

Diversity of passions and equality in terms of the capacity to kill others leads to the state of 'mutual fear' of death. The same argument is also found in *De Cive* and *Leviathan*.[16] Here, in the state (or condition) of nature, men's life would be miserable, like that of the savage.[17]

   This picture produces the basic tenor of Hobbes's argument, and he

---

[12] *The Elements of Law*, II. 8. 13. 177.   [13] Ibid. I. 7. 6. 30.
[14] Ibid. I. 14. 2. 70.   [15] Ibid. I. 19. 5. 102.
[16] *De Cive*, I. 3–5. 93–4 [E: pp. 45–6]; v. 4. 131–2 [E: pp. 86–7]; *Leviathan*, IV. 31 [p. 17]; VIII.. 53 [p. 35], XIII. 86–8 [pp. 60–2].
[17] *The Elements of Law*, I. 14. 12. 73; *De Cive*, I. 13. 96 [E: p. 49]; *Leviathan*, XIII. 89 [p. 63].

maintains this tenor through the three works. In order to construct a theory of power and obedience upon that basis, he plants the notion of right. Men have a 'blameless liberty' to preserve their own lives. Hobbes calls it 'a right of nature'.

According to Hobbes, a man has a natural right 'to use all means and do whatsoever action is necessary for the preservation of his body'. This natural right includes a man's right to judge what is necessary for self-preservation, and to judge what endangers his life.[18] Now, the causes of *bellum omnium in omnes* can be articulated in a slightly different way: every man has a right to exercise his force, which can be powerful enough to kill others. In doing so he follows his private judgement, which derives from his passions.

It is physically impossible to deprive a man of his force unless he is killed. But it is possible to make him give up his private judgement. Hobbes chooses the latter. If every man ceases to follow his private judgement concerning social and political action, and accepts only one judgement by one man or one council (assembly), peace and order will prevail. This transformation is explained in legal terms. Since every man has a natural right, he is considered to be eligible for a legal contract. By a contract, he renounces his right to all, and accepts judgement made by the one man or one council (assembly) as his own judgement. This process is called making 'union' or 'one Person'.[19] The representative alone retains his (or its) natural right and is called the sovereign. Since everyone had a right to all before the contract, no sovereign-to-be could receive any more than that—*nouum ius dare non potuit*. The scope and nature of the sovereign's right itself is not altered by the contract, but there is no longer anyone entitled to contest his right, so that his right to everything becomes effective.[20]

---

[18] *The Elements of Law*, I. 14. 6–12. 71–2. In *De Cive*, 'Natura dedit *unicuique ius in omnia* [Nature hath given to *every one a right to all*]' (I. 10. 95 [E: p. 47]). And in *Leviathan*, 'THE RIGHT OF NATURE, which Writers commonly call *Jus Naturale*, is the Liberty each man hath, to use his own power, as he will himselfe, for the preservation of his own Nature; that is to say, of his own Life; and consequently, of doing any thing, which in his own Judgement, and Reason, hee shall conceive to be the aptest means thereunto' (XIV. 91 [p. 64]).

[19] *The Elements of Law*, I. 19. 7. 103–4; *De Cive*, V. 7. 133–4 [E: pp. 88–9]; *Leviathan*, XVI. 114 [p. 82]; XVII. 120 [p. 87]. What is the significance of using the word 'Person' in *Leviathan* in the place of the word 'union'? Perhaps one of the reasons Hobbes used the word was that he was anxious to establish a clear contrast with the idea of popular sovereignty, which the Levellers claimed to be formed by popular suffrage. '[I]t is the *Unity* of the Representer, not the *Unity* of the Represented, that maketh the Person *One*' (ibid. XVI. 114 [p. 82]). See Richard Tuck, *Hobbes* (Oxford, 1989), 66–7; J. P. Sommerville, *Thomas Hobbes: Political Ideas in Historical Context* (London, 1992), 60. Yet Hobbes's argument remains the same because sovereign power by representation (or authorization) is made by way of covenant as in the other two works. For a view from a different perspective, see D. P. Gauthier, *The Logic of Leviathan* (Oxford, 1969), 112–28.

[20] *De Cive*, II. 4. 100 [E: p. 53].

The sovereign monopolizes all sorts of judgement. The powers of legislature, administration, judicature, making war and peace, and anything else concerning the safety of his commonwealth, lie in his hands.[21] He decides what is good and what should be done, and controls religious doctrine. Even what does not seem to be directly related to political power can be under his control. No one other than the sovereign may decide who is witty, or who is worthy, etc.[22] The monopoly of such judgement is the first step by which the sovereign minimizes men's envy.

As long as every man relinquishes his private judgement concerning political obedience, there remains no room for resistance, and the sovereign power is absolute. More correctly, the power of any government has to be absolute in Hobbes's theory, because otherwise the state of war will return. Absoluteness—absence of resistance—is what logically belongs to the sovereign power. He does not argue that absoluteness would better secure the power of government over the subjects. Rather, the supremacy of government over individuals is attained only by the absence of resistance itself, since everyone had a right to all in the first place. The duty of obedience to the government solely *derives* from the renunciation of private judgement, and it is not the case that renunciation *tightens* duty which has its basis in something else. A large implication of Hobbes's message is this: one must concede that the power of government must be absolute if one wants to escape the state of war.

For Hobbes, the idea of mixed government, which asserted that the power of government should be divided, was a logical absurdity. As we shall see in detail in the next chapter, Hobbes acknowledged the rise of the English Polybian theory of mixed government through the 1640s, and escalated his hostility towards it accordingly. Yet his hostility seems odd when we recall the intentions of the writers involved in the debate over that theory between 1642 and 1644. After all, they shared Hobbes's concern. Their primary fear, like his, was not tyranny but anarchy. They deployed the Polybian idea so as to try to end a civil war, not to moderate the king's absolute power. Like Hobbes's theory of sovereignty, the English Polybian mixed government was a theory for peace in the crisis of the civil war. Together with Hobbes's *The Elements of Law*, those writings marked the opening of the new era of the history of English political theory in the early 1640s.

Although the two approaches shared a concern for internal peace, they

---

[21] *The Elements of Law*, II. 1. 8–11. 111–12; *De Cive*, VI. 6–10. 138–40 [E: pp. 94–5]; *Leviathan*, XX. 139 [p. 102].

[22] *Leviathan*, XXVII. 205 [p. 154].

conflicted in a radical manner. Hobbes's departure from mixed government will be better explained by his basic view of human nature than by the way he operated legal terms to construct absolute sovereignty. To get a better view of the gap between the two sides, we should now concentrate on Hobbes's starting-point, *bellum omnium in omnes.*

3. Private Judgement and Conscience

The heart of Hobbes's argument of *bellum omnium in omnes* was his unique view of private judgement. In that view, what things are is totally different from what we conceive them to be. The world we have in our mind is far removed from the external world because our internal world is constructed by imagination caused by motions of the nerves. Perfect knowledge of the external world is not, and should not be, the object of our intellectual activity. Rather, what is crucial for human activity is not 'truth' but 'image':

not truth, but image, maketh passion; and a tragedy affecteth no less than a murder if well acted. (*The Elements of Law*, I. 13. 7. 68)

What leads men to sedition and wars is passion caused by 'image'. The right usage of names and words, asserts Hobbes, does not consist in conveying the truth but in avoiding any unnecessary ambiguity.[23]

This clear distinction between the world outside our mind and the world of imagination in our mind is the basis of his refutation of the existence of a common standard of good and evil. Moreover, if men were allowed to compete against each other in judging what we should do and should not do in politics and religion, their competition of wits, caused by vainglory, would explode in a hellish manner.[24]

Hobbes does not believe that there is any point concerning the public good about which men could be expected to agree. The distinction between good and bad must not be left to individuals. As we have seen, the refutation of judgement by individuals—private judgement—is the basic tenet in Hobbes's argument. Once private moral judgement is rejected, and moral criteria are lost, the Aristotelian distinction between good governments and bad ones becomes meaningless.[25] Hobbes reduces the number of the forms of government from six (Aristotle's three good and three bad ones) to three. As long as the purpose of government is the peace and preservation

---

[23] *The Elements of Law*, I. 5. 8. 21; *Leviathan*, VI. 36 [p. 22].
[24] *De Cive*, I. 4–5. 93–4 [E: p. 46].
[25] *The Elements of Law*, II. 5. 1. 138.

of the subjects, there are only three sorts of government: monarchy, aristocracy, and democracy.[26]

Hobbes offers a bold challenge to the Aristotelian idea that man is a moral creature and should lead a good life in political society. Aristotle wanted to see men not merely live, but live well. If we cease to judge what we should do and what we should not do, or what is good and what is bad, we cannot ask how to live well. For instance, Christian theologians had discussed for centuries whether disobedience to a tyrant is allowed. They did so because the matter was morally important. They considered that the problem directly concerned the question how to lead a good life. The question whether obedience to a tyrant is morally good had been examined under the name of 'conscience'.

Hobbes did not hesitate to denounce the notion of conscience, since he believed that conscience is nothing but judgement: 'a mans Conscience, and his Judgement is the same thing'.[27] Hobbes explains why this particular word has been used to denote 'judgement':

men, vehemently in love with their own new opinions, (though never so absurd,) and obstinately bent to maintain them, gave those their opinions also that reverenced name of Conscience, as if they would have it seem unlawfull, to change or speak against them.   (*Leviathan*, VII. 48 [p. 31])

Since private judgement and (private) conscience are the same, the diversity of conscience causes disaster:[28]

if every man were allowed this liberty of following his conscience, in such difference of consciences, they would not live together in peace an hour.   (*The Elements of Law*, II. 5. 2. 139)

At this point, Hobbes emerges as a figure who has fundamentally questioned a premise shared by Ferne and Hunton. Can 'conscience' be trusted as a peacemaker?

As we saw in the previous chapter, conscience is given a key position by Ferne and Hunton. Admittedly, they do not resort to conscience as an

---

[26] *The Elements of Law*, II. 1. 3. 109; *De Cive*, VII. 1–2. 150–1 [E: pp. 106–7]; *Leviathan*, XIX. 129–30 [p. 95]; XLVI. 469–71 [pp. 376–7].

[27] *Leviathan*, XXIX. 223 [p. 168]. Yet it should be remembered that 'conscience' may survive as 'faith' under Hobbesian sovereignty, even if 'conscience' as 'private judgement' which concerns any outward political actions must not be a dictate to the individual. In fact, when it comes to Christian religion, Hobbes defends liberty of conscience in *Leviathan*. For this, see Appendix A below.

[28] An individual's conscience or judgement is sometimes called 'private conscience' or 'private reason'; judgement by the sovereign is 'public conscience' or 'public reason'. See *The Elements of Law*, II. 6. 12. 157; *Leviathan*, XXIX. 223 [p. 169]; XXXVII. 306 [p. 238].

instrument with which to examine the moral credibility of obedience in general. Even Ferne, who virtually denies any right to armed resistance, does not claim that disobedience to a tyrant is a sin. Hunton is further still from doing so. Equally, Hunton does not assert that to obey a tyrant is to commit a sin. Neither Hunton nor Ferne needs to introduce conscience into his discourse as long as the constitution works properly. Both writers resort to conscience in a very specific case. When the constitution breaks down—when the king and parliament are in serious conflict—the subjects are expected to follow their consciences 'as if there were no government'.[29] Philip Hunton calls on the subjects to follow their consciences because, in his eyes, that is the only way to restore 'the frame of the government',[30] that is, the English constitution. Henry Ferne makes the same appeal, in the confidence that the conscience of an individual will not fail to instruct him to obey the king.[31] Though Hunton allows the subjects to fight for the parliamentarians, while Ferne claims they should fight for the king, both men think that conscience alone can restore order and peace to the land. In other words, they cannot find any force other than conscience to bind men's obedience now that the government has collapsed. They believe that men would work for the maintenance and restoration of peace and order if they were left to their own private judgements.

Hobbes takes an opposite approach. He considers private judgement to be not the saviour from anarchy, but its cause. Hobbes attacked what Ferne and Hunton believed to be the fortress of peace and order. If the subjects were allowed to follow their conscience, wrote Hobbes, 'they would not live together in peace an hour'. Hunton and Ferne were in favour of mixed government, and Hobbes was a theorist of indivisible sovereignty. But well before they came to the question of mixed government, Hobbes and the two theorists had taken opposite directions. Hobbes started his theory at the point where Ferne and Hunton finished theirs.[32]

How, then, does Hobbes make his fresh start? How does he construct peace and order, after having destroyed the fortress of conventional theorists? More specifically, how does he expect to guarantee obedience to the sovereign?

---

[29] Philip Hunton, *A Treatise of Monarchie* (London, 1643), 29.
[30] Ibid. 63.
[31] Henry Ferne, *The Resolving of Conscience* (London, 1642), 4–5.
[32] Hunton and Ferne wrote after Hobbes's *The Elements of Law* circulated in 1640. But I have not found any evidence that either of them had read Hobbes before they wrote the pamphlets discussed above.

4. Fear and Covenant

In place of 'conscience', Hobbes gave the crucial role to 'fear'. In spite of the diversity of men's passions, there is one thing everybody shares, which is the fear of wounds and death. 'The Passion to be reckoned upon, is Fear.'[33] The sovereign has the common power, and obedience to the sovereign is to be secured by the fear caused by the common power.[34]

While punishment guarantees the obedience of the subject, the effect of punishment has a certain limit by its nature. Since there is '*gradus quidam timiditatis summus* [a certain most prominent degree of fear]' which supersedes the degree of fear of punishment, we cannot expect obedience from men who are threatened by a present imminent danger of death or wounds. If one asserts that men can be compelled to obey the sovereign by fear of punishment, one has to concede that men can be forced, by an imminent danger, to ignore the commands of the sovereign. When the subjects are exposed to a present danger, the sovereign is left with no means to prevent them from resisting.[35] That is why 'no covenant bindeth farther than in endeavour'.[36]

---

[33]   *Leviathan*, XIV. 99 [p. 70]. S. A. Lloyd denies the primary importance of the fear of death in Hobbes's scheme of peace and order in *Leviathan*, and claims that coercive power was less significant than education. To substantiate that claim, Lloyd repeatedly quotes a passage from *Behemoth*: 'if men know not their duty, what is there that can force them to obey the laws? An army, you will say. But what shall force the army?' (*Ideals as Interests in Hobbes's Leviathan* (Cambridge, 1992), 39, 101, 209, 254, 318; Hobbes, *English Works*, ed. Molesworth (1839–45), vi. 237). Yet that passage, written after the Restoration, is distant from the Hobbes of *Leviathan*.

[34]   *The Elements of Law*, I. 19. 6. 103.

[35]   'Mortem, vel vulnera, vel aliud damnum corporis inferenti, nemo *pactis* suis quibuscunque obligatur non resistere. Est enim in vnoquoque gradus quidam timiditatis summus, per quem, malum quod infertur apprehendit vt maximum, ideoque necessitate naturali quantum potest fugit, intelligiturque aliter facere non posse. Ad talem gradum metûs cùm peruentum fuerit, non est expectandum, quin vel fugâ, vel pugnâ sibi consulat. Cum igitur nemo teneatur ad impossibile, illi quibus *mors* (quod maximum naturæ malum est,) vel quibus vulnera, aut alia corporis damna inferuntur, nec ad ea ferenda constantes satis sunt, ea ferre non obligantur. . . . pacto non resistendi obligamur, *duorum malorum præsentium* eligere illud quod majus videbitur. Nam mors certa majus malum est quam pugna. Sed duorum malorum impossibile est non eligere minus. Tali ergo pacto teneremur ad impossibile, quod naturæ pactorum repugnat. [No man is oblig'd by any *Contracts* whatsoever not to resist him who shall offer to kill, wound, or any other way hurt his Body; for there is in every man a certain high degree of fear, through which he apprehends that evill which is done to him to be the greatest, and therefore by naturall necessity he shuns it all he can, and 'tis suppos'd he can doe no otherwise: When a man is arriv'd to this degree of fear, we cannot expect but he will provide for himself either by flight, or fight. Since therefore no man is tyed to *impossibilities*, they who are threatened either with *death*, (which is the greatest evill to nature) or wounds, or some other bodily hurts, and are not stout enough to bear them, are not obliged to endure them. . . . by the contract of not resisting, we are oblig'd of *two Evills* to make

[*See opposite page for n. 35 cont. and n. 36*]

Hobbes's claim that the right of defending cannot be transferred is derived from this limit to the fear of punishment.[37] Except in the case of the death penalty, the government will lose the obedience of its subjects when they are exposed to imminent danger. Thus 'a man is released of his subjection by conquest', since he is 'out of the protection of the sovereignty'.[38] As long as the sovereign protects the subjects from such danger, the obedience of the subjects is secured.[39] 'The end of Obedience is', therefore, 'Protection.'[40]

Here, what should be noted is that Hobbes does not make the obedience conditional. If it is conditional, private judgement must be ready to be exercised at any time in order to decide whether the condition has been kept or violated.[41] But if private judgement is given scope, the initial contract itself collapses. In Hobbes's theory, it must not be private judgement that tells the subject when the claim of obedience ceases. It may happen that men are set free from the duty of the contract, but only when the performance of the duty becomes impossible. Hobbes concedes nothing more than that in an emergency an escape from the duty of obedience is unavoidable. He

choice of that which seems the greater; for certaine Death is a greater evill then Fighting; but of two Evills it is impossible not to chuse the least: By such a Compact therefore we should be tyed to impossibilities, which is contrary to the very nature of compacts]' (*De Cive*, II. 18. 105 [E: pp. 58–9]). In the English translation, 'two Evills' should rather be 'two *present* Evills'. In the Hobbesian world, a man in normal circumstances chooses the lesser evil from a calm calculation made with his free will. Yet in this citation, the word 'present' is crucial, since the circumstances around the subject are not normal but constitute an emergency. This passage does not imply a rational and calm assessment of 'two' predictable 'Evills'. The subject here is forced to flee by the 'present' danger. Fleeing is a result not of calculation but of a response without deliberation, because the other choice, fighting, is 'impossible'. There is no room for the exercise of private judgement, and the subject's private judgement remains asleep at the moment of flight.

[36] *The Elements of Law*, II. 7. 14. 159.

[37] Ibid. I. 17. 2.88; *De Cive*, II. 18. 105 [E. pp. 58–9]; *Leviathan*, XIV. 93 [p. 66]; XXI. 153 [p. 114]; XXVII. 208 [p. 156].

[38] *The Elements of Law*, II. 2. 14–15. 126.

[39] 'The Obligation of Subjects to the Sovereign, is understood to last as long, and no longer, than the power lasteth, by which he is able to protect them' (*Leviathan*, XXI. 153 [p. 114]).

[40] *Leviathan*, XXI. 153 [p. 114]. Quentin Skinner is right to claim that the mutual relation between obedience and protection 'is not stated absolutely explicitly until the Review and Conclusion of *Leviathan* in 1651'. See Quentin Skinner, 'Conquest and Consent', in G. E. Aylmer (ed.), *The Interregnum* (London, 1972), 97. Skinner focuses upon the change in the presentations of Hobbes's idea of conquest, and not particularly upon the change in that idea itself: the change to which we shall turn in the following chapter, and in which we shall locate the uniqueness of *Leviathan*. For Skinner's more recent account, see Ch. 4, nn. 31, 40.

[41] Cf. Perez Zagorin, *A History of Political Thought in the English Revolution* (London, 1954), 185.

makes this concession because he thinks it impossible for human beings to resist such 'a certain most prominent degree of fear'.

That escape is based not upon a calculation of a lesser evil, but upon an instinctive response to the imminent greatest fear. In the case of the institution of a commonwealth in the state of nature, it is true, Hobbes argues that men would act upon a rational calculation of a lesser evil. A man in the state of nature, asserts Hobbes, is rationally expected to renounce his natural right since he is very likely to judge that he will better off if he gets rid of the state of mutual fear. Yet in the matter of the termination of obedience, Hobbes never argues in the same way. In this matter, the subject can be set free from the duty of obedience, but Hobbes does not argue that the subject is likely to judge that he will better off if he escapes. Unlike a man in the state of nature, the subject is not allowed to exercise his private judgement.

After the initial contract, which renounces private judgement as far as the question of political obedience is concerned, that judgement stays asleep until the contract becomes void. It is true that private judgement only sleeps, never dies. But in Hobbes's theory it cannot wake itself. Under the contract, private judgement can never tell itself that it is the right time to wake up. Only when overwhelmed by imminent danger does a man forget the contract. What Hobbes concedes is that there is a limit to men's capacity for fear-bearing. There exists a certain degree of fear beyond which a man will lose his rational thinking. When the imminent fear facing a man goes beyond a certain point, he ceases to be a rational creature who understands the idea of obligation and punishment. Following an instinctive response, he escapes from fear without any calculation. After his escape, he will come to himself, and will begin to exercise his private judgement. His private judgement, which fell asleep by the covenant, wakes only after it has been forced to rise and has begun to walk. As long as a man is forced by fear—first by fear of punishment, and secondly by the greater imminent fear—any exercise of his private judgement remains excluded from the process of emancipation from his previous obedience. The sovereign has the common power for punishment: the conqueror has the power which gives rise to the imminent greatest fear.

But how does the sovereign acquire the common power in the first place? If the common power derives from the obedience of the subject, the argument will fall into an endless circle. How is the making of the sovereign possible? How does the covenant making the sovereign power become effective? This is the problem which perplexes everyone reading Hobbes. It is fair to say that Hobbes's own explanation is far from clear. Perhaps the fundamental circularity of argument was a problem left unresolved even in his own mind.[42]

This predicament of Hobbes's sovereign-making contract theory has been discussed a great deal in modern Hobbes scholarship. Two points need to be suggested here.

First, his effort to justify that contract, if not very successful, does alter in the course of the three works. We may learn more about Hobbes from an analysis of this subtle difference than from an examination of the failure of his theory. Particularly, there can be found a clear cleavage upon this issue between, on the one hand, the two works of the 1640s, and, on the other, *Leviathan*. In the early works, in the process of instituting a commonwealth in the state of nature, the weight of the covenant and that of the common power are kept even, and this even relationship makes his argument unclear and gives a strong impression of circularity. But this was because, particularly in *De Cive*, Hobbes made every effort to find a logical exit from the state of nature, where no fear of punishment by the common power is available to defend the sovereign-making contract.[43] In *Leviathan*, however, he seems to have abondoned this sort of effort. The common power gains weight in his argument, and becomes superior to the covenant.

Secondly, Harrington, who was so keen to find fault with Hobbes, somehow overlooked the circularity of his argument. He could have exploited this weakness of his opponent to great effect, but did not.

Those two points are closely linked together. In *Leviathan*, Hobbes corrected his previous understanding of the relationship of the common power to the covenant. That correction, which was made in response to the events of the time, was a solution to the problem of circularity. In fact, his argument in *Leviathan* was less complicated than that in his early writings. Yet this clarity in *Leviathan* cost him something valuable, and opened the door to the criticism made by Harrington. In the next chapter we shall analyse the Hobbes of *Leviathan*.

---

[42] Tuck, *Hobbes*, 68. For different views, see Gauthier, *The Logic of Leviathan*, 59; Noel Malcolm, 'Hobbes and Spinoza', in J. H. Burns (ed.), *The Cambridge History of Political Thought, 1450–1700*, 540–1; Sommerville, *Thomas Hobbes: Political Ideas in Historical Context*, 54.

[43] For this effort of Hobbes's, see Appendix C below. Hobbes used the notion of 'mutual fear' to end the circularity of his argument.

4
LEVIATHAN AND THE
ENGLISH REPUBLIC,
1649–1653:
Sword, Victory, Conquest

1. Anarchy and Mixed Government

In the 1640s, when the constitution of the king-in-parliament broke down, the 'modern prudence' of Fortescuian mixed government offered no effective formula for unity and piece. Two alternative solutions were proposed: the Polybian idea of mixed government—'ancient prudence'—and Hobbes's idea of sovereignty.

Both of them failed. War broke out and proved long and bitter. In 1649 King Charles was executed, the House of Lords abolished, and England declared to be a Commonwealth. The English constitution, to which the writers of the *Answer* and others had adapted the Polybian idea, disappeared.

Yet in the years 1650–1, when Hobbes wrote *Leviathan* in Paris, he was still able to use the argument he had set out in *The Elements of Law* in 1640 to describe what had happened in England. Sovereignty had now been transferred from 'one man', King Charles, to 'one council (assembly)', the Rump Parliament.[1] His theory could urge the English people to obey the Rump on the same grounds as those on which he had told them to obey Charles. In his eyes, no more than the government of Charles I was that of the Rump mixed.

Hobbes took the Fortescuian mixed government and the Polybian mixed government to be different things. Even so, he believed that both had been contrived to limit sovereignty and were therefore fallacious and dangerous. In his eyes, 'ancient prudence' was as damaging as 'modern prudence'.

In *The Elements of Law*, Hobbes, in defending the king's absolute sovereignty, denounced two types of critics of it. The first were those who tried

---

[1] *The Elements of Law*, I. 19. 6. 103; *Leviathan*, XIX. 132 [p. 97].

to limit and moderate the sovereign power by subjecting it to the people's consent. The second were those who conceived of a functional division within the government.[2] Apparently, Hobbes thought that those who appealed to 'consent' were different people from those who appealed to 'mixed government'. Hobbes's understanding of consent corresponded to the position taken by Fortescue and Henry Parker; his understanding of mixed government, to the position taken by Polybius and by the authors of the *Answer to the Nineteen Propositions*. Both ideas were harmful, in Hobbes's account, for both endorsed the exercise of private judgement.

Hobbes maintained that the renunciation of private judgement by the subjects amounts to the making of sovereignty. He reduces the question of the scope and nature of the supreme power to a simple one: a choice between the two extremes, all or nothing. Assertions that the power of government can be limited or divided are logically absurd, and therefore require no discussion. Suppose the power of government is limited by 'fundamental law'. If the subjects think that the government has violated the limitation, they will be set free from the duty of obedience, and be allowed to decide what to do regardless of the dictate of the government. At this point, private judgement returns, and the state of war will be resumed accordingly.[3] Similarly, in the case of mixed government, as long as the three parts agree, the government is absolute. When the three disagree, private judgement returns, and the government will fall into anarchy.[4]

Certainly, admits Hobbes, no one would welcome the condition of subjects under absolute sovereignty. But the choice men face is not between absolute sovereignty and moderate sovereignty, but between civil government and the state of war. We have to accept absolute sovereignty, '*quoniam res humanæ sine incommodo esse non possunt* [because humane affairs cannot possibly be without some inconveniences]'.[5] Indeed, theorists of mixed or limited government do not know how miserable the state of war is. Hobbes in *The Elements of Law* deplored the fact that

men that have not had the experience of that miserable estate, to which men are reduced by long war, think so hard a condition that they cannot easily acknowledge, such covenants and subjection, on their parts, as are here set down, to have been ever necessary to their peace. (*The Elements of Law*, II. 1. 13. 113)

[2] Ibid. II. 1. 13–16. 113–15.
[3] Ibid. II. 1. 14. 114.
[4] Ibid. II. 1. 16. 115.
[5] *De Cive*, 'Preface', p. 83 [E: p. 36]. And see also ibid. VI. 13, 'Annotation', p. 143 [E: p. 99]. Both passages are added in the Amsterdam edition which was published in 1647—after the first English civil war.

In 1640 Englishmen had not had 'the experience of that miserable estate'. Perhaps, by 'long war', he meant the wars of religion on the other side of the Channel, in which case 'men' would have been Continental men. In *Leviathan*, however, his words had a clear application to England.

> But a man may here object, that the Condition of Subjects is very miserable ... not considering that the estate of Man can never be without some incommodity or other; and that the greatest, that in any forme of Government can possibly happen to the people in generall, is scarce sensible, in respect of the miseries, and horrible calamities, that accompany a Civill Warre.   (*Leviathan*, XVIII. 128 [p. 94])

Hobbes condemns ideas which favour the subject's liberty: these are 'seditious doctrines' whose poison causes 'the *Diseases* of a Commonwealth'.[6] Those who dislike tyranny are merely infected by '*Tyrannophobia*', just as dogs go mad from '*Hydrophobia*, or *fear of Water*'.[7]

For Hobbes, the Polybian idea of mixed government, no less than the Fortescuian mixed government of prerogative and liberty, was a vain attempt to defend fanciful liberty under an absolute sovereign. The main tenor of his criticism of mixed government remained the same from 1640.[8] Yet between 1640 and 1651 that criticism became more specific and gained in weight. How it became specific can be seen from a comparison between the two passages below, the first from *The Elements of Law*, and the other from *De Cive*. In *The Elements of Law*, Hobbes points to those who, hating 'absolute subjection', 'have devised a government as they think mixed of the three sorts of sovereignty'.

> As for example: they suppose the power of making laws given to some great assembly democratical; the power of judicature to some other assembly; and the administration of the laws to a third, or to some one man; and this policy they call mixed monarchy, or mixed aristocracy, or mixed democracy, according as any of these three sorts do most visibly predominate.   (*The Elements of Law*, II. 1. 15. 115)

Here, Hobbes attacked a general model of mixed government rather than the particular model of mixed monarchy. Apparently, it was not an English model, for in it the law-making power belongs to 'some great assembly

---

[6] *Leviathan*, XXIX. 223 [p. 168].

[7] Ibid. XXI. 149–50 [pp. 110–11]; XXIX. 226 [p. 171]. See also *The Elements of Law*, II. 5. 1. 137; II. 8. 10. 174; *De Cive*, VII. 3. 151 [E: p. 107].

[8] '[T]he sovereignty is indivisible; and that seeming mixture of several kinds of government, not mixture of the things themselves, but confusion in our understandings, that cannot find out readily to whom we have subjected ourselves' (*The Elements of Law*, II. 1. 16. 115); 'what is it to divide the Power of a Common-wealth, but to Dissolve it? for Powers divided mutually destroy each other'; 'although few perceive, that such government, is not government, but division of the Common-wealth into three Factions' (*Leviathan*, XXIX. 225 [p. 170]; 228 [p. 172]).

democratical' rather than, as in the English constitution, to all the three components. No English theorist of mixed government had insisted that the law-making power ought to be confined to the House of Commons.

Yet in *De Cive*, the passage corresponding to the above quotation from *The Elements of Law* reads:

For example, if the naming of Magistrates, and the arbitration of War, and Peace, should belong to the King, Judicature to the *Lords*, and contribution of Monies to the *People*, and the power of making Lawes too *altogether*, this kind of State would they call a *mixt Monarchie* forsooth.   (*De Cive*, VII. 4. 152 [E: p. 108])[9]

Here, the model Hobbes criticizes is specifically applicable to England. The model is a 'mixed monarchy' rather than a 'mixed government'. In *The Elements of Law*, the division of the functions of government is explained by resort to general terms: the legislative, the judicature, and the administrative power. But the model in *De Cive* is more specific. The functions allotted to the king are detailed, and are exactly the same as those described by Sir Thomas Smith.[10] At the same time, the power of raising money is given to '*populus* [the people]' rather than '*omnes* [altogether]'. '*Magnates* [the Lords]' are given the judicature. These features coincide with those of the English constitution described in the *Answer to the Nineteen Propositions*.[11] The distinguishing feature of this model is that the law-making power is given to *omnes*, that is the king-in-parliament, and not to *populus*.

In 1640, it seems, Hobbes saw the main threat to his arguments in the theory of government by consent. That theory was the weapon of the defenders of the subjects' property, who used it to justify resistance to the king.[12] Hobbes, who noticed the danger of that prevalent theory, bitterly denounced it in *The Elements of Law*. But what of the Polybian theory of mixed government? It is possible that in *The Elements of Law*, Hobbes criticized it not with the current political situation in mind but in order to endorse the familiar objection to mixed government raised by Jean

---

[9] The Latin passage reads: 'Exempli causa, si nominatio Magistratuum, & Arbitrium belli & pacis, penes *Regem* esset, iudicia apud *magnates*, pecuniarum contributio penes *populum*, & legum ferendarum potentia, penes omnes simul. Huiusmodi statum vocarent *Monarchiam mixtam*.' John Sanderson quotes the same passage from *De Cive*, but does not point to the difference between *De Cive* and *The Elements of Law*: 'The *Answer to the Nineteen Propositions* Revisited', *Political Studies*, 32 (1984), 629. See also Ch. 2, n. 5.

[10] Smith summarizes the functions given to the king himself as two: 'making of battell and peace, or truce with forraine nations' and 'choosing and election of the chiefe officers and magistrates', *De Republica Anglorum*, ed. Mary Dewar (Cambridge, 1982), 88.

[11] *Historical Collections*, ed. John Rushworth, part III. vol. i (London, 1691), 731–2. See Sect. 2.2 above.

[12] See J. P. Sommerville, *Politics and Ideology in England, 1604–1640* (London, 1986), 69–77.

Bodin.[13] In *De Cive*, however, Hobbes's fear of the Polybian idea may have extended from the world of bookish political thought to that of practical politics.[14]   Perhaps the attempt to redefine the English constitution in terms of the Polybian idea of mixed government had already become powerful enough for Hobbes to feel the need to attack it in a precise manner. This would be why he had to attack an Anglicized version of Polybian mixed government in *De Cive*.

Hobbes had become alert, it seems, to the rise of the English idea of Polybian mixed government through the 1640s. After the English constitution had vanished, he wrote in *Leviathan*:

> If there had not first been an opinion received of the greatest part of *England*, that these Powers were divided between the King, and the Lords, and the House of Commons, the people had never been divided, and fallen into this Civill Warre; first between those that disagreed in Politiques; and after between the Dissenters about the liberty of Religion; which have so instructed men in this point of Soveraign Right, that there be few now (in *England*,) that do not see, that these Rights are inseparable.   (*Leviathan*, XVIII. 127 [p. 93])[15]

While it is a matter for argument whether that idea was really the main cause of the civil wars, there is no mistaking Hobbes's antagonism to the English theory of mixed government.[16] But when he wrote *Leviathan*, the new English government was not mixed. It consisted of a single chamber.

[13] Hobbes invokes Jean Bodin when condemning mixed government, but never refers to him again in *De Cive* or in *Leviathan*. In *The Elements of Law*, Hobbes wrote 'if there were a commonwealth, wherein the rights of sovereignty were divided, we must confess with Bodin, Lib. II. chap. I. *De Republica*, that they are not rightly to be called commonwealths, but the corruption of commonwealths' (II. 8. 7. 172–3). Sir Robert Filmer cited the same passage of *De Republica* in his *The Anarchy of a Limited or Mixed Monarchy . . .*, published in 1648. For this, see *Patriarcha and Other Writings*, ed. J. P. Sommerville (Cambridge, 1991), 163.

[14] Yet as I emphasized in Sect. 2.1, we cannot tell where Hobbes first encountered the Polybian definition of the English constitution. *De Cive* was written well before the *Answer to the Nineteen Propositions* appeared.

[15] Richard Tuck explains that, in the place of 'those that disagreed in Politiques . . . Religion', the manuscript reads, 'the temporall factions of parliamentarians and royalists, by the name of Roundheads and Cavaliers, and since between the doctrinall factions of presbyterians and Independents': See Tuck's footnote on that page.

[16] Another indication of Hobbes's increasing antagonism to the idea of mixed government in *Leviathan* is found in his description of republican Rome. Though, earlier, he writes that Rome was a democracy, where the people had the sovereignty, in *Leviathan* Rome is regarded as an example of seditious government where no one could claim the sovereignty: 'if we should suppose the people of Rome to have had the absolute sovereignty of the Roman state, and to have chosen them a council by the name of the senate, and that to this senate they had given the supreme power of making laws, reserving nevertheless to themselves, in direct and express terms, the whole right and title of the sovereignty, . . . I say, this grant of the people to the senate is of no effect, and the power of making laws is in the people still' (*The Elements of Law*, II. 8. 7. 173); 'whereas the stile of the antient Roman Common-wealth, was, *The*

Thus Hobbes did not need to amend his idea of undivided sovereignty. Yet when he applied his theory to the current events in England, he seems to have tilted a delicate balance in his theory, and to have deprived his earlier argument of its strength.

2. Word and Sword

In *Leviathan*, of course, Hobbes maintained his basic formula that the renunciation of private judgements by the subjects leads to the making of sovereignty. The subjects' obedience to the sovereign is due to two factors, the binding force of the sovereign-making covenant itself, and (the fear of punishment caused by) the common power. As is suggested above, the contract and the common power—which will be depicted as 'word' and 'sword' in *Leviathan*—overlap and assist each other. Those two factors are in an even partnership in his system, and Hobbes does not say which one should come first.[17]

Yet in *Leviathan* the relationship between the two has been changed. The notion of 'word' in his theory lost its weight against that of 'sword'. This shift of balance leads to the change of the relationship between 'institution' and 'conquest' accordingly. This section focuses upon that shift, which may look a small one, but was to have a significant consequence.

In his early writings—in *The Elements of Law* and *De Cive*—Hobbes emphasized the role of 'covenant' in determining how the sovereign acquired the common power in the state of nature. Although Hobbes had reservations about the effectiveness of a covenant in general, he gave a covenant a certain weight in the making of the common power. The common power was assumed to be held as a result of a covenant, the binding force of which derived from the promise itself. In *Leviathan*, however, the binding force of a covenant was discredited. A covenant generates no binding force, Hobbes argues in 1651, unless it is substantiated by the common power.

Senate, and People of Rome; neither Senate, nor People pretended to the whole Power; which first caused the seditions, of *Tiberius Gracchus, Caius Gracchus, Lucius Saturninus*, and others; and afterwards the warres between the Senate and the People, under *Marius* and *Sylla*; and again under *Pompey* and *Caesar*, to the Extinction of their Democracy, and the setting up of Monarchy' (*Leviathan*, XXIX. 222 [p. 168]).

[17] If the sovereign-making covenant and the common power seem to make for a chicken-and-egg relationship, and if Hobbes's argument looks circular, it is because he had held the two notions in so even a balance in *The Elements of Law* and *De Cive*. In fact, he seems to have found an exit from the trap of circularity. See Appendix C below.

As far as *The Elements of Law* is concerned, two sorts of distinction, which indicate his high regard for the binding force of covenant, need to be pointed out. First, Hobbes distinguishes government 'by consent' from that 'by covenant', only the latter of which was reliable in his view.[18] Secondly, he distinguishes a covenant from a law. They differ, he claims, because 'a covenant is the declaration of a man's own will'.[19] A law is considered to be valid only after the common power has been established by the sovereign-making covenant. That distinction between covenant and law is also found in the first edition (Paris, 1642) of *De Cive*, where he criticizes Aristotle's view of law.[20] Beneath his distinction between covenant and law, there lay the idea that 'covenants oblige us (*Pacto obligamur*)'. He believed that 'the verbal bonds of covenant' can secure obedience no less firmly than 'natural bonds', that is, 'chains, or other like forcible custody'.[21] He had surely been committed to the idea that 'covenants oblige us' as late as 1647, when he added a note to support it in the second edition of *De Cive* published in Amsterdam.[22]

In *Leviathan*, however, he seems to have abandoned those two distinctions. First, he deprived the notion of covenant of its special status. When

---

[18] '[C]onsent (by which I understand the concurrence of many men's wills to one action) is not sufficient security for their common peace, without the erection of some common power, by the fear whereof they may be compelled both to keep the peace amongst themselves, and to join their strengths together, against a common enemy. And that this may be done, there is no way imaginable, but only union; which is defined . . . to be the involving or including the wills of many . . . in the will of one man, or of one COUNCIL. . . . The making of union consisteth in this, that every man by covenant oblige himself' (*The Elements of Law*, I. 19. 6–7. 103).

[19] '[W]hatsoever is a law to a man, respecteth the will of another, and the declaration thereof. But a covenant is the declaration of a man's own will. And therefore a law and a covenant differ . . . a covenant obligeth by promise of an action, or omission, especially named and limited; but a law bindeth by a promise of obedience in general, whereby the action to be done, or left undone, is referred to the determination of him, to whom the covenant is made' (*The Elements of Law*, II. 10. 2. 185).

[20] '[Aristotle] confounds *Contracts* with *Lawes*, which he ought not to have done; for *Contract is a promise, Law a command. In Contracts we say, I will do this; In Lawes, Doe this. Contracts* oblige us, Lawes *tie* us fast, being obliged. A *Contract* obligeth of *it self*, The *Law* holds the party obliged by vertue of the universall *Contract* of yeelding obedience' (*De Cive*, XIV. 2. 206 [E: p. 169]). In this quotation the word 'contract', used in place of 'covenant', is the choice of the translator, not of Hobbes. The original Latin word is '*pactum*'.

[21] *The Elements of Law*, II. 3. 3. 128.

[22] The newly attached note in the 1647 edition reads: '*Clarius ergo hoc dico. Pacto obligari hominem, id est, propter promissionem præstare debere. Lege vero obligatum teneri, id est, metu pœnae quæ in Lege constituitur ad præstationem cogi.* [*More cleerly therefore, I say thus, That a man is obliged by his contracts, that is, that he ought to performe for his promise sake; but that the Law tyes him being obliged, that is to say, it compells him to make good his promise, for fear of the punishment appointed by the Law*]' (*De Cive*, XIV. 2, 'Annotation', p. 207 [E: p. 170], Hobbes's italic).

he explains the notions of covenant and civil law in *Leviathan*, the distinction between covenant and law has vanished.[23]

The other distinction has been eroded, too. In *Leviathan*, when he attacked an idea of limiting the sovereign power by subjecting it to the people's consent, he no longer distinguished between government by consent and that by covenant. Previously, when he denounced that idea, he had allocated the word 'consent' to his opponent, and appropriated the word 'covenant' for his own argument of sovereignty. Yet the Hobbes of *Leviathan* did not hesitate to use the word 'covenant', and openly denied that a covenant could have any binding force, unless it is substantiated by the sword.

The opinion that any Monarch receiveth his Power by Covenant, that is to say on Condition, proceedeth from want of understanding this easie truth, that Covenants being but words, and breath, have no force to oblige, contain, constrain, or protect any man, but what it has from the publique Sword. (*Leviathan*, XVIII. 123 [p. 89])

Here the well-known contrast between word and sword appears. 'The force of Words', Hobbes maintains, is 'too weak to hold men to the performance of their Covenants'. 'Covenants, without the Sword, are but Words, and of no strength to secure a man at all.' By his repetitive use of this contrast, the binding force held by a covenant alone in his earlier works has been discredited.[24] He has given up his commitment to the idea that 'covenants oblige us'.

Thus the Hobbes of *Leviathan* delivers a serious blow to his own notion of 'a commonwealth by institution'. If words themselves have no force, no one will keep the sovereign-making contract to establish a commonwealth, since at the moment of its institution 'the public sword' is not yet available. If a sword has to be established before a covenant is made, no commonwealths can be instituted in the state of nature. In *Leviathan* the notion of the institution of commonwealth can hardly be a credible exit from the state of nature. Yet in spite of that, the Hobbes of *Leviathan* was still able to explain to himself what had happened in England. Even though 'institution' was dropped, 'conquest' offered an alternative.

From the beginning of his political writing, Hobbes had described two methods of creating sovereigns: a commonwealth by institution, and a commonwealth by acquisition; that is, by conquest.[25] The crucial difference between the two is that the power of punishment is, in the latter category,

---

[23] See *Leviathan*, XIV. 94 [p. 66]; XXVI. 183–4 [pp. 136–7].

[24] Ibid. XIV. 99 [p. 70]; XVII. 117 [p. 85].

[25] *The Elements of Law*, II. 1. 1. 108; *De Cive*, V. 12. 135 [E: p. 90]; *Leviathan*, XVII. 121 [p. 88].

given *before* the covenant is made. In the case of a commonwealth by acquisition, the conquered make a covenant in which they accept the conqueror
as the sovereign. The conqueror has by definition, before the covenant is
made, a formidable power which enables him to kill the people at his
mercy. As soon as the covenant is made, the conqueror, now the sovereign,
is to use the formidable power, now the common power, to force the subjects to keep the covenant by fear of punishment by death.

In this case, unlike in the case of a commonwealth by institution, Hobbes
was not troubled by the question of the power-basis of punishment at the
very moment the covenant is being made. By definition in his argument,
the power-basis of punishment is given to the conqueror in advance.[26]
Thus as far as a commonwealth by acquisition is concerned, Hobbes is
able to bypass the awkward circular argument around the initial sovereign-
making covenant. Now the common power gives the covenant its binding
force, and never vice versa.

'The Rights and Consequences' of a sovereign by acquisition 'are the very
same with those of a Soveraign by Institution', he assures us in *Leviathan*.[27]
Admittedly, it was not until in 'A Review, and Conclusion' that he
employed the notion of a commonwealth by acquisition to acknowledge
who newly conquered England. However, well before writing that
'Review' the Hobbes of *Leviathan* seems to have resolved to use that
notion to interpret current events. The old government, he believed, had
been dissolved by the civil wars, and the subjects were thus set free from
all obligations. The Rump Parliament and Charles II were still fighting,
and the outcome was not yet foreseeable. But no matter who might finally
emerge as the conqueror, Hobbes was ready, without any reservation, to
recognize the conqueror to be the new sovereign.

This explains his cynical view of 'covenant'.[28] As far as the interpretation of
the civil wars is concerned, he no longer felt any need to emphasize the binding
force of the covenant itself. Rather, once he dared to recognize that the govern-

---

[26] Here Hobbes smartly excuses himself from explaining why and how the conqueror
acquired the conquering power in the first place.

[27] *Leviathan*, XX. 142 [p. 104]. The equivalents in the early writings read: 'So that whatsoever rights be in the one, the same also be in the other' (*The Elements of Law*, II. 4. 10. 135);
'yet being constituted, it hath al [*sic*] the same properties, and the Right of authority is every
where the same, insomuch as it is not needfull to speak any thing of them apart' (*De Cive*,
IX. 10. 168 [E: p. 126]).

[28] That cynicism seems to me to undermine the interpretations of *Leviathan* as a royalist
tract which have been proposed by Glenn Burgess, 'Contexts for the Writing and Publication
of Hobbes's *Leviathan*', *History of Political Thought*, 2 (1990), 682–3, and Hans-Dieter
Metzger, *Thomas Hobbes und die Englische Revolution 1640–1660* (Stuttgart and Bad
Cannstatt, 1991), 149–50.

ment had been dissolved by the civil wars, he had to eliminate all legal terms which had created obligations to the former government. That was what he did in *Leviathan* when he denied that any binding force can derive from a word. By contrast, until 1647, he was ready to approve any covenants requiring obedience to Charles I, unless the subjection were conditional.

Yet Hobbes's attack upon 'covenant' virtually involves an assault on the basis of his own notion of a commonwealth by institution. As a result, in *Leviathan*, Hobbes struck a delicate balance between the two notions, word and sword, and, consequently, between institution and conquest. In fact, he had sustained that balance in his early writings. The Hobbes of *Leviathan* eloquently defended the notion of a commonwealth by acquisition, but at the expense of that by institution.[29]

Perhaps Hobbes felt that if only he could successfully defend 'conquest', he need no longer trouble himself with the fate of 'covenant'. It is true that he still held the notion of a commonwealth by institution, but its primary role in his argument was now to explain 'the Rights and Consequences' of a sovereign by 'conquest'. That notion no longer offers an exit from the state of nature.[30] His withdrawal from the notion of a commonwealth by institution simplified his argument and made it less ambiguous. The relationship between the common power and the covenant was no longer circular. What was required first was not the covenant but the common power. In the case of a commonwealth by acquisition, this requirement would be fulfilled with no difficulty. Hobbes concentrated his argument on conquest when he tried to understand recent events in England. But that attempt proved less easy than it seemed, as we shall now see.

3. Conquest and Victory

Hobbes endorsed the new government of the English Commonwealth in an explicit manner in 'A Review, and Conclusion' of *Leviathan*.[31] Yet even before that the Hobbes of *Leviathan* was waiting for the civil wars to be

[29] In *The Elements of Law* (II. 1. 1. 108), when Hobbes explains 'two ways of erecting a body politic', one, by 'institution', is said to be 'like a creation out of nothing by human wit', and the other, by 'compulsion', to be like a generation 'out of natural force'. But in the corresponding section of *Leviathan* (XVII. 121 [p. 88]), the phrase 'out of nothing by human wit' vanishes: 'The attaining to this Soveraigne Power, is by two wayes. One, by Naturall force; as when a man maketh his children . . . The other, is when men agree amongst themselves, to submit to some Man, or Assembly of men, voluntarily, on confidence to be protected by him against all others.'

[30] This might be the reason the Hobbes of *Leviathan* used the phrase 'the condition of nature' in place of 'the state of nature'.

[31] See Quentin Skinner, 'Conquest and Consent', in G. E. Aylmer (ed.), *The Interregnum*

settled by a conquest. This attitude of his was shown in his frequent equation of 'conquest' and 'victory' as well as in his contrast between 'word' and 'sword'. Earlier, in *The Elements of Law* the way of making a commonwealth other than by 'institution' (or 'mutual agreement') was explained to be 'a conquest'. But in *Leviathan*, the word 'victory' is used as often as the word 'conquest'.[32] A victory in a civil war, that is, an internal invasion, appears, alongside a conquest by foreign invasions, as a main factor deciding the location of sovereignty.[33] The victor of a civil war would acquire the public sword in exactly the same manner as a foreign invader. There is no reason to distinguish between those two in terms of the obedience due to the victor. On the other hand, when Hobbes rejected the exercise by the subjects of private judgements concerning political obedience, the prevention of civil war was far more important to him than the prevention of foreign invasion.

Particularly, in the early writings, he deliberately failed to make a clear distinction between real civil wars and a war in the state of nature, and threatened that a war in the state of nature would last forever unless the exercise of private judgements were banned. '[A] War of all men, against all men', he warned in *De Cive*, is 'perpetuall in its own nature', and 'cannot be ended by Victory'.[34] In *Leviathan*, however, the idea of 'the

(London, 1972), 79–98. For the debate concerning obedience to *de facto* authority, see John M. Wallace, *Destiny His Choice: The Loyalism of Andrew Marvell* (Cambridge, 1968), ch. i. More recently Skinner has refined his interpretation. In *Leviathan*, he believes, Hobbes emphasized that the concepts of conquest and consent were not incompatible, and insisted that a man who had submitted to the Rump must have done so 'freely'. That man was thus not the Rump's 'slave' but its 'subject': 'Thomas Hobbes on the Proper Signification of Liberty', *Transactions of the Royal Historical Society*, 40 (1990), 145–51. I concur with this judgement, but am not persuaded that the position Skinner describes is, as he suggests, 'a revision of [Hobbes's] earlier arguments'. Even in *The Elements of Law* conquerors are said to obtain the sovereign power through covenants, which Hobbes consistently regards as the products of free choice (ibid. II. 3. 2. 128). Moreover, in *The Elements of Law* Hobbes distinguishes 'servants' from slaves, for servants are tied to the master 'by the bonds of covenant', slaves only by 'natural bonds' (ibid. II. 3. 3. 128). The distinction between servants and slaves, which Skinner seems to overlook, reappears in *Leviathan*: 'after such Covenant made, the Vanquished is a SERVANT, and not before: for by the word *Servant* . . . is not meant a Captive, which is kept in prison, or bonds, . . . (for such men, (commonly called Slaves) have no obligation at all . . .)' (ibid. XX. 141 [p. 104]). See also J. P. Sommerville, *Thomas Hobbes: Political Ideas in Historical Context* (Cambridge, 1992), 181–2.

[32] 'Dominion acquired by Conquest, or Victory in war, is that which some Writers call DESPOTICALL . . . It is not therefore the Victory, that giveth the right of Dominion over the Vanquished, but his own Covenant. Nor is he obliged because he is Conquered; that is to say, beaten, and taken, or put to flight; but because he commeth in, and Submitteth to the Victor; Nor is the Victor obliged by an enemies rendering himselfe' (*Leviathan*, XX. 141 [pp. 103–4]).

[33] '[W]hen in a warre (forraign, or intestine,) the enemies get a finall Victory' (*Leviathan*, XXIX. 230 [p. 174]).

[34] '[T]he naturall state of men, before they entr'd into Society, was a meer War, and that not simply, but a War of all men, against all men. . . . But it is perpetuall in its own nature,

equality of those that strive' is virtually denied. He claims that fear of men, unlike fear of 'Spirits Invisible', cannot enforce the performance of covenants 'before Civill Society', 'because in the condition of meer Nature, the inequality of Power is not discerned, but by the event of Battell'.[35] Hobbes, it seems, has changed his original position. He emphasizes, at least in this passage, that inequality of power does exist. Now, a civil war can even be a process in which this inequality of power, having been obscure, will be revealed. If a man has more power than others, he will be the victor. If it is wrong to think that a civil war 'cannot be ended by Victory', *bellum omnium in omnes* may involve the making of the public sword rather than its disintegration.

His argument then proceeds in a strange direction. What makes war perpetual, he asserts, is not the nature of civil war itself but the attitude of those people who refuse to accept the victor as their sovereign. Hobbes claims that people addicted to Greek philosophy never know

(till perhaps a little after a Civill warre) that without such Arbitrary government, such Warre must be perpetuall; and that it is Men, and Arms, not Words, and Promises, that make the Force and Power of the Laws. (*Leviathan*, XLVI. 471 [p. 377])

The English civil wars began as a dispute over the power of the sovereign against the danger against which Hobbes had warned in 1640. The war was a hellish and abhorrent experience, as he predicted in 1640 and 1642 that it would be, and as he reflected in 1651 that it had been. However, the war did not last forever. The parliament emerged as the victor of the civil war. Or, more correctly, at the very end of *Leviathan* Hobbes considered the war to have been won by the parliament in 'A Review, and Conclusion'.

The famous passage which follows is certainly a clear endorsement of the new government. But more significantly in our perspective, it also acknowledges the shortcomings of his former account of conquest.

I find by divers English Books lately printed, that the Civill warres have not yet sufficiently taught men, in what point of time it is, that a Subject becomes obliged to the Conquerour; nor what is Conquest; nor how it comes about, that it obliges men

---

because in regard of the equality of those that strive, it cannot be ended by Victory' (*De Cive*, I. 12–13. 96 [E: p. 49]). The equivalent in *Leviathan* reads, 'it is manifest, that during the time men live without a common Power to keep them all in awe, they are in that condition which is called Warre; and such a warre, as is of every man, against every man' (*Leviathan*, XIII. 88 [p. 62]).

[35] *Leviathan*, XIV. 99 [p. 70]. Similarly, as for the question whether a child belongs to the father, 'there is not alwayes that difference of strength, or prudence between the man and the woman, as that the right can be determined without War' (*Leviathan*, XX. 139 [p. 102]).

to obey his Laws: Therefore for farther satisfaction of men therein, I say, the point of time, wherein a man becomes subject to a Conquerour, is that point, wherein having liberty to submit to him, he consenteth, either by expresse words, or by other sufficient sign, to be his Subject.   (*Leviathan*, 'A Review, and Conclusion', 484 [p. 390])

Here, Hobbes concedes the existence of the question at what point of time the earlier sovereign is replaced by the new sovereign by conquest, and recognizes that this question has arisen in England. In his early account of conquest, the question was left untackled. Indeed, it could not be properly handled within that theory of conquest.

In many places, particularly before *Leviathan*, Hobbes wrote as if a government would be replaced overnight by conquest, and a new government would seize power as soon as the old one collapsed. But in fact, especially in the case of a civil war, there comes a certain grey-zone period of time in which people have to choose which government they should obey. While no one around Hobbes had seen how William I conquered England, everybody knew how the English civil wars were fought. In the latter case, very few people felt compelled to change their allegiance on the spot, as Hobbes's early writings implied that they would. Most English people had to face several choices—which side they should take when the wars broke out, and to which government they should owe allegiance thereafter. The grey-zone period of time lasted many years for them.

In *Leviathan*, for the first time, Hobbes makes an attempt to define the moment at which defeat is to be recognized, and at what point obedience to the defeated power ceases. When a man's means of living is in the power of the enemy, Hobbes says, he may obey the enemy.[36] As a soldier, if his old government fails either to keep the field, or to give him the means of subsistence, he may submit himself to the new one.[37]

According to Hobbes's (original) theory of obedience by fear, a man will be set free from obedience only if the fear of imminent death or wounds overwhelms fear of punishment. In the case of conquest, there can be, in the process of termination of the obedience to the former sovereign,[38]

---

[36] *Leviathan*, XXI. 154 [p. 114]; 'A Review, and Conclusion', 484 [p. 390]. Yet the conditions for the termination of obedience seem to have been more relaxed in 'A Review, and Conclusion'. In ch. 21, a man might terminate his obedience 'because he had no other way to preserve himself' (ibid. 154 [p. 114]). But in 'A Review, and Conclusion' he is described as free to 'refuse' to submit if he wants (ibid. 485 [p. 391]).

[37] Ibid. 485 [pp. 390–1].

[38] See Sect. 3.4 above. Of course, after the termination of the obedience to the former sovereign, the man who is no longer a subject to any sovereign is to exercise his private judgement in making a covenant with the sovereign-to-be.

between the earlier and the new obedience, no room for the grey-zone period, since in such a period private judgements have to be exercised on the very question of obedience.

But in either of the cases specified above, the grey zone remains grey. When his means of living is under the enemy's control, a man may suffer death or wounds if he does not obey the enemy. Yet he may not be exposed to that sort of imminent danger. He is not yet endangered by 'a certain most prominent degree of fear'.[39] He has to think for himself which is the better means to survive: resistance or surrender. When a soldier's army loses control of the field, the soldier may be killed if he does not surrender. But how can he rule out the possibility that his army will recapture the field? The soldier has to assess the circumstances and decide whether to resist or to surrender. Virtually, private judgement is now allowed to work *before* he faces the imminent fear, that is, *before* the obedience becomes impossible. It is not an instinctive response, but the exercise of private judgement which terminates the obedience.[40]

In *Leviathan*, when Hobbes tried to specify the condition of being defeated, he seems to have relaxed the notion of the imminent greatest fear—that crucial requirement of his concept of conquest.[41] In other words, he eased the condition under which the obligation of obedience

---

[39] *De Cive*, II. 18. 105 [E: p. 58]. See Sect. 3.4 above.

[40] As far as the issue of the termination of obedience is concerned, Hobbes's notion of liberty remains unclear. From *The Elements of Law* to *Leviathan*, Hobbes allows subjects to terminate their obedience in an emergency. Does Hobbes mean that they do so freely? Has he allowed them that sort of liberty? The Hobbes of *Leviathan* does so. The notion of 'liberty to submit' to a conqueror has two meanings: to terminate their obedience; and to make a new covenant with the sovereign-to-be ('A Review and Conclusion', 484–5 [pp. 390–1]). But, while the second of these liberties is granted in *The Elements of Law* and *De Cive*, those earlier writings are silent on the first. I suspect that that silence reflects Hobbes's unwillingness to confront a potential contradiction between two positions: the first, we may say, when the subjects terminate their obedience in an emergency, they do so freely, for they are exercising their 'right of defending'; the second, that because they do not have options between which to choose, they are not free (see Sect. 3.4 above). Some critics seem to me to miss that ambiguity: e.g. Skinner, 'Thomas Hobbes on the Proper Signification of Liberty', 147–51; see also n. 31 above. All we can safely say is that in his earlier works Hobbes grants men no liberty to follow their private judgements when terminating their obedience. The term 'liberty' (like 'right') is not a useful instrument in examining the particular issue of the termination of obedience. In this book I have instead employed the terms 'private judgement' and 'fear'.

[41] Compare the following passage with its equivalent of *De Cive* cited in Ch. 3, n. 35: 'man by nature chooseth the lesser evill, which is danger of death in resisting; rather than the greater, which is certain and present death in not resisting' (*Leviathan*, XIV. 98 [p. 70]). In *De Cive*, Hobbes claimed that we are *obliged* by the contract of no resistance to choose the lesser of the two *present* evils, and that it is *impossible* not to do so. The room for private judgement is ruled out since the other choice is said to be impossible. But in *Leviathan* he merely says 'man by nature chooseth'.

ceases. When he elaborated his answer to the question at what point a conquest becomes effective, he virtually conceded that a man's recognition
that he has been conquered can itself be a question of private judgement. If
people are *really* forced to obey the conqueror in a Hobbesian sense, the
matter cannot be one for argument. Nor can it be one of choice. It must be
one of instinctive response caused by fear.

Hobbes, making every effort to save his concept of conquest, even distinguishes conquest from victory in 'A Review, and Conclusion'. He writes
that conquest is achieved by a contract after victory.[42] But this claim
merely shows his recognition that to decide which is the decisive victory is
a matter of judgement. In 'A Review, and Conclusion', certainly, Hobbes
was able to imply that the conquest of England by parliament would be
achieved if 'the Oath of Engagement' were subscribed to by all men over
18 as required by parliament. Yet still Hobbes would not have been able to
explain at what point in time, and in what manner, parliament had established its decisive victory. He simply took the victory by parliament as a premise of his argument. In doing so, he neglected to analyse the power-basis
of the new government, and tacitly conceded that private judgement had
been exercised in the process by which the people acknowledged the victory.
He conceded that parliament could not claim its victory to be decisive
until the people, exercising their private judgements, had decided that the
parliamentarians would provide better protection than the royalists would
do. Hobbes's theory of conquest in *Leviathan* could not rule out the possibility of the exercise of private judgement.

Thus ironically enough, the Hobbes of *Leviathan* cannot maintain the
notion of a commonwealth by acquisition unless the exercise of private
judgement is smuggled into the argument. When Hobbes criticized mixed
government, his quarrel with theorists of mixed government was that they
endorsed private judgement by the subjects concerning political obedience.
Hobbes's starting-point was to submit a theory which creates peace and
order *without* recourse to 'conscience', which Ferne and Hunton expected

---

[42] 'Conquest, is not the Victory it self; but the Acquisition by Victory, of a Right, over the
persons of men. He therefore that is slain, is Overcome, but not Conquered . . . *Conquest* (to
define it) is the Acquiring of the Right of Soveraignty by Victory. Which Right, is acquired,
in the peoples Submission, by which they contract with the Victor, promising Obedience, for
Life and Liberty' (*Leviathan*, 'A Review, and Conclusion', 485–6 [p. 391]). Compare this passage with the following extract from ch. 20 of *Leviathan*, where victory and conquest had
both been handled as matters of fact, not of right: 'Dominion acquired by Conquest, or Victory
in war, is that which some Writers call DESPOTICALL . . . It is not therefore the Victory, that
giveth the right of Dominion over the Vanquished, but his own Covenant. Nor is he obliged
because he is Conquered; that is to say, beaten, and taken, or put to flight; but because he commeth in, and Submitteth to the Victor' (ibid. XX. 141 [pp. 103–4]).

to save the nation from anarchy. Hobbes made a fresh start with the word 'fear'. Yet in *Leviathan*, when he explicitly urged the people to obey the new English republic, his theory of obedience from fear left room for conscience. In the world of Ferne and Hunton, when the king and the parliament could not agree, the people were expected to exercise their private judgements and to decide which would be more likely to restore the constitution. In the world of *Leviathan*, when the royalists and the parliamentarians were at war, the people were to exercise their private judgements and to decide which would offer them better protection. Hobbes, as much as the theorists of mixed government, needed the peacemaker, conscience, to restore peace.

Moreover, Hobbes's endorsement of the new government undermined the notion of obedience he had established in *The Elements of Law* and *De Cive*. In *Leviathan* obedience due to the government becomes fragile, since men are allowed to exercise their private judgements in seeking better protection at any time. A man might disobey the government and support an enemy even before a battle if he thinks that this course will increase his chances of survival. Hobbes says that what the government can rely upon is not 'the word' but only 'the sword'. But the sword of the new English republic apparently fell short of what could impose an imminent danger to force the people to renew their obedience, even though the government might be able to win several decisive victories in battle. If the people saw that the common power of the government was inadequate to keep them 'in awe', they would desert the government, and the common power itself would disintegrate. In *De Cive* a sovereign by acquisition has the common power regardless of the subjects' attitude, since the sovereign has maintained the formidable power which was used for the conquest. Yet in *Leviathan*, a sovereign by acquisition has the common power just as long as the people believe that the sovereign will offer them sufficient protection. In *De Cive* a conqueror has the military power to force the people to change their allegiance overnight. But in *Leviathan* his military power may fall short of that. In fact, in Hobbes's eyes, parliament has sufficient military power only to make the people find that parliament will offer better protection. The parliament has the common power to govern, but that power depends totally on the people's private judgements. 'Word' itself is said to be unreliable, and is not available to the parliament. Nor is 'sword' sufficiently possessed by them. In short, the Hobbes of *Leviathan* could not provide any basis of the common power for the new English republic.

The theorist of sovereignty, who appeared to have succeeded in bridging the events of 1640–51, left a gap open between having won the victory and having the common power in the civil war. He equated parliament's victories with a conquest. He did not analyse the question whether parliament had a sword powerful enough to carry 'the public sword' in the meaning defined in his theory. When, two years after *Leviathan*, the sole sovereign assembly fell for the lack of the common power, the shortcoming of his position in *Leviathan* was revealed. Three years later, Hobbes's theory would be challenged for the weakness of its very notion of common power.

5

THE CHALLENGE OF JAMES HARRINGTON, 1653–1656:
Fear, Necessity, Equality

1. Introduction

In April 1653 the Rump Parliament was dissolved by Cromwell's army. The first English republican government had broken down despite its absolute sovereignty and its monopoly of both legislative and executive power. The Rump fell short of playing the part of the first English Leviathan, and proved to lack 'the common power' to keep the subjects 'in awe'.[1] The parliament which had won the civil wars by its army was put down by the same army. The sole sovereign assembly, which emerged after the abolition of the kingship and the House of Lords, was powerless to prevent the military coup. Of course, Hobbes himself was not involved in the political process of the failure of the Rump. While he defended the new duty of obedience to that government, he himself was by no means an architect of the regime. However, there would emerge a critic whose argument implied that the dissolution of the Rump had proved the failure of Hobbes's political theory. Although Hobbes laid emphasis on the notion of 'the public sword', he did not pay attention to the relationship between a government and its army. When he defended the Rump's cause, he neglected to examine the military power-basis of the government. This critic, sharing Hobbes's concern for peace and order, analysed the basis of military power, and articulated a new theory, which explained both the defeat of the royalists during the civil wars and the failure of the Rump Parliament. The critic was James Harrington.[2]

[1] *The Elements of Law*, I. 19. 4. 111; *Leviathan*, XVII. 118 [p. 86].

[2] The classic accounts of Harrington are to be found in H. F. Russell Smith, *Harrington and his Oceana* (Cambridge, 1914); Charles Blitzer, *An Immortal Commonwealth* (New Haven, 1960); and particularly John Pocock's 'Historical Introduction', *The Political Works of James Harrington* (Cambridge, 1977). See also J. C. Davis, *Utopia and the Ideal Society*

Among critics of Hobbes, Harrington alone raised one question about Hobbes's thought: he raised no objection when Hobbes gave a conqueror the absolute sovereignty; but he did object when Hobbes considered a victor of a civil war to be a conqueror. Equally, Harrington did not oppose Hobbes's decision to give a conqueror the lawful claim to govern. But he was dissatisfied when Hobbes considered a victor to have sufficient military power to govern. As far as events in England were concerned, the question for Harrington was not whether parliament had a legitimate claim to govern when it inaugurated the Commonwealth. Instead, the question had to be whether parliament had a sufficient military basis to govern after it won the war. This was the question Hobbes neglected, and the one Harrington tackled. The answer was 'No'.

Harrington's aim was, of course, not restricted to this criticism of Hobbes. He intended to provide the means of saving the nation from anarchy. Consequently, he was among those who invented various plans for political institutions in the post-Rump period. However, as far as absolute sovereignty is concerned, Harrington had much more in common with Hobbes than many writers of the Interregnum had. In addition, his prescription was tightly bound by his diagnosis of the situation of his country, a diagnosis at its strongest in its criticism of Hobbes. Thus Harrington started his discussion by raising a unique question about Hobbes's thought.[3]

James Harrington published *The Commonwealth of Oceana* in the autumn of 1656 under the Protectorate government.[4] The publication may have been intended to support those who in the parliamentary election

(Cambridge, 1981), ch. viii; Blair Worden, 'James Harrington and "The Commonwealth of Oceana", 1656', *Republicanism, Liberty, and Commercial Society, 1649–1776* in David Wootton (ed.), (Stanford, Calif., 1994), 82–110. For *Oceana*, I was also much helped by S. B. Liljegren's meticulous notes in his *James Harrington's Oceana* (Heidelberg, 1924).

[3] For Harrington's relation to Hobbes, see Paul A. Rahe, *Republics Ancient and Modern* (Chapel Hill, NC, 1992), 409–26; Jonathan Scott, 'The Rapture of Motion', in Nicholas Phillipson and Quentin Skinner (eds.), *Political Discourse in Early Modern Britain* (Cambridge 1993), 139–63. I agree with Rahe and Scott that Harrington shared Hobbes's concern with peace and order. But where they maintain that Harrington betrayed the tradition of ancient prudence and joined Hobbes against it, I shall argue that Harrington located his argument firmly within that tradition. See also Pocock, *The Machiavellian Moment* (Princeton, 1975), 397–8.

[4] After *Oceana* Harrington wrote and published a number of political treatises and pamphlets until he was arrested in 1661. All his writings, except for *The System of Politics*, were published during the Interregnum. While some differences can be found among his many writings, his idea of 'absolute' and 'balanced' sovereignty remains unchanged from *Oceana* to his later works. As far as that idea is concerned, his political works will be treated *en bloc*, and differences among them will not be explored. When, later in Appendix B, we come to another idea of Harrington, the immortality of the commonwealth which he designs, the difference between *Oceana* and his later works will be addressed.

campaign held in the summer of that year opposed the current direction of the Protectorate.[5] Yet behind the failings of the Protectorate there lay, in Harrington's mind, another, perhaps larger, target. It was the Rump Parliament. In *Oceana* he suggested that the failure of the Rump Parliament, a single assembly, was inevitable, and that it should have been replaced by a government consisting of two chambers, the senate and the popular assembly. He may have welcomed the dissolution of the Rump, for its expulsion offered an occasion to create a new and healthy government. Yet instead of creating the two-chamber government which Harrington wanted, Cromwell had replaced the Rump with another single assembly, the short-lived Barebone's Parliament, and later made himself Lord Protector. It is possible that Harrington thought that a second opportunity to create a two-chamber government had arrived in 1656 and that he published *Oceana* in the hope of exploiting it. In 'The Second Part of the Preliminaries' of *Oceana*, Harrington ended his narrative of English history at the point of the dissolution of the Rump Parliament. From 1653, it seems, Harrington had remained concerned by the failure of the first English republican government. He expounded his constitutional scheme at every point during the Interregnum when he saw an opportunity to secure its implementation.

We saw in Chapter 3 that the main tenet of Hobbes's argument was formed by 1640. The argument appearing in *Leviathan* cannot therefore be assumed to have been freshly constituted to defend the new English government born in 1649. Yet Harrington read *Leviathan* as an apologia for the Rump Parliament. Admittedly, Harrington had access to Hobbes's earlier writings, which were written well before the rule of the Rump and in which his distinctive arguments were first advanced.[6] However, Harrington

---

[5] For the formation and the publication of *Oceana*, see Blair Worden, 'Harrington's "Oceana": Origins and Aftermath, 1651–60', in *Republicanism, Liberty, and Commercial Society, 1649–1776*, 110–26.

[6] It seems certain that Harrington studied *The Elements of Law* (though not necessarily in any of the manuscripts of 1640). In *Oceana* (171 [p. 21]), 'as often as reason is against a man, so often will a man be against reason' is a quotation from 'the Epistle dedicatory' in *The Elements of Law* (See Liljegren, *James Harrington's Oceana*, 245). In 1650 this 'Epistle' was attached to *Human Nature; or the Fundamental Elements of Policy . . .*, the first thirteen chapters of *The Elements of Law*. The rest of the book, published under the title *De Corpore Politico; or the Elements of Law*, is mentioned in Harrington's *Politicaster* (712) as 'De cor. polit.' Harrington's claim that 'Mr Hobbes holdeth democracy to be of all governments the first in order of time' would have been based upon chapter 3 of *De Corpore Politico* (part 2, ch. 2 of *The Elements of Law*), although Pocock suggests *De Cive*. The first paragraph of ch. 3 of *De Corpore Politico* has a headline, 'Democracy precedeth all other institution of government'. As to *De Cive*, Harrington refers to its title, saying '*Leviathan* affirms the politics to be no ancienter than his book *De Cive*' (*Oceana*, 183 [p. 36]). Yet it may merely mean that Harrington had access to *De Corpore* (1655), at the outset of which Hobbes made that boast about *De Cive*.

explicitly regarded the theory of sovereignty in *Leviathan* as a defence of the new English republican government, as we shall later see in detail.[7] That perception led him to feel at odds with Hobbes mainly on two points: Hobbes approved the Rump's rule by considering it to be the conqueror, and also by finding it to consist of a single assembly.

First, Harrington examined the basis of the military power in general which can be deployed for a conquest. While Hobbes defended the new English government as the victor—and therefore, as the conqueror—he did not explain how or why parliament had won the civil wars. He took parliament's victory as a premise of his argument, and did not ask whether the parliament had the power which in his theory is essential to government. Harrington did explore that question. As modern commentators often explain, he offered a theory which explained that parliament's victory was inevitable in the social conditions which prevailed in mid-seventeenth-century England, and which gave the people good reason to renounce their former allegiance to the king. However, the significance of his theory goes further than that. He showed the relationship between a government and its military power. In doing so, he warned that the achievement of victory in the civil war was not the same as the ability to govern the country. In his eyes, the Rump Parliament was not the conqueror.

Secondly, if the Rump did not have sufficient military power to govern, it should instead have adopted the principle of mixed government, and should have equipped itself with constitutional arrangements which satisfied that principle. Harrington and Hobbes both saw the Rump as government by a single assembly. That was the ground on which Hobbes endorsed it, and on which Harrington believed it to have been doomed.

In this chapter we shall focus on the first of Harrington's two objections. Why, in Harrington's mind, was the Rump not the conqueror?

2.   The Two 'Preliminaries' of *Oceana*

Harrington's *Oceana* begins with 'The Preliminaries, showing the Principles of Government' and 'The Second Part of the Preliminaries'. It may seem strange that he wrote more than one introduction, but his elaborate arrangement of the introductory parts reflects the complexity of his task in *Oceana*. He had to fight on two very different fronts at once: in defence of 'ancient prudence', he wrote both against Hobbes and against 'modern prudence'.

---

[7] *Oceana*, 205 [p. 65].

As emphasized at the outset of this book, the first 'Preliminary' starts with the distinction between the two sorts of prudence.[8] Following this distinction, Harrington refers to Hobbes, and then discusses 'the principles of government' to vindicate the classical idea of mixed government—ancient prudence—against Hobbes. In 'The Second Part', on the other hand, Harrington narrates the history of the rise and fall of modern prudence. Modern prudence, having ascended with the Roman Empire, established 'Gothic' monarchies in Europe. In the latter half of the second 'Preliminary', the history of English monarchy is followed from the age of the Saxons to the age of the civil wars in the seventeenth century. At the end of the narrative an imaginary legislator appears. He makes up his mind to erect, in the midst of the confusion, a new republic. So he dissolves the parliament and summons 'the Council of Legislators', where 'the archives of ancient prudence should be ransacked' to design a new regime.[9]

Harrington employs the two 'Preliminaries' to discuss two sorts of prudence. The first considers ancient prudence, the second modern prudence. His treatment of the two kinds of prudence is not even-handed. While 'the principles of government' were examined at length in the first part, there is no equivalent discussion in the second.[10] He is almost silent upon the question of the principles of government in modern prudence; instead modern prudence is discussed in terms of its history. There is little history in the account of ancient prudence in the first 'Preliminary'. It is true he supplies a catalogue of commonwealths which have embodied ancient prudence in the past and the present; but he does not trace the fate of those commonwealths chronologically. In short, the first part examines the principles from a theoretical point of view, the second part from a historical one. Harrington might equally well have analysed the principles of both forms of prudence in the former part and written the histories of both in the latter. If he had done so, the two forms could have been treated in parallel. But he did not.

This unevenness reflected Harrington's evaluation of modern prudence, which was very low. The principles of modern prudence did not deserve theoretical examination. How had ancient prudence, so superior to modern prudence, come to give way to it? So grave a change could be explained only by the intervention of 'something of necessity' in history. His narrative of modern prudence aims to identify that 'something'.[11]

---

[8] Ibid. 161 [pp. 8–9].   [9] Ibid. 207–8 [pp. 67–9].

[10] '[T]he first treating of the principles of government in general, and according to the ancients; the second treating of the late governments of Oceana in particular, and in that of modern prudence' (*Oceana*, 162 [p. 10]).

[11] 'The date of this kind of policy is to be computed, as was shown, from those inundations

In Harrington's judgement, modern prudence has far less theoretical sophistication than ancient prudence. His judgement is shown by his careful wording at the beginning of the first 'Preliminary'. In the two parallel definitions of government, the crucial difference concerns the notion of 'a civil society':

government (to define it *de jure* or according to ancient prudence) is an art whereby a civil society of men is instituted and preserved upon the foundation of common right or interest . . . And government (to define it *de facto* or according unto modern prudence) is an art whereby some man, or some few men, subject a city or a nation, and rule it according unto his or their private interest.[12]

In the world of modern prudence, some may rule and some may be ruled, but there is no 'civil society of men'. Only by ancient prudence could a civil society be 'instituted and preserved'. Modern prudence lacks any political principles which bind together a certain number of people into 'a well-ordered commonwealth'.

That is why his opponent, when Harrington vindicated ancient prudence in the first part of 'the Preliminaries', was not modern prudence but Thomas Hobbes. Most of the first 'Preliminary' is devoted to showing the superiority of the classical idea of mixed government to Hobbes's idea of undivided sovereignty by a single holder. Hobbes's argument merited criticism in detail, thought Harrington. That criticism, although a mark of disagreement, was also a mark of respect. For Hobbes had tried, if not very successfully in Harrington's eyes, to find 'an art' to construct 'a well-ordered commonwealth'.[13] In Harrington's perspective, Hobbes, like Harrington himself, offered a new vision of politics at a time when modern prudence—the conventional political wisdom—had collapsed in England. The two writers, however, headed in opposite directions: whereas Harrington returned to ancient prudence, Hobbes rejected ancient and modern

of Goths, Vandals, Huns and Lombards that overwhelmed the Roman Empire. But as there is no appearance in the bulk or constitution of modern prudence that she should ever have been able to come up and grapple with the ancient, so something of necessity must have interposed, whereby this came to be enervated and that to receive strength and encouragement' (*Oceana*, 188 [p. 43]).

[12] Ibid. 161 [pp. 8–9]. Other contrasts which he drew in making those definitions, like that between *de jure* and *de facto*, that between 'common interest' and 'private interest', and that between 'empire of laws' and 'empire of men', are less important, even if more conspicuous.

[13] In the passage of *Oceana*, 341 [p. 244], where he writes 'For in the art of man, being the imitation of nature which is the art of God, there is nothing so like the first call of beautiful order out of chaos and confusion as the architecture of a well-ordered commonwealth', Harrington refers to Hobbes by name. As is remarked by Pocock, he is alluding to the 'Introduction' of *Leviathan*. See also Harrington, 'The Epistle Dedicatory' of *The Prerogative of Popular Government* (London, 1658), 390.

prudence alike and wanted to leap forward. Hobbes's new idea disrupted and delayed the transition from modern to ancient, for which Harrington longed.

3. Fear and Necessity

In the first 'Preliminary' of *Oceana*, immediately following the distinction between the two sorts of prudence, Harrington lays down his criticism of Hobbes. When he does so, the matter over which he takes issue with Hobbes is the notion of 'fear'.

The notion of fear is often associated by critics only with Hobbes, and not with Harrington. Yet as far as the notion of fear is concerned, Harrington is Hobbes's disciple. Hobbes's claim that fear is the origin of obedience was certainly part of 'what he taught' Harrington.[14] Having accepted that claim, Harrington 'opposed the politics of Mr Hobbes', insisting that another notion has to be introduced before fear can be satisfactorily discussed. That is the notion of 'necessity'. Though a people can be ruled by fear, an army, the cause and object of fear, cannot. An army must be impelled by necessity.

In the previous chapter we found that Hobbes contrasted 'word' with 'sword' in some passages of *Leviathan*.[15] Harrington launched his criticism of Hobbes with a quotation from one of those passages:

another error of Aristotle's *Politics*, that in a well-ordered commonwealth, not men should govern but the laws. What man that hath his natural senses, though he can neither write nor read, does not find himself governed by them he fears, and believes can kill or hurt him when he obeyeth not? Or who believes that the law can hurt him, which is but words and paper without the hands and swords of men?[16]

In that passage, Hobbes, discussing 'law', focuses not upon the binding force of any particular laws made by the sovereign, but upon the obedience due to the sovereign in general. The duty of obedience derives solely from the fear caused by the sovereign, claims Hobbes. To this, Harrington replies:

I confess that *magistratus est lex armata*; the magistrate upon his bench is that unto the law, which a gunner upon his platform is unto his cannon. Nevertheless I should not dare to argue with a man of any ingenuity after this manner. An whole

---

[14] *The Prerogative of Popular Government*, 423.
[15] See Sect. 4.2 above.
[16] *Oceana*, 161–2 [p. 9]. As quoted by Harrington. The original was from *Leviathan*, XLVI. 471 [pp. 377–8].

army, though they can neither write nor read, are not afraid of a platform, which they know is but earth or stone, nor of a cannon which, without a hand to give fire unto it, is but cold iron; therefore a whole army is afraid of one man.[17]

Here, Harrington does not oppose Hobbes's claim that obedience derives from fear. Indeed he accepts it. Because he agrees with Hobbes, he wants to discuss it further. What causes fear? The answer, says *Leviathan*, is 'the public sword'. But Harrington cannot be satisfied with that answer, since Hobbes has said nothing about what controls the sword. The sword may be controlled by the 'word'. But Hobbes in *Leviathan* clearly denies this possibility. How, then, should a Hobbesian sovereign handle the sword? Harrington is concerned with that question, because he is no less concerned with the notion of fear than Hobbes was. Since he is disappointed by his master's answer, Harrington's comment on Hobbes's account of word and sword sounds cynical:

Leviathan, . . . hath caught hold of the public sword, unto which he reduceth all manner and matter of government; as where he affirms 'the opinion that any monarch receiveth his power by covenant, that is to say upon condition, to proceed from want of understanding this easy truth, that covenants, being but words and breath, have no force to oblige, contain, constrain or protect any man, but what they have from the public sword'. But as he said of the law that without this sword it is but paper, so he might have thought of this sword that without an hand it is but cold iron.[18]

Thus Harrington, as a disciple of Hobbes, wants to carry the study of 'fear' further than his master, by investigating the basis of sword.

Yet before we watch Harrington developing his argument, we should note that it was the Hobbes of *Leviathan* with whom Harrington took issue. In *The Elements of Law* and *De Cive*, 'covenant' was considered to be as important as 'fear' in terms of the means which secure obedience. But the passage of *Leviathan* Harrington cited in the quotation above is the same I quoted in the previous chapter in order to show the difference between the Hobbes of *The Elements of Law* and the Hobbes of *Leviathan*. In that passage, the Hobbes of *Leviathan* did not hesitate to discredit the binding force of 'covenant' itself, whereas the Hobbes of *The Elements of Law* appropriated that word for his notion of 'a commonwealth of institution'. One of the conclusions we reached in the previous chapter was that the emphasis on 'victory' in *Leviathan* tilted the delicate balance between

---

[17] *Oceana*, 162 [p. 9].
[18] Ibid. 165 [p. 13]. Harrington's quotation slightly differs from the original. The original words of Hobbes from Tuck's edition (*Leviathan*, XVIII. 123) are found in my citation in Sect. 4.2 above.

'institution' and 'conquest', and made his idea of a commonwealth by institution implausible. Owing to the contrast, deliberately drawn in *Leviathan*,
between word and sword, only the idea of a commonwealth by acquisition,
or more correctly, the idea of a commonwealth by victory, could maintain
the coherence of Hobbes's argument. What Harrington attacked was Hobbes's position of 1651, not his original one.[19] Harrington showed little interest either in Hobbes's notion of covenant or in that of a commonwealth by
institution.

Perhaps that is why he did not remark on the circularity of the argument
around that notion. Perhaps too that is why Harrington called Hobbes
'Leviathan' in *Oceana*. Harrington believed that Hobbes himself had discredited the notion of a commonwealth by institution by arguing in
Leviathan that what was needed was the common power rather than the
word. Harrington felt no need to repeat Hobbes's criticism of that notion.
His attention was devoted to the criticism of the notion of a commonwealth
by acquisition. In Harrington's view, neither of Hobbes's categories of commonwealths could be maintained: commonwealth by institution had been
rejected by Hobbes himself, and Harrington himself disproved commonwealth by acquisition.

Harrington begins by asking what the basis of the common power is. If
the common power originates from the victory rather than the covenant,
where does the victory originate? In claiming, with Hobbes, that obedience
is caused by fear, Harrington returns to chapter 10 of *Leviathan* and supplements Hobbes's account of 'power'.[20] In that chapter Hobbes discussed
power in a broad sense: power as the 'means to obtain some future apparent
Good'. Harrington's concern is more specific. He does not consider
'natural strength, beauty, and health' to be reliable sources of power, since
'if a man or an army acquire victory or empire, it is more from their discipline, arms, and courage'. Here he analyses the notion of power in terms of
its utilization for conquest or victory. It is a power which can force obedience by fear. That is why 'a man or an army (or a 'militia')'—rather than 'a
man, or an assembly'—comes into the focus of his argument.[21]

Having linked 'power' and 'army' in this way, Harrington next connects

---

[19] Harrington concentrated on *Leviathan*, although he had access to *The Elements of Law*
and *De Cive*. See n. 6 concerning this point in the first section of this chapter.

[20] 'There be goods also of the body, as health, beauty, strength, but these are not to be
brought into account upon this score, because if a man or an army acquire victory or empire,
it is more from their discipline, arms, and courage, than from their natural health, beauty, or
strength, in regard that a people conquered may have more of natural strength, beauty and
health, and yet find little remedy' (*Oceana*, 163 [pp. 10–11]).

[21] Cf. *Leviathan*, x. 62 [p. 41], xix. 132 [p. 97].

'army' with 'lands'. 'An army is a beast that hath a great belly and must be fed.' The question whether you have control over an army, therefore, 'will come unto what pastures you have'.[22]

What is an army for? If asked, Hobbes and Harrington would have given the same answer: it is to cause a fear which will secure the obedience of the people. What then secures the obedience of the army? This was the question Hobbes did not raise. Even if the people fear the army, the army fears nothing, since it monopolizes military power by definition. Fear cannot be the answer to this question. Here Hobbes's key notion of fear ceases to work. Harrington did raise that question, and thought he had found the answer. He deployed another notion which guarantees obedience. This was the notion of 'necessity'.

To begin with riches, in regard that men are hung upon these, not of choice as upon the other, but of necessity and by the teeth: for as much as he who wanteth bread is his servant that will feed him, if a man thus feed an whole people, they are under his empire.[23]

In Harrington's account, a man's obedience can be guaranteed by meeting his necessity as well as by threatening him with fear. Those who are fed by a man with his land, no less than those who are conquered by his army, are considered to be 'under his empire'. Harrington's innovation was to find a link between obedience and 'riches'—particularly, between obedience and 'lands'. The more land a man has, therefore, the more people he has under his empire.

From this account there derives his well-known formula that political power follows landownership. How a certain territory is governed depends upon how the landed property is distributed in that territory. This is 'the doctrine of the balance of the land'. Employing two causes of obedience, 'fear' and 'necessity', Harrington presents a new classification of the forms of government:

If one man be sole landlord of a territory, or overbalance the people, for example, three parts in four, he is grand signor, for so the Turk is called from his property; and his empire is absolute monarchy.

If the few or a nobility, or a nobility with the clergy, be landlords, or overbalance the people unto the like proportion, it makes the Gothic balance (to be shown at large in the second part of this discourse) and the empire is mixed monarchy, as that of Spain, Poland, and late of Oceana.

And if the whole people be landlords, or hold the lands so divided among them, that no one man, or number of men, within the compass of the few or aristocracy,

---

[22] *Oceana*, 165 [p. 13].   [23] Ibid. 163 [p. 11].

overbalance them, the empire (without the interposition of force) is a common-wealth.[24]

On the other hand, there could emerge a temporary government which is not supported by 'the balance'.

If force be interposed in any of these three cases, it must either frame the government unto the foundation, or the foundation unto the government, or, holding the government not according unto the balance, it is not natural but violent; and therefore, if it be at the devotion of a prince, it is tyranny; if at the devotion of the few, oligarchy; or if in the power of the people, anarchy; each of which confusions, the balance standing otherwise, is but of short continuance, because against the nature of the balance which, not destroyed, destroyeth that which opposeth it.[25]

The premise of this classification is that a landlord can organize those who are under his empire into his army. The more land he has, the more people he has under his empire; and therefore the more military power he has, since they are 'at his command'.[26] As far as Harrington's account of conquest is concerned, military power is the only source of political power. Thus, when he maintains that the location of political power can be determined according to 'the balance of the land', his analysis of political power deploys only two notions, 'necessity' and 'fear'.

For instance, in the case of the Turk, where the empire is 'absolute monarchy', the structure of the political power can be analysed by those two notions as follows. There are three sorts of men in the territory of the Turk: the landlord; the people living upon the landlord's land (who are the majority); and the people living in their own land (the minority). In this case everybody obeys the landlord for the following reasons. First, the dependent majority obeys him because 'of necessity' they are his servants. They will starve if they lose his favour. Secondly, the independent minority obeys him because of 'fear'. They are, it is true, free in terms of 'necessity'. They can live by themselves and do not need the landlord's support. Even so, the landlord is able to deploy his army which consists of his servants, the dependent majority. The minority cannot but obey him from 'fear', since they are easily outnumbered by the army, which is made up of the majority. Thus obedience is guaranteed universally by 'necessity' and

---

[24] Ibid. 163–4 [pp. 11–12]. Interestingly, Harrington made an insertion, '(without the interposition of force)', only in the paragraph for 'commonwealth'.

[25] Ibid. 164 [p. 12].

[26] '[I]f a man, having one hundred pounds a year, may keep one servant or have one man at his command, then, having one hundred times so much, he may keep one hundred servants and, this multiplied by a thousand, he may have one hundred thousand men at his command' (*The Prerogative of Popular Government*, 404).

'fear', and the landlord is 'grand signor' accordingly. His rule is 'absolute monarchy'.[27]

In his sixfold classification of government, Harrington must have thought he had outwitted Hobbes. Hobbes, having rejected the distinction between good and bad forms of government, removed the categories of 'tyranny', 'oligarchy', and 'anarchy', and so reduced the number of categories from six to three. His criticism of the Aristotelian classification was that it defined 'Good, and Evill, by the Appetite of men', and that the 'bad' forms are nothing more than what men 'misliked'.[28] Seeing this, Harrington replaced the old criterion of good and bad by a new one which relates to the distribution of the land. Apparently 'the balance of the land' is not a matter of 'appetite'. Forms of government which are classified by the number of the ruler(s) first, are then judged satisfactory if they are supported by 'the balance of the land', unsatisfactory if they are not. There are thus six forms, three satisfactory ones and their three unsatisfactory counterparts. 'The doctrine of the balance' was thus a revision of the traditional sixfold classification, carried out in response to Hobbes's protest.

Yet we should remember that Harrington shares with Hobbes a premise which aligns the two writers against the traditional classification. Harrington accepts, without reservation, Hobbes's provocative dismissal of the distinction between good and bad forms. In Harrington's account the difference between monarchy and tyranny does not lie, as it did for classical writers, in the question whether the prince governs for himself or for all. If a prince overwhelms the people in terms of property, his government is a monarchy, not a tyranny. He does not need to care for the public good in order to be called king. On the other hand, if his property cannot overwhelm the people, he is a tyrant no matter how keenly he may care for them. Nor does Harrington say, as theorists opposed by Hobbes did, that the people are entitled to resist the ruler if they consider him a tyrant. Subjects cannot rise up against a monarch, for they are forced to obey him by fear and necessity. By contrast, in the case of tyranny, the people do not need to obey the tyrant from the beginning, because the tyrant cannot overwhelm them and lacks the means to exact obedience from them.

Harrington, no less than Hobbes, was writing in order to secure obedience. The three unsatisfactory forms—tyranny, oligarchy, and anarchy—

---

[27] To what extent must the servants outnumber the independent minority for the landlord's 'absolute monarchy' to be secure? Harrington could not, it seems, answer this question convincingly. His tentative answer, offered 'for example', is that they have to be more than 'three parts in four' (*Oceana*, 163 [p. 11]).

[28] *Leviathan*, XLVI. 469 [p. 376]; XIX. 130 [p. 95]. See Sect. 3.3 above.

all fail to secure obedience by either fear or necessity, and are all synonymous with 'confusion'. In effect they are not 'government' at all, for confusion is something less than government. The three unsatisfactory forms are mere quasi-governments, transitory and insubstantial. For Harrington as for Hobbes, therefore, there are only three valid forms. Like Hobbes, Harrington concentrated his attention on the stability of government. For both writers, a stable government is one which is obeyed absolutely and to which there is no resistance.

Yet there is a difference.[29] Hobbes's classification of governments allowed no place for tyranny or oligarchy. Harrington preserved those terms even though he took them to be equivalent to anarchy. Hobbes eliminated tyranny and oligarchy to refute Aristotle. Harrington preserved them to refute Hobbes. By mentioning them early in the first 'Preliminary' he prepared the ground on which to challenge Hobbes at a later stage in 'The Second Part', where he claims that the Rump, which Hobbes regarded as government by 'an assembly' and then as an aristocracy, was really an oligarchy.[30] It was an oligarchy because it was, in Harrington's judgement, unstable. In the same way, Harrington implied that what Hobbes called government by 'a man' was a tyranny if, in Harrington's judgement, it was unstable. Thus did Harrington equip himself to examine Hobbes's application of the idea of government by 'a man, or an assembly'.

Now perhaps we can have a better view of Harrington's approach in his criticism of Hobbes. Harrington's 'doctrine of the balance of the land' and Hobbes's account of sovereignty by conquest have a provocative claim in common: the acquisition of political power derives solely from superiority in terms of military power. Military power secures the obedience of the people by fear. In Harrington's account a man who has an overwhelming military power is automatically entitled to rule. Hobbes requires a covenant as well as the military power. Yet in the Hobbes of *Leviathan*, military power and a covenant are not, as they were in the earlier Hobbes, mutually supportive. Military power now has to precede the covenant. Once military power is lost, the covenant cannot maintain obedience. In this sense, for the Hobbes of *Leviathan* as well as for Harrington, overwhelming military power is essential to the maintenance of political power. If Hobbes and Harrington are asked who rules in a certain region, therefore, they give the

[29] Rahe sees the similarity between Hobbes and Harrington's classifications of governments but misses the significance of the differences. Rahe, *Republics Ancient and Modern*, 413.

[30] In Hobbes's terminology, if the sovereign is 'one man', its government is 'monarchy'. If it is 'one assembly', the government is either aristocracy or democracy. If the assembly consists of only some of the men of the commonwealth, it is 'aristocracy'. When the assembly consists of all, it is 'democracy'. See *Leviathan*, XIX. 129 [p. 94].

same reply: the one who has the overwhelming military power. Harrington breaks with Hobbes in answering the further question who, then, has the military power. Hobbes cannot reply. Harrington can, thanks to the notion of 'necessity'. The landlord who owns the greater part of the region has it. Harrington offered a test to decide who is qualified as a Hobbesian conqueror. The conqueror has to be the landlord. Hobbes is mistaken if he considers anyone other than the landlord to be the conqueror, for 'the public sword is but a name or mere spitfrog' without 'the balance of property'.[31] This perception enables Harrington to attack Hobbes's interpretation of particular events. To see how he does so, we shall look at Harrington's interpretation of English history.

4. Conquest and Equality

The first 'Preliminary', which discussed 'the principles of government', attacked Hobbes's theory and defended ancient prudence against him. 'The Second Part', however, which narrates the history of modern prudence, seems on first acquaintance to have nothing to do with Hobbes. But in reality that part, too, involves Harrington in a criticism of Hobbes. For the history of modern prudence included the fall of the Stuart monarchy and its replacement by the Rump Parliament, subjects which, in Harrington's view, Hobbes misunderstood.

The beginning of modern prudence, says Harrington, was to be found in the politics practised by Sulla, Caesar, and the Roman emperors, who distributed conquered lands to their private soldiers and ruled with those private armies, *milites beneficiarii*. As long as the benefices of the soldiers were given only for life, the emperors could manage to maintain their rule. But after they were made hereditary and the soldiers became less dependent on them, they found it difficult to hold their empire without the assistance of the Goths and other tribes. Finally when Rome was sacked and the (Western) Roman Empire disintegrated, 'ancient languages, learning, prudence, manners, cities' were 'overwhelmed' and 'the transition of ancient into modern prudence' was completed.[32]

The Roman Empire was succeeded by the 'Gothic' world: that is, by a feudal society consisting of three hierarchical orders of *feudum*, namely, the nobility of the first class with such titles as marquesses and earls, barons who are inferior to them, and the tenants of those superiors. In this system of feudal landownership, the balance of the land is called 'the Gothic

---

[31] *Oceana*, 165 [p. 13].   [32] Ibid. 190 [p. 46].

balance, by which all the kingdoms this day in Christendom were at first erected'. France, Spain, Poland, and England (Oceana) are among them. These observations are consistent with 'the doctrine of the balance of the lands' in the first 'Preliminary', which also classified those kingdoms into a 'mixed monarchy' upon 'the Gothic Balance'.[33]

In the second 'Preliminary', Harrington deployed this doctrine to illustrate the political changes in England. The English mixed monarchy, which the Gothic balance supported, was formed through the conquests and invasions made by the Romans, the Saxons, the Danes, and the Normans. The Tudors, a family of nobles, overcame other noble families and acquired the crown. To strengthen their position they weakened the power-basis both of their noble rivals and of the other competitor for their authority, the Church. They dissolved the abbeys and deregulated the sale of land by the nobility. These measures worked for a time. The nobility and clergy lost their lands and their power decreased accordingly. The power of the crown rose, at least in relative terms. In Harrington's eyes, however, the real consequences of those policies were disastrous for the crown. The lands sold by the nobility went to the hands of the commons, and thus became more equally distributed among the majority of the people. Because of this change of the balance of the lands, the power of the commons was accordingly strengthened at the crown's expense. By the reign of Elizabeth the balance of power had shifted in favour of the commons. Though her reign appeared stable, this was only because the queen, by 'a kind of romance', contrived to postpone the inevitable clash between the crown and the people.[34]

As early as her reign 'the balance of the land' in England was such that 'no one man, or number of men, within the compass of the few or aristocracy, overbalance them [= the people]'.[35] The Stuarts, who inherited this balance of the land, could not retain the kingly power. The brutal confrontation between king and people was a reflection of the new balance. The civil wars were a natural consequence of the change of the balance: *'Wherefore the dissolution of this government caused the war, not the war the dissolution of this government'*.[36]

Harrington explains that the English monarchy collapsed because it lost the Gothic balance. According to the definition in the first 'Preliminary', 'mixed monarchy' emerges when there is no 'sole landlord' and when a small number of landlords still overwhelm the people. At first sight, the condition of 'mixed monarchy' may appear the same as that of 'absolute

---

[33] Ibid. 189–91, 164 [pp. 44–7, 11–17].   [34] Ibid. 191–8 [pp. 48–56].
[35] Ibid. 164 [p. 12].   [36] Ibid. 198 [p. 56] (Harrington's italic).

monarchy', except that the 'grand signor' is replaced by 'a nobility'. In fact the situation is quite different. In Harrington's world, a group of landlords cannot rule as successfully as a single landlord, because neither 'necessity' nor 'fear' can work upon them. Among the few landlords, no one is forced to obey the others. They may work together, but their co-operation cannot be guaranteed, since they are independent of each other in terms of food and military power. The best they can do is to reach a compromise by which one of them takes the crown as their head, and is allowed to rule in their interests.[37]

Because they appoint a king, Harrington calls this government 'mixed monarchy' rather than 'aristocracy'. But that monarchy rests upon the nobility. It is insecure, because the compromise reached by the nobility in creating it is provisional and fragile. Some of the nobility may confront others at any time. As long as the nobility have only a king, not a 'grand signor', above their heads, there is no necessity or fear to impel them to solve their conflicts. The king cannot make peace and order, since the nobility are not his tenants. He may deploy his own tenants and raise a faithful army, but he will be unable to force the nobility to obey him. The people would also be able to fight against the king, for they too are not his tenants, and his private army cannot overwhelm them. In mixed monarchy—unlike in absolute monarchy—no one can control the situation through necessity and fear. Mixed monarchy is, it follows, intrinsically unstable, even when the Gothic balance is suited to sustain it. That is why Harrington bitterly denounced the Fortescuian dualism of prerogative and liberties, which Henry Parker and others inherited and deployed in the 1640s.[38] Even at its best, the English monarchy, 'the masterpiece of modern prudence', was 'no other than a wrestling match' among the king, the nobility, and the people. Among the nobility the wrestling match consisted of the 'setting up and pulling down of their kings, according to their various interests'.[39]

The historical account which Harrington illustrated with the doctrine of the balance has more than one implication. First, it nullifies the distinction, dear to Fortescue and Parker, between the English monarchy and the French one. In Harrington's view those monarchies were the same as long as they rested on that Gothic balance which is common to 'all the kingdoms

---

[37] '[T]hey may make whom they please king or, if they be not pleased with their king, down with him, and set up whom they like better, . . . For as not the balance of the king, but that of the nobility, in this case is the cause of the government, so not the estate or riches of the prince or captain, but his virtue or ability, or fitness for the ends of the nobility, acquires that command or office' (*The Prerogative of Popular Government*, 405).

[38] See Sect. 1.4 above.

[39] *Oceana*, 196–7 [pp. 53–4].

this day in Christendom'.[40] Secondly, he showed why modern prudence was defective by nature: it had produced no theories to tackle the problem of obedience among the feudal landlords. Certainly, modern prudence had formed the government in England, but that was 'natural and easy, being in no other direction than that of the respective balance'.[41] This is, it seems, the reason he considered modern prudence to have little to do with the institution of 'a civil society'. Fortescue and his followers had talked about liberties, but had said little about how to secure obedience.

Harrington's narrative of English history involves not just a criticism of the Fortescuian idea but a defence of his own account of landed property against Hobbes. Harrington applied the relationship of power to landed property to the historical experience of England. In the first 'Preliminary', while asserting that landed property creates power by meeting 'necessity', he does nothing to explain either the origins or the security of landed property. If property is protected by power, his logic is circular, and remains vulnerable to a Hobbesian criticism.[42] Had he confined himself to the abstract level of argument, where he disagreed with Hobbes's claims about the origins of power, he would have confronted the question of the origin of landed property, and would have lost the argument. Since Hobbes maintained that the distinction between *meum* and *tuum* does not exist before the sovereign power is established, Harrington's argument would have seemed pointless to him. In the Hobbesian state of nature, no property can be securely held. Servants who live upon their master's land may at any time kill their master and seize his land.

Harrington handles the notion of 'necessity' on the assumption that a servant will not kill his master. For Harrington, however, that assumption was far from absurd, because he set his discussion of property and necessity within the historical process which Hobbes ignored. What he discussed in the second 'Preliminary' was not a servant in the Hobbesian state of nature, but a tenant in English feudal society. Thus Harrington could have pointed out that very few tenants fought against their landlords even during the English civil wars.

Yet Harrington's decision to cast necessity in feudal terms has a further implication. No principles other than feudal obligations, in his scheme, can organize men into an army which can be guaranteed to obey its

[40] Ibid. 191 [p. 47].

[41] *The Prerogative of Popular Government*, 398.

[42] See Matthew Wren, *Considerations on Mr. Harrington's Common-wealth of Oceana: Restrained to the first part of the Preliminaries* (London, 1657), 13; *Monarchy Asserted or The State of Monarchicall & Popular Government in Vindication of the Considerations upon Mr Harrington's Oceana* (Oxford, 1659), 19.

commander. When the Gothic balance has been lost, and the mighty feudal lords have fallen, there is no one left capable of controlling the army. In the post-feudal—the post-Gothic—world, the governing power can no longer be maintained by military power, for now 'the whole people be landlords, or hold the lands so divided among them, that no one man, or number of men, within the compass of the few or aristocracy, overbalance them'. This is the 'balance of the land' which is said to be favourable to 'a commonwealth'.[43]

Under this new balance of the land, Harrington's account of necessity and fear comes close to Hobbes's account of 'equality'. All men—except for a small minority who are still alienated from landownership even under this balance—become equal in terms of military power. To Hobbes, men are naturally equal before the civil government is established: to Harrington, men are equal under a certain balance of the land. Hobbes's man always has the power to kill others, a power which is equal to the power of other men: Harrington's man has a power to do so if only he has land. Most people will be independent if the land is equally distributed, 'for equality of estates causeth equality of power'.[44] What should be noted is that Harrington here agreed with Hobbes in thinking that equality of power leads to anarchy. Both men have as a main concern the problem of equality of power.[45] To avoid the worst scenario, anarchy, Hobbes elaborated his theory of sovereignty; Harrington, as we shall see later, his theory of mixed government: the theory of the proper form of government under the balance of the land which is favourable to a commonwealth.

Nevertheless, perhaps the most crucial difference between the two writers lies here. In Hobbes's theory, equality of power among men is a starting-point of the argument. For Harrington, equality of power is one of the conclusions that derive from his doctrine of the balance of the land. The way in which Hobbes intended to remove the state of equality was to erect an absolute sovereign by institution or by acquisition. Yet the Hobbes of *Leviathan* allowed only one exit from the state of equality. This was a sovereign by conquest. What terminates the state of war in *Leviathan* is the emergence of a conqueror who excels others in terms of military power, and has power strong enough to keep the others silent. The implication of Harrington's account of fear and necessity is that he has blocked Hobbes's loophole.

As we saw in the previous section Harrington claimed that a Hobbesian conqueror must be the landlord. This thesis had a simple but serious implication for his idea of the state of equality. A Hobbesian conqueror may

---

[43] *Oceana*, 164 [p. 12].   [44] Ibid. 170 [p. 20].

[45] *The Rota or a Model of a Free State* (London, 1660), 808.

emerge in Harrington's scheme, if only he is the overwhelming landlord in a region. Yet there can be no conqueror in the Harringtonian state of equality where the land is equally distributed.

Hobbes is wrong, implies Harrington, if he expects a conqueror to emerge from the English civil wars. No one can form a powerful army and become a conqueror in a state of equality. A conqueror who becomes a sovereign in England must be a feudal landlord having the greater part of the land, but there can be no such person in the state of equality. Hobbes's notion of a commonwealth by acquisition cannot be applied to the post-feudal world. A civil war may produce a victor, but not a sovereign. Harrington's doctrine of the balance of the land strictly excludes any possibility of the emergence of such a conqueror from the condition of 'equality of estates'—the balance of the land in mid-seventeenth-century England.

Like Hobbes, Harrington acknowledges that the parliamentarian army won the civil wars. Yet his understanding of 'victory' is different from Hobbes's. In 'A Review, and Conclusion' of *Leviathan*, Hobbes approximated the fact that parliament had won the civil war to the assertion that parliament had a capacity to protect its subjects. Harrington opposes that approximation. For him, what matters is the present balance of the land, not the result of the civil war. The Rump Parliament, which is not an overwhelming feudal landlord, cannot be a conqueror. It could become a conqueror by the massive confiscation of lands from the people. But to seize lands from 'a people that never fought against you, but whose arms you have borne', is 'against any example in human nature'. In the period of the Protectorate the situation remains basically the same. Cromwell is not a conqueror, and his military power is no more than a 'force', which is not supported by the balance. His government is not 'a single person and a parliament, but a single person and an army'. Being supported only by 'force', his government, according to the doctrine of the balance, 'can be of no long continuance'.[46]

Yet Harrington's reference to the Protectorate is a mere deviation. He returns from it to focus on the Rump Parliament. 'The government of Oceana (as it stood at the time whereof we discourse) consisting of one single council of the people, to the exclusion of the king and of the lords, was called a parliament.' The rule of the Rump was recognizable neither as a feudal landlord of modern prudence nor as a constituent of the mixed government required by ancient prudence. Harrington, for whom an

---

[46] *Oceana*, 198–201 [pp. 56–9]. In the first 'Preliminary', Harrington claimed that tyranny, oligarchy, and anarchy are 'but of short continuance'. See ibid., 164 [p. 12].

immediate transition from modern to ancient prudence should have taken place after the execution of the king, saw the Rump as an interruption of that process. The Stuart monarchy had been succeeded by 'So new a thing that neither ancient nor modern prudence can show any avowed example of the like'.[47]

Even so, Harrington identified an apologist for the Rump, who, too, belonged to 'neither ancient nor modern prudence'. This, of course, was Hobbes, 'who is surer of nothing than that a popular commonwealth consisteth but of one council', and who 'transcribed his doctrine out of this assembly'.[48] But that doctrine could not be justified by the experience of the Rump, believed Harrington, since the Rump's rule was only a short-lived one.

We saw in the previous section that Harrington equated 'oligarchy' (as he equated 'tyranny') with 'confusion'. He applies that definition to the refutation of Hobbes. In Harrington's judgement, the Rump Parliament, which Hobbes considered to be the conqueror after the civil wars, was an oligarchy, for the Rump could not control the army by 'necessity'.[49]

If the emphasis of Hobbes's notion of equality was upon the 'mutual fear' among men, Harrington's equality features independence among them. When they are independent of each other, they can use their sword at their will—not 'of necessity' but 'of choice'. Because of this, they will never form the army, disciplined by necessity, which is needed to keep peace and order. When Hobbes said that a sovereign needs the common power in order to punish those who do not obey him, the common power must mean a military power which is rigidly controlled by the sovereign's will. It cannot mean a military power which happens to be formed by the will of individuals who are independent of each other. In Harrington's view, in fact, the Rump Parliament had the latter sort of army, to which he applied the word 'force'. Hobbes was wrong to consider the Rump to be a sovereign.

The royalists were defeated in the civil wars, thought Harrington, because under the new balance of the land the king deployed only limited military power and his arms were 'as ineffectual as his nobility'. Many independent individuals fought together for the parliament and formed 'the victorious army'.[50] But winning victory was not the same as having military

---

[47] *Oceana*, 205 [pp. 64–5].   [48] Ibid.

[49] '[T]here being nothing of this kind that I can find in story but the oligarchy of Athens' (ibid. 205 [p. 65]); 'A council without a balance is not a commonwealth, but an oligarchy' (ibid. 206 [p. 66]).

[50] Ibid. 198 [p. 56].

power to govern. Hobbes was wrong to infer, from parliament's victory in the civil wars, that the new English government had the basis for the common power. The Rump Parliament, argued Harrington, did not have a sufficient military power to govern the country. In reality, under the Rump, the people were divided into parties. No wonder, for the Rump was not the conqueror, and therefore, despite Hobbes's endorsement of it, 'there [was] not any common ligament of power sufficient to reconcile or hold them'.[51]

Harrington was a writer who appeared not only after the English monarchy but also after the failure of the first English republican government. His narrative of English history in the 'The Second Part of the Preliminaries' shows why the Stuart monarchy collapsed and why modern prudence was obsolete. But at the same time it also claims that the failure of the Rump Parliament was inevitable. If the fall of the Stuart monarchy underlined the failure of modern prudence, the dissolution of the Rump revealed the deficiency of Hobbes's theory of sovereignty.

When the balance of the lands is favourable to a commonwealth, there emerges a state of equality where neither fear nor necessity can make for political order. We may feel tempted to conclude that Harrington's 'commonwealth', too, is another name for 'confusion', no less than 'tyranny' and 'oligarchy' are. Nevertheless he maintains his distinction between a commonwealth and the three unstable forms, tyranny, oligarchy, and anarchy.[52] In the state of equality, any government which achieves stability under this balance will, in his scheme, be called a commonwealth. Something other than military power is needed if a commonwealth is to make 'a civil society of men'. That is, in Harrington's view, a certain set of political institutions. Now his message to Hobbes is clear enough: there can be no conquest in the state of equality. What is needed in mid-seventeenth-century England is to construct proper political institutions without

---

[51] Ibid. 202 [p. 61].

[52] Tyranny, oligarchy, and anarchy appear, argues Harrington, when 'force' is 'interposed'. It follows that absolute monarchy, mixed monarchy, and commonwealth appear only when force is not interposed. However, his real interest is in the distinction between commonwealth and the three unstable forms. This becomes evident during his explanation of the sixfold classification of government. Harrington inserts a reservation, '(without the interposition of force)', into the paragraph in which he explains commonwealth, but not in those which explain absolute monarchy and mixed monarchy. See the previous section above and *Oceana*, 163–4 [pp. 11–12]. It may be that when he inserted that reservation, 'force' particularly referred to the New Model Army, or Cromwell's musketeers, who dissolved the Rump, and that Harrington's major concern was how to end the interventions of the force by introducing a new form of government. His solution of this problem was to deploy Cromwell's military power to introduce the new constitutional arrangements rather than to govern the country. See *Oceana*, 207 [p. 67]; *Valerius and Publicola* (London, 1659), 784.

presupposing the existence of any military power sufficient to govern. Should 'fear' and 'necessity' not be available to keep the subjects obedient to the government, another principle of obedience has to be found. That is the challenge Harrington meets by turning to ancient prudence, the classical idea of mixed government.

Like Hobbes, Harrington wanted to eradicate resistance to the government in which sovereignty is established. For Harrington, as for Bodin and Hobbes, sovereignty had to be absolute. Yet if we follow Bodin and Hobbes, Harrington's idea may seem eccentric. For Bodin and Hobbes, to establish sovereignty is to unify different wills into a single will, and this singularity is guaranteed by the fact that the sovereign himself (themselves) has only one will. The single will of the sovereign will end anarchy and restore peace and order. In this unifying process, some measures of coercion are needed, for the subjects must be forced to give up their will and accept the will of the sovereign. In Hobbes's case, the subjects are forced by the covenant and the fear of punishment to abandon their right to follow their private judgements. Harrington's argument is different. He did not think that the acceptance of the sovereign's will by the subjects was absolutely necessary to avoid anarchy. The need was to eradicate resistance. If there are not the conditions of resistance, and the government is stable, sovereignty is established, he believes. As long as resistance remains a possibility, the government has to maintain a means of coercion. If there is no such possibility, there is no need for an instrument of coercion. Even when the government does not have any means of coercion, thinks Harrington, the eradication of resistance is still possible.

Harrington transforms Hobbes's meaning of obedience. To Harrington's mind obedience, in the state of equality, is not—and cannot be—obedience by command. It is merely the absence of resistance, which is sufficient for the ending of anarchy. This transformation enables Harrington to put forward a new notion as the source of obedience. What replaces the combination of 'fear' and 'necessity' is 'interest'.

Harrington's deployment of the word 'interest' derives from his unique approach toward the controlling of military power. The common way to control a 'sword' is to suppress it by a greater one. But what if no greater one is available? This is the predicament in the Harringtonian state of equality. He provides an alternative approach, which reflects his novel view of obedience. When a sword is exercised by individual people, each individual is held to have his 'will' to exercise it. In Harrington's terms, military power is considered to be used under the individual's will, that is, his 'reason'.[5] A man draws his sword and rises up against the government because he wants to advance his ends, his 'interest'. Without an 'interest' in doing so, he will not draw his sword. If the government can prevent him from having any interest in using his sword against it, therefore, the

---

[5] Ibid. 171 [p. 21]; *The Prerogative of Popular Government*, 401.

government can virtually disarm him against it. This is the basic point of creating a government which is not supported by military power.

To control the sword of the people, Harrington does not try to place the law 'above' it, for he believes that to be impossible. Rather, he claims that the sword should be placed 'in' the law.[6] His aim is to wrap it with constitutional arrangements. 'A sword; but that rust, or must have a scabbard, and the scabbard of this kind of sword is a good frame of government.'[7] Thus Harrington's approach turns the focus of his argument away from the balance of the lands to constitutional arrangements; that is, from the domain of power to that of authority. When the government does not have a proportion of lands large enough to rule by power, its capacity to maintain order wholly depends upon what it offers rather than what it possesses. If what it offers meets the interests of all, resistance will be eradicated. In Harrington's account, what the government offers wholly depends on its constitutional arrangements. If the government is perfectly framed, it is able to put an end to anarchy.

His definition of perfect government summarizes the basic tenet of his new political theory.

the perfection of government lieth upon such a libration in the frame of it, that no man or men, in or under it, can have the interest or, having the interest, can have the power to disturb it with sedition.[8]

When no one has an interest 'to disturb' the government 'with sedition', the government is considered to represent 'the common interest'. Even when the government does not possess the Hobbesian 'common power' to keep the people in 'awe', it can still offer 'the common interest' to keep them quiet. Harrington replaces Hobbes's notion of the common power with his own concept of the common interest.[9]

The assertion that a stable government is a perfect government would have raised the eyebrows of Plato, Aristotle, and their successors (if not those of Polybius).[10] To them, a perfect government had to be more than a merely stable one. It had to promote virtue and the good life. However, Harrington claimed that his equation of stability with perfection 'requireth no proof'.[11] His claim makes sense when we see that he makes it as a reply not to Plato or Aristotle but to Hobbes. It is Hobbes whom he 'invite[d]' to discuss 'the perfection of government'.

The notion of perfection of government may seem characteristic of

---

[6] *Oceana*, 174 [p. 25].

[7] *The Prerogative of Popular Government*, 391.

[8] *Oceana*, 179 [pp. 30–1].

[9] Ibid. 171–2 [p. 22].

[10] For Polybius, see Sect. 1.2 above.

[11] *Oceana*, 179 [p. 31].

Harrington and not of Hobbes. But Hobbes, who used the phrase 'the imperfection of policy', thus implied—on Harrington's reading of that phrase—that there could be perfection of government. It is in reply to Hobbes's reference to the imperfection of policy that Harrington discussed the perfection of government. Hobbes, blaming 'the Reading of the books of Policy, and Histories of the antient Greeks, and Romans' as 'the most frequent causes' of rebellion against monarchy, claims that that reading has led young men to praise '*Tyrannicide*' without 'considering the frequent Seditions, and Civill warres, produced by the imperfection of their Policy'.[12] Harrington's definition of the perfect government is a direct response to that claim. He agrees with Hobbes in equating perfection with stability. Harrington's concern, even when he discusses constitutional arrangements and the common interest, is Hobbes's concern: the prevention of 'Seditions and Civill warres', and the restoration of peace and order.[13]

Harrington defines the condition of the perfection of government as 'an equal commonwealth'.[14] When Harrington claims that 'an equal commonwealth cannot be seditious', his claim is tautologous, since he has already equated equality with stability.[15] An equal commonwealth is one which is equipped with the perfect constitutional arrangements. It has to have Harringtonian features of government: a bicameral legislature, and 'rotation'. These features guarantee stability.[16]

Earlier in this section, we saw that among the four forms of government—commonwealth, tyranny, oligarchy, and anarchy—Harrington considers only commonwealth to be a stable one, and that a commonwealth must be a mixed government. But when Harrington defines the perfect form of government, he describes it not merely as a commonwealth but as

[12] *Leviathan*, XXIX. 225–6 [pp. 170–1].

[13] Harrington quotes from *Leviathan*, XXIX. titled 'Of those things that Weaken, or tend to the DISSOLUTION of a Common-wealth' at *Oceana*, 178 [p. 30].

[14] '[A]n equal commonwealth is that only which is without flaw and containeth in it the full perfection of government' (*Oceana*, 180 [p. 32]); 'if a commonwealth be perfectly equal, she is void of sedition, and hath attained unto perfection, as being void of all internal causes of dissolution' (*The Art of Lawgiving* (London, 1659), 613).

[15] *The Prerogative of Popular Government*, 426. The real question should not be whether an equal commonwealth cannot be seditious, but whether it exists in reality. Harrington is sure that it exists, and we shall examine the basis of his confidence in the next chapter.

[16] *Oceana*, 180–1 [pp. 33–4]. Harrington claims that besides rotation, an agrarian law, which fixes the balance of the land, is required to make a commonwealth equal. However, in what follows, as far as the idea of equal commonwealth is concerned, we shall concentrate upon the rotation, and later turn to an agrarian law in Appendix B. For unlike the rotation, an agrarian law is not at the heart of Harrington's idea of mixed government. Rather, the aim of an agrarian law is to support the rotation, and the function of that law is to stop an equal commonwealth from becoming an unequal one.

an equal commonwealth. We should note, therefore, that the notion of an equal commonwealth contains two different types of argument concerning mixed government.

First, a stable government must be a commonwealth. To create a commonwealth, the principle of mixed government must be adopted. In terms of constitutional arrangements, this principle is embodied as a bicameral legislature of 'the senate' and 'the popular assembly'.

Secondly, a stable government must be equal. To create an equal commonwealth, the principle of mixed government must be operated 'equally'—in a proper way. In terms of constitutional arrangements, the members of the legislature have to be frequently and regularly reshuffled by 'rotation', so that a large number of people have equal opportunities to be elected.

Thus two steps are required to create an equal commonwealth.[17] The first step, which shows that any simple forms of government will inevitably fail, was needed to repudiate Hobbes's idea that 'a commonwealth consisteth of a single person, or of a single assembly'.[18] But that step was not enough to attain stability. After all, not all failed commonwealths had been ruled by single assemblies. Many commonwealths which had been mixed governments had fallen into confusion, as Hobbes pointed out. So Harrington needed to take the second step. He needed to show that mixed government never fails provided it is properly constituted. The commonwealths which had fallen, the Roman republic among them, had been imperfectly constituted. We examine that first step in the next section, before we follow his argument further.[19]

2. Interest and Authority

For peace and order to be achieved in the state of equality, the principle of mixed government has to be adopted at the outset, Harrington claims. This first step requires a bicameral legislature, which embodies that principle. The failure of the Rump illustrated Harrington's point. The Rump

[17] In the first step, commonwealth is contrasted against tyranny, oligarchy, and anarchy; in the second step, equal commonwealth against unequal commonwealth. The Roman republic is used as a good example in the former case, as a bad example in the latter one. Yet in taking both steps, he uses the same single criterion—stability—to distinguish between different forms of government. This makes Harrington's argument sound complicated. As a result, an unequal commonwealth is often described as if it were no less factious and unstable than oligarchy, tyranny, etc.

[18] *Oceana*, 184 [p. 38].

[19] This second step—discussion of the equality of a commonwealth—involves Harrington in criticism of Machiavelli, as we shall see in Sect. 7.2 below.

was not a conqueror, and did not have 'the common power' to govern. But it could have survived if it had only located 'the common interest' instead. It could have done so by 'framing the government unto the foundation'—by adopting the principle of mixed government.[20] The Rump failed to take that step. It was 'an oligarchy, which is a single council both debating and resolving, dividing and choosing'.[21]

The common interest can never be found in a single council, Harrington believes. It can only be found in a bicameral legislature—a combination of two assemblies with separate functions, 'debating' and 'resolving'. The 'debating and proposing' chamber is called 'the senate', and the 'resolving and deciding' one 'the people', or 'the popular assembly'.[22] That functional division is, in his account, the core of the principle of mixed government, which ancient prudence endorses. Since the common interest is to be represented in the form of a law, the law-making body is to be the heart of Harrington's scheme. In the law-making process a senate makes a bill, which is to be tabled in a popular assembly later. If only this functional division is introduced, argues Harrington, the common interest will prevail, and peace and order will be restored.

If Hobbes's readers are confused by the circularity of his argument about 'the covenant' and 'the common power', Harrington's may be puzzled by the simplicity of his confidence in the efficacy of the division between 'debating' and 'resolving'. He demonstrates his principle by an analogy: the well-known analogy of a 'common practice' of two girls when they share a cake. This image offers a peaceful and literally sweet contrast to the dark and complicated reality of the civil wars. Perhaps this is one of the reasons why Harrington was sometimes regarded as a dreaming utopian.

However, the story of the cake was not the source of his confidence in the principle of the bicameral legislature, as we shall see in the next chapter. It is not the case that he thought out the idea of 'dividing' and 'choosing' first, and translated it into the combination of the senate and the popular assembly only afterwards. Rather, as we shall see, he extracted that principle from his examination of commonwealths in ancient prudence. He was sure of that principle because it had worked in the experience of antiquity and that of Venice, in the practice of ancient prudence.

In his mind, the principle was sanctioned not only by 'experience' but by 'reason'. 'Reason and experience', he believed, always support each other.[23] Hobbes, by contrast, far from bringing 'experience' to the aid of 'reason',

---

[20] *Oceana*, 164 [p. 12]. [21] Ibid. 206 [p. 65].
[22] Ibid. 173–4, 266, 278, 284 [pp. 23–4, 146–7, 163, 170–1], etc.
[23] Ibid. 180, 184 [pp. 32, 38], etc. See Sect. 7.2 below.

ignored it. He turned in the domain of reason alone. In order to meet Hobbes's argument, Harrington took him on within that circumscribed territory. The story of the girls who cut and choose the cake was used by Harrington in reply to a statement of Hobbes, which confines itself to logical abstraction. In 'The Epistle dedicatory' to *The Elements of Law*, Hobbes wrote:[24]

FROM the two principal parts of our nature, Reason and Passion, have proceeded two kinds of learning, mathematical and dogmatical. The former is free from controversies and dispute, because it consisteth in comparing figures and motion only; in which things truth and the interest of men oppose not each other. But in the later there is nothing not disputable, because it compareth men, and meddleth with their right and profit; in which, as oft as reason is against a man, so oft will a man be against reason.[25]

Harrington, who likewise acknowledges the difficulty of achieving a consensus in the world of politics, quotes the conclusion of Hobbes's statement in *Oceana*:

'*as often as reason is against a man, so often will a man be against reason.*' This is thought to be a shrewd saying, but will do no harm; for be it so that reason is nothing but interest, there be divers interests, and so divers reasons.[26]

Why do different people perceive 'divers reasons'? Harrington explains:

a man doth not look upon reason as it is right or wrong in itself, but as it makes for him or against him.[27]

This account looks close to Hobbes's.

Every man, for his own part, calleth that which pleaseth, and is delightful to himself, GOOD; and that EVIL which displeaseth him.[28]

In this account, Hobbes asserts that no one could ever be persuaded to unite with others under the banner of the common good. Harrington concurs. Any attempt to persuade men to advance 'the common interest' at the expense of their own interests will fail:

all this is to no more end than to persuade every man in a popular government not to carve himself of that which he desires most, but to be mannerly at the public table, and give the best from himself unto decency and the common interest.[29]

---

[24] See S. B. Liljegren, *James Harrington's Oceana* (Heidelberg, 1924), 245.
[25] *The Elements of Law*, 'The Epistle Dedicatory', p. xv.
[26] *Oceana*, 171 [p. 21]. The italic is Harrington's.
[27] Ibid. 172 [p. 22].
[28] *The Elements of Law*, I. 7. 3. 29.   [29] *Oceana*, 172 [p. 22].

Hobbes, who thought that even to attempt such persuasion would cause civil war, never tried to identify the real content of the common interest beyond the most basic need, peace and order. Harrington, too, steers clear of any such persuasion. Nevertheless he does stick to the notion of the common interest. For him, 'to persuade' by words is one thing, 'to constrain' by the 'orders of a government' another. Where persuasion is useless, constitutional arrangements can constrain people to care for the common interest. It is upon this basis that Harrington introduces the analogy of two girls.

According to Harrington, where one of the two girls is to cut the cake into two parts, and the other is free to choose which part she will take, the cake will be shared equally. The one realizes that she needs to divide the cake equally, for otherwise the other would take the bigger part.[30] The point to note here is the relationship between the two girls. The relationship correctly reflects that which prevails among men in the Harringtonian state of equality. Neither of them is a tenant of the other, or is capable of snatching the whole cake by military power. Because neither necessity nor fear is capable of settling their dispute over the cake, the argument reaches deadlock.

What breaks the deadlock, claims Harrington, is the separation of dividing from choosing. The crucial role in the analogy is taken not by the girl who chooses the cake but by the one who cuts. For as long as the cake is cut equally, the one who chooses cannot affect the outcome. Yet the girl who cuts restrains her appetite for a larger part of the cake, and divides it equally, since she knows that otherwise she will be rewarded with a smaller part. So she cuts the cake according to the common interest of the two. But she was not 'persuaded' to do so by anybody. She was 'constrained' to behave like that by the separation of dividing from choosing. This separation is equal to that of 'proposing' and 'resolving', Harrington maintains. A senate in a commonwealth, he believes, will be led by the separation of proposing and resolving to attempt to discover where the common interest lies, and to propose it in the form of a bill.

[30] '[T]hat such orders may be established as may, nay must, give the upper hand in all cases unto common right or interest, notwithstanding the nearness of that which sticks unto every man in private, and this in a way of equal certainty and facility, is known even unto girls, being no other than those that are of common practice with them in divers cases. For example, two of them have a cake yet undivided, which was given between them. That each of them therefore may have that which is due, "Divide", says one unto the other, "and I will choose; or let me divide, and you shall choose." If this be but once agreed upon, it is enough; for the divident dividing unequally loses, in regard that the other takes the better half; wherefore she divides equally, and so both have right' (*Oceana*, 172 [p. 22]).

His constitutional arrangements create a space where the members of the senate will find the granting of any favour to their private interests useless. Every senator may want to see his private interest advanced first. But this is impossible, for he is forbidden to 'choose'. Senators know that if they propose a bill 'such as would be advantageous' to them 'but prejudicial to the many' (= if they cut the cake unequally), it will be thwarted by the popular assembly (= the bigger part will be taken away by others). The senators, 'perceiving that they cannot impair the common interest, have no other interest left but to improve it'.[31] In this case, they do not need to be persuaded to prefer the common interest. They merely give up their hope of advancing their own interest because they know it is impossible. The essence of the institutional division of debating and resolving is to produce an area where men are allowed to think about the common interest without being distracted by their own interests.

In the senate a man ceases to 'look upon reason' 'as it makes for him or against him'. Instead he does so 'as it is right or wrong in itself'. This is the response to the statement Hobbes had made in 1640.

Yet the people may feel tempted to debate and to make a bill on their own, as the Athenian people did. What hinders them from violating the functional division? Taking an oath is pointless, since the people has 'the sword'—'an oath . . . is a weak tie for such hands as have the sword in them'.[32] Again, Harrington remains faithful to his master, who claimed that the sword cannot be controlled by the word. Only the authority of the senate makes the people refrain from debating, he believes. When the senate guarantees a space where the common interest will prevail, it is said to have authority. Authority is a function of articulating the common interest, which is represented by a bill to 'propose'. The authority is compared with the power of the popular assembly, which is expected to 'resolve' the proposal. In the maintenance of domestic peace, the essential function is authority rather than power, for the popular assembly will never fail to resolve a bill, if only the bill really suits the common interest. Authority, not power, matters in Harrington's argument after he has shifted it from the balance of the lands to constitutional arrangements.

Harrington strengthens the authority of the senate by ensuring that the personal quality of the senators is above that of the average citizens. When we 'take any number of men, as twenty', and allow them discussion, Harrington writes, 'a third will be wiser, or at least less foolish, than all the rest'. By the guidance of 'the six', 'the fourteen discover things that they

---

[31] *The Prerogative of Popular Government*, 416–17.
[32] *Oceana*, 268 [p. 149]. See also ibid. 167 [p. 16].

never thought on'. Like those six wise men in the twenty, the wiser sort of people should be the senators and should form 'a natural aristocracy' of the commonwealth.[33] Eligibility for the senate is restricted to men with a certain minimum of real property, since Harrington believes property to reflect the level of political intelligence.[34]

Thus 'the nobility or gentry' is considered to be indispensable to Harrington's commonwealth.[35] The senate forms 'the natural aristocracy', and the popular assembly 'the natural democracy'.[36] Those two elements form 'the natural mixture of a well-ordered commonwealth'.[37] Yet no matter how wise a senator may be, he will be no less selfish than the ordinary people. If he is selfless in the debating chamber, that is solely because of the separation of debating from resolving.

Of course, to prevent the senators from being distracted by their private interests is not necessarily the same as to make them care for the common interest. Harrington's argument will have to be developed if he is to show why his system will work. However, he believes that he has already shown what is indispensable to the identification of the common interest. Without the Harringtonian bicameral system, the representation of the common interest is impossible. When the separation of the functions of dividing and choosing is ignored, mere confusion follows. Indeed that was what happened after 1649. The Rump Parliament had tried both to divide and to choose a cake:

if she that divided must have chosen also, it had been little worse for the other, in case she had not divided at all, but kept the whole cake unto herself, in regard that being to choose too, she divided accordingly. . . . in a commonwealth consisting of a single council, there is no other to choose than that which divided; whence it is, that such a council faileth not to scramble, that is to be factious, there being no other dividing of the cake in that case but among themselves.[38]

The Rump failed to provide a space where its members would discuss the interests of the nation without being distracted by their own private interests. The parliament neither had the common power as a conqueror nor held authority by representing the common interest. No government by a single assembly can end an anarchy in the state of equality. When a single assembly monopolizes 'both debating and resolving', 'what that must come

[33] Ibid. 172–3 [pp. 23–4].
[34] This restriction leads to the issue of an agrarian law. See Appendix B.
[35] *Oceana*, 257 [pp. 135–6]. See also pp. 166–7, 173, 183 [pp. 14–15, 23–4, 36–7].
[36] *The Prerogative of Popular Government*, 416
[37] *Oceana*, 259 [p. 138].
[38] Ibid. 173 [p. 24].

to was shown by the example of the girls, and is apparent through all experience'.[39] The impermanence of the Rump was inevitable in the light of its constitutional arrangements.

Thus what Harrington requires as the criterion of mixed government is the bicameral legislature. Yet readers familiar with earlier notions of mixed government may feel at odds with him, since his legislature consists only of two elements, not of three. He is ready to answer that objection. A law made by the legislature has to be executed, and consequently the magistracy is needed. Since the magistracy represents the monarchical element, the classical triad of monarchy, aristocracy, and democracy will be completed in the Harringtonian commonwealth.[40] However, he did not think the completion of the triad to be essential, since the magistracy was not as vital as the legislature. In any commonwealth, believed Harrington, the magistracy derived from 'necessity', not from 'prudence'. No commonwealth can survive without a magistracy. So he took issue with the ancients, saying 'if there be such a thing as pure monarchy, yet that there should be such an one as pure aristocracy or pure democracy is not to my understanding'. The magistracy is simply required to carry out its function 'according unto the law'.[41] It had nothing to do with identifying the common interest. Harrington's commonwealth may appear to be a mixture of that triad, but the core is the mixture of aristocracy and democracy. He felt no unease about this, and did not stick to the beauty of the triad. Like Polybius, he merely tried to learn from the constitutional architecture of republican Rome. The bicameral system of the senate and the popular assembly was coherent with the phrase *senatus populusque Romanus*, which he invoked against Hobbes's criticism of mixed government.[42]

3. Faction and Equality

Harrington, in adopting the principle of mixed government, knows that it does not by itself guarantee peace and order. While any simple forms of government will fail, a commonwealth which has a bicameral legislature sometimes fails, too. A commonwealth must be 'equal' to attain stability, Harrington claims. Why is this second step necessary? How does an equal commonwealth locate the common interest which secures peace, while an unequal one does not? These questions cannot be tackled satisfactorily until we have examined Harrington's account of the relationship between private interests and the common interest. How are private interests,

[39] *Oceana*, 206 [p. 65].   [40] Ibid. 174 [p. 25].
[41] Ibid.   [42] Ibid. 163 [p. 10].

which are bound to contradict each other, integrated under the common interest in his scheme? This section examines the manner in which he, in contrast to his contemporaries, treats private interests and explains why he adheres to his equal commonwealth.

Harrington's attitude towards the relationship between private interest and the common interest is not straightforward. On the one hand, the two look incompatible, since Harrington claims that members of the senate should be set free from all consideration of private interests. But on the other, the common interest is supposed to satisfy all men's interests, for otherwise the government might be threatened by rebellion.[43]

Of course, Harrington was not the only writer of the Interregnum to use the term 'interest' in the debate about forms of government: it was often used by contemporary pamphleteers. John Pocock suggests that *Oceana* should be considered alongside the literature published in 1656 by Marchamont Nedham, Sir Henry Vane, and 'R.G.' That literature, published between May and July, shared the dissatisfaction within the army against the Protectorate government. It had in common the language of the Good Old Cause.[44]

In addition, those authors are 'interest' theorists, too.[45] They share the belief that a split between private interest and common interest has entered the government. They take this split to be the source of political division and faction.

Nedham's contribution to the literature of 1656, *The Excellencie of a Free State*, is a collection of editorials published in *Mercurius Politicus* in

[43] This relationship between the two has been one of the vital issues of Harrington scholarship. See J. A. W. Gunn, *Politics and the Public Interest in the Seventeenth Century* (London, 1969); K. Toth, 'Interpretation in Political Theory: The Case of Harrington', *Review of Politics*, 37 (1975), 317–39. Gunn was particularly concerned with the manner in which Harrington treated the concept of 'interest'. He properly pointed to the tension between 'diverse private interests' and 'a public interest' (Gunn, *Politics and the Public Interest*, 140). However, his conclusion is not very persuasive. Gunn suggests that Harrington's argument about the public interest ends up by adopting the majority principle and by failing to satisfy the minority to which the diversity of interests inevitably gives birth (pp. 140–2). In fact, Harrington's aim was to invent a machinery that would never allow a cleavage between the majority and the minority in the commonwealth.

[44] Marchamont Nedham, *The Excellencie of a Free State* (London, 1656); Sir Henry Vane the Younger, *A Healing Question Propounded and Resolved upon Occasion of the Late Publique and Seasonable Call to Humiliation* (London, 1656); 'R.G.', *A Copy of a Letter from an Officer of the Army in Ireland, to his Highness the Lord Protector, concerning his changing of the Government* (London, 1656; and a modern reprint: Exeter, 1974). For this see Pocock, 'Historical Introduction', in *Works*, 36–42. See also Blair Worden, 'Marchamont Nedham and the Beginnings of English Republicanism, 1649–1656', in David Wootton (ed.), *Republicanism, Liberty, and Commercial Society, 1649–1776* (Stanford, Calif., 1994), 60–81.

[45] On the term '"interest" theorist', see Jonathan Scott, *Algernon Sidney and the English Republic, 1623–1677* (Cambridge, 1988), 110.

1650–2. Nedham emphasizes the tension between 'particular', 'private' interests and that of 'the Publique' in the passages below.

> it being usual in Free-States to be more tender of the Publick in all their Decrees, than of particular Interests: whereas the case is otherwise in a Monarchy, because in this Form the Princes pleasure weighs down all Considerations of the Common good.[46]

> how unsafe it is in a new alteration, to trust any man with too great a share of Government, or place of Trust; for such persons stand ever ready . . . upon any occasion of discontent, or of serving their own Interests, to betray and alter the Government.[47]

> Not to let two of one Family to bear Offices of High Trust at one time . . . The reason is evident, because a permission of them, gives a particular Family an opportunity, to bring their own private Interest into competition, with that of the Publique.[48]

In the other two writers, we find the view that the private interest is represented by 'the head of the army', while the common interest is guarded by 'the Honest party', who have stood firm to 'the good old cause'. Sir Henry Vane's contribution, *A Healing Question*, uses the term 'interest' in those ways:

> some-thing rising up that seems rather accommodated to the private and selfish interest of a particular part (in comparison) then truly adequate to the common good and concern of the whole Body engaged in this Cause.[49]

> the standing Army and their Governours . . . in a divided interest from the rest of the Body of Honest men, . . . By this mutual and happy transition which may be made between the party of Honest men in the Three Nations virtually in Arms, and those actually so now in power at the Head of the Army, how suddenly would the union of the whole Body be consolidated.[50]

> The matter which is in question among the dissenting parts of the whole body of honest men, is not so trivial and of such small consequence, as some would make it.[51]

> To remove out of the minds and spirits of the Honest party, that still agree in the reason and justice of the good old Cause, all things of a private Nature and selfish Concern (the tendency whereof serves but to foment and strengthen wrath and divisions amongst them) and in place thereof to set before them that common and publique interest, which (if with sincerity embraced) may be the means of not only procuring a firm union amongst them, but also of conserving them herein.[52]

---

[46] Nedham, *The Excellencie*, 19–20. [47] Ibid. 21–2.
[48] Ibid. 167. [49] Vane, *A Healing Question*, 3.
[50] Ibid. 11. [51] Ibid. 15.
[52] Ibid. 'Postscript'.

The third author, 'R.G.', employs the same vocabulary. He writes in *A Copy of a Letter*:

the best and most limited *Monarchies* are but perpetuall contests between the interest of Mankind, and that of one person, each striving industriously which shall ruine and undermine the other.[53]

what I did originallie look at, was the justness and honestie of the cause, the excellencie of libertie, the glorie of advancing and promoting the interest of mankind, the making my Nation more wise, vesiant [? *sic*], happie, and honest then before, as well as more free.[54]

that life of yours [= Cromwell's life] like to be, which hath been hitherto so precious to all the honest partie in these Nations.[55]

the only firme States men, for sticking to their principles these must now be called the honest partie, whilst those who were so the last year stiled factious fellows.[56]

when you have made it the interest of honest men, . . .on this arbitrary Soveraignty.[57]

Harrington shared the concern of these writers about the tension between the common interest and private interest, tension which, in his view as in theirs, causes factional divisions:

if we have anything of piety or of prudence, let us raise ourselves out of the mire of private interest unto the contemplation of virtue, and put an hand unto the removal of this evil from under the sun: this evil against which no government that is not secured can be good.[58]

Yet his approach to private interest is not so straightforward as that of the other three writers. In the following passages, for all his concern about private interests and factions, he does not necessarily take private interest to be incompatible with the common interest. It is these passages, rather than the passage above, which distinguishes his approach from those of the other writers.[59]

Whereas the people, taken apart, are but so many private interests, but if you take them together they are the public interest; the public interest of a commonwealth . . . is nearest that of mankind, and that of mankind is right reason.[60]

every man hath an interest what to choose, and that choice which suiteth with every

---

[53] 'R.G.', *A Copy of a Letter*, 4.   [54] Ibid. 11.   [55] Ibid. 12.
[56] Ibid. 14.   [57] Ibid. 19.   [58] *Oceana*, 169 [p. 19].
[59] Pocock and Worden take a different view, and consider that passage to be strong evidence that 'virtue' plays a key role in Harrington's argument. See Pocock, 'Historical Introduction', in *Works*, 64; Worden, 'James Harrington and "The Commonwealth of Oceana", 1656', in *Republicanism, Liberty, and Commercial Society*, 106.
[60] *Oceana*, 280–1 [p. 166].

man's interest excludeth the distinct or private interest or passion of any man, and so cometh up unto the common and public interest or reason.[61]

that which is the interest of the most particular men, the same, being summed up in the common vote, is the public interest.[62]

These passages are not easy to follow, but we may at least say that they show Harrington to have double standards of private interest. There seem to be two types of private interest in his mind. One is assumed to be compatible with the common interest: another is denounced as incompatible with it. What sort of private interest, then, is acceptable in his world?

A clue lies in the difference which separates Harrington from Sir Henry Vane and 'R.G.' For Vane and 'R.G.', who took the side of 'the honest party' against the army grandees, the common interest was the interest of 'the honest party'. They used the phrase 'the common interest' to speak for a particular group under the name of 'the common interest'. Yet Harrington never identifies the common interest with the interest of any one party. He believes that there can be no party whose interest can be endorsed as the common interest, because 'a commonwealth consisting of a party will be in perpetual labour of her own destruction'.[63] Even if there should emerge a party constituting the majority of the people, its interest is not the common interest. Upon this point he remains uncompromising:

so it is ever, that the humours or interests of predominant parties hold themselves to be national; and that which fitteth them can never fit a nation, nor that which fitteth a nation ever fit them.[64]

A party constituting the majority is not a welcome prospect to Harrington, for what he most fears is not a clash between the common interest and private interests but one between 'the interest of the many' and 'the interest of the few'.[65] For Harrington, the problem is not how to exclude the minority from the government, or even how to reconcile them with the majority, but how to prevent such a division in the first place.

As we saw earlier, Harrington employs the notion of the common interest to end the deadlock where the government has no common power to exclude dissidents. He does not believe that reconciliation between the majority and the minority can succeed. The primary task of his bicameral system is the prevention of factional division. It was Sir Henry Vane who feared that those at 'the Head of the Army' would 'assume and engross the

---

[61] *The Prerogative of Popular Government*, 416.   [62] *Politicaster*, 719.

[63] *Oceana*, 203 [p. 62].   [64] *Brief Directions . . .* (1658), 590.

[65] *A Discourse upon this saying . . .* (London, 1659), 740.

office of soveraign rule and power' at the expense of 'the whole body of honest men'.[66] This was not Harrington's major concern.

Admittedly, there is one view of what anarchy looks like which Harrington does share with Nedham, Vane, and 'R.G.' Anarchy, for him as for them, is a state of divisions and factions. He agrees with them too that different factions pursue different interests. But, though all three writers regret the polarization of interests, Harrington alone asks how it may be prevented.

For Harrington, the interest of faction is an unacceptable form of private interest: the interest of an individual is an acceptable one. That is his double standard. The private interest of an individual can be reconciled with the common interest, but the interest of a faction cannot. Compared with the writers above, the unique feature of his account of 'interest' is clear: he perceives that a private interest can belong to an individual as well as to a group, and that these two sorts of private interest are distinguishable.

When the private interests of individuals collide, he believes, there is a hope that those interests can be 'summed up in the common vote' into 'the public interest'. Of course, there will be no hope if individuals, when presented with a proposal which the senate believes to represent the common interest, stick to interests which conflict with each other. There is hope only if they think beyond what they have taken to be their interests and weigh the merits of that proposal. A man who does so may relinquish his former judgement about what options will satisfy his private interest. Instead he may come to think that the senate's proposal will satisfy his private interest at least as well as the options he previously favoured.

A man will only accept the senate's proposal if he is given the freedom to judge where his interest lies. In order for this freedom to prevail in the popular assembly, Harrington strictly prohibits discussion and demagogy, that is, interferences by others in the process of judgement by each man in his own mind.[67] In addition, he insists that voting in the assembly be secret, a provision which, he believes, will 'increase[s] the freedom of . . . judgment'.[68]

---

[66] Henry Vane, *A Healing Question*, 11, 16.

[67] *Oceana*, 251, 267 [pp. 126, 148]; *The Prerogative of Popular Government*, 479; *Valerius and Publicola*, 800. See also *Valerius and Publicola*, 799, where Harrington confirms that 'the whole people' are allowed to 'debate six weeks together upon the matter' before the popular assembly is convened.

[68] *Oceana*, 181 [p. 34]. Harrington acknowledges that he learnt the secret ballot from Venice. Venetian too are his extraordinarily detailed voting procedures, which prohibit debate, and require golden balls and silver ones (used as lots to choose 'electors', who nominate 'competitors'), urns, and linen rags (used as votes, which are to be cast in silence to

When different factions clash, however, there is no remedy. Factions deprive men of their freedom to determine where their true interests lie. If a certain number of men are already united in a faction under a particular private interest, they cannot be contained within the common interest. Once different interests have taken concrete shape, and the polarization of the people has been created, Harrington's bicameral legislature cannot reconcile them.[69] Harrington uses the phrase 'distinct interests' to describe a desperate situation where irreconcilable factions have emerged.[70]

What polarizes the citizens into factions, then? We have already been warned that a commonwealth of 'a single council' like the Rump will be 'factious' because its members try to 'divid[e] the cake . . . among themselves'. Yet he warns that factions can form even in a commonwealth which has adopted the principle of mixed government and has a bicameral legislature. In explaining why, he advances an original view, which is reflected in his insistence upon the idea of an equal commonwealth. 'To make a commonwealth unequal is to divide it into parties.' It is inequality which causes factions.[71]

He believes that neither social circumstances, nor differences of religious or political belief, have anything to do with the origins of factions. It is solely defects in constitutional arrangements which give birth to factions. Unequal treatment of men in the constitutional arrangements is the origin of factions, and inevitably brings a clash of factional interests.[72] His well-known remark 'Good orders make evil men good, and bad orders make good men evil'[73] could be paraphrased as follows: 'equal orders make men free from factions, and unequal orders make men into factions'.

That is why the setting up of two different assemblies for 'debating' and 'resolving' is not enough for peace and order. A Harringtonian bicameral legislature is required to treat the citizens equally. Otherwise, the common-

---

assure the secrecy of voting). See Gasparo Contarini, *The Commonwealth and Government of Venice*, tr. Lewis Lewkenor (London, 1599), 22–33; also *Oceana*, 218–19, 221–7, 285 [pp. 83–5, 88–96, 172]. Though Harrington's voting arrangements may seem complicated, even comically so, they are less complicated than those described by Contarini. As for secret balloting, according to Contarini, it was invented because otherwise 'through a priuate regard the common good might receiue preiudice' (*The Commonwealth and Government of Venice*, 70).

[69] Harrington wanted to introduce an agrarian law into his model in *Oceana*, but had to face the problem of the polarization of the citizens which its introduction might cause. See Appendix B.

[70] *The Prerogative of Popular Government*, 426.

[71] *Oceana*, 180, 321 [pp. 32, 218–19].

[72] This view is derived from his study of the Roman republic, Lacedaemon, and Venice, as we shall see in the next chapter.

[73] *A System of Politics*, 838 [p. 274]. See also *Oceana*, 205 [p. 64].

wealth will become an unequal one, and the government will collapse into divisions and factions.

If equal opportunities for offices are to be open to a large number of people, the office of senator must not be hereditary. In his terminology, senators must be elected by the people and their tenure must be limited. They must be subjected to 'rotation' of office:[74] 'if you allow not a commonwealth her rotation, in which consists her equality, you reduce her to a party'.[75] Rotation will prevent the formation of 'a distinct interest' of the senate which would lead the senate to usurp the right of 'resolving'. When the members of the senate remain unshuffled for a long time, they may become aware of a certain particular interest which can be shared only among themselves. They may be irresistibly tempted to advance it by defying the division between debating and resolving.[76]

So far as the bicameral principle is concerned, Harrington praises the Roman republic. When it comes to rotation, however, that republic is repeatedly criticized. Having a hereditary senate, it was an unequal commonwealth which ruined herself 'through her native inequality'.[77] In Harrington's mind, it seems, the civil wars and confusions of the England of his time were linked with and paralleled by the turmoil of the final years of the Roman republic: 'the late monarchy, being rightly considered, was indeed no more than an unequal commonwealth'.[78]

In England between 1653 and 1659 several political experiments were tried in the search for political stability.[79] Harrington criticized each of them according to the same criterion, the notion of an equal commonwealth. Not only the combination of the hereditary senate and the popular assembly in Rome, not only that of the House of Lords and the

---

[74] *Oceana*, 181 [pp. 33–4].

[75] *Oceana*, 249 [p. 123].

[76] *The Art of Lawgiving* (London, 1659), 696.

[77] *Oceana*, 321 [p. 219].

[78] 'Rome was a seditious commonwealth because the perpetual feud that was between the senate and the people sprung out of her orders, and was that to which there was no remedy to apply. England was not a seditious government because it had a Vaux or a Felton, but because the power, anciently of the nobility and late of the people, was such by the orders of the same as might at any time occasion civil war' (*The Prerogative of Popular Government*, 428); 'what hath any man to do in this place to tell me of the feuds between the senate and the people of Rome, or those of the states in regulated or Gothic monarchies?' (*Politicaster*, 724); 'the late monarchy, being rightly considered, was indeed no more than an unequal commonwealth; only here is the fault of all unequal commonwealths . . . which fault was the cause of perpetual feud, or at least jealousy, between our kings and our parliaments' (*Pour Enclouer le Canon*, 729).

[79] For the period between the publication of *Oceana* and the Restoration, see Blair Worden, 'Harrington's "Oceana": Origins and Aftermath, 1651–60', in *Republicanism, Liberty, and Commercial Society*, 126–38.

House of Commons in England, but also the parliaments which ruled or met in the 1650s, failed to meet the condition of an equal commonwealth.[80]

[80] Political arrangements denounced by Harrington were as follows: the 'single council' of the Rump Parliament (*The Art of Lawgiving*, 647, 675; *Pour Enclouer le Canon*, 730; *A Discourse upon this saying*, 737); the 'single person and single parliament' of the Protectorate (*Oceana*, 201 [p. 59]; *Pour Enclouer le Canon*, 730); 'the nobility of the new [House]' (*The Art of Lawgiving*, 678); or 'an house of new peers' (ibid. 702), i.e. the Other House of *The Humble Petition and Advice* (1657).

7

HARRINGTON'S THEORY OF BALANCED SOVEREIGNTY, 1656–1660 (II):

Interest, Sovereignty, Mixed Government

1. Matthew Wren's Criticism

'An equal commonwealth cannot be seditious, and an unequal commonwealth can be no other than seditious', claims Harrington.[1] In the previous chapter we saw why an unequal commonwealth fails. It is because it polarizes the people into factions. What we have not seen is why an equal commonwealth never fails to locate 'the common interest'. What is the basis of his confidence in the claim that 'an equal commonwealth cannot be seditious'? In this chapter, we search for that basis and examine the nature of his notion of 'balanced' and 'absolute' sovereignty.

Harrington argued, as we saw, that an equal commonwealth is free from factions, the private interests of which cannot be reconciled with each other, and therefore cannot be compatible with the common interest. Yet even if we accept his claim, there still remain the private interests of individuals. He believed that the private interests of individuals are acceptable in an equal commonwealth. But how can those private interests be reconciled with each other and be integrated into the common interest? Different men, surely, will have different and sometimes competing interests. Can such a thing as the common interest, which takes in the interests of all individuals, really exist in the world of politics?[2] While he claims that 'Where

---

[1] *The Prerogative of Popular Government*, 426.

[2] Apparently, Harrington does not expect that private religious concerns can be accommodated by the common interest. Rather, they are distinguished from private interests, and are called 'private conscience', which is to be satisfied by a policy of toleration. In this sense a policy of toleration, together with that of the bicameral legislature, is indispensable to satisfy everybody for peace and order. For this, see Appendix A.

there is a well-ordered commonwealth, the people are generally satisfied', is it possible for any government to satisfy everybody?[3] Among Harrington's contemporaries, it was Matthew Wren who raised those objections to his thesis.[4] In the rest of this section and the following one, by examining the exchange between Wren and Harrington, we shall arrive at the basis of Harrington's belief in an equal commonwealth.

While Hobbes remained silent in the face of Harrington's criticism, Wren attacked his discussion of interest in *Considerations* (1657). Harrington responded quickly by writing *The Prerogative of Popular Government* (1658). In 1659 Wren launched his second attack in *Monarchy Asserted*, which was to be refuted in the same year by Harrington in the last part of *The Art of Lawgiving* and in *Politicaster*.[5]

Wren denies that such a thing as the common interest, which satisfies everybody, can easily be found, since conflicting interests cannot be held together.[6] In England, different regions have different interests apparently in conflict.

The Concernments of the Severall Parts of this Nation are very different in Reference to Propriety and Riches; some Parts subsist upon Mines and Cole, Others upon Manufacture, Some upon Corne, Others upon the Profits of Cattle, London and the Sea Ports upon Exportation and Importation; And it is not possible but that when those severall things come to be regulated by Lawes, the Different Parts of the Nation must necessarily espouse very Different Interests.[7]

No legislation which regulates people's social and economic activities can satisfy everyone since any such legislation inevitably divides them into 'Gainers' and 'Loosers [*sic*]'.[8] Therefore:

---

[3] *Aphorisms Political* (London, 1659), 764.

[4] Matthew Wren, *Considerations on Mr. Harrington's Common-wealth of Oceana: Restrained to the first part of the Preliminaries* (London, 1657); *Monarchy Asserted or The State of Monarchicall & Popular Government in Vindication of the Considerations Upon Mr Harrington's Oceana* (Oxford, 1659). See Pocock, 'Historical Introduction', *The Political Works of James Harrington*, 83–9.

[5] In *The Art of Lawgiving*, Harrington argued against only a limited part of *Monarchy Asserted*, i.e., pp. 84–7, 97–107, 178–83 of a work of 185 pages. Yet *Politicaster*, in which Harrington had planned to examine the whole of *Monarchy Asserted* chapter by chapter, abruptly ended after he had refuted chapter 2 (which ended on p. 18 of *Monarchy Asserted*). His initial plan seems to have been dropped, perhaps because of the restoration of the Rump in May 1659. See Pocock, 'Historical Introduction', 105. For the last phase of Interregnum politics, see also Austin Woolrych's historical introduction in *The Complete Prose Works of John Milton*, ed. Robert W. Ayers, vii (New Haven, 1980).

[6] *Considerations*, 20, 32.   [7] *Monarchy Asserted*, 87–8.

[8] 'It is to be remembered also that the greatest Part of Lawes concern such Matters as are the continuall Occasion of Controversie between the People of a Nation; Such are the Lawes which respect the Regulation of all Contracts and Bargains, the Privileges of Companies and

They [=the people] cannot where their Interests are thus divided be so fitly qualified for Legislators, as is a Prince who having no private Concernment going, can
have no aime but the Common good.[9]

Yet Harrington, in replying to Wren, retains every confidence in his
scheme:

Sir, if a man know not what is his own interest, who should know it? And that which
is the interest of the most particular men, the same, being summed up in the
common vote, is the public interest.[10]

Even when Wren provided concrete illustration of the inevitable conflict of
private interests, Harrington remained content to argue in abstract terms.
The two writers make a sharp contrast here. How should the contrast be
explained?[11]

If we take the view that the analogy of the cake-dividing girls was the
centre of Harrington's idea, he appears to be a simple-minded thinker,
naïve about the real world of politics.[12] Wren, it seems, took that view of
him. He mocked Harrington's analogy, saying 'the stronger of the two
Girles would have eaten up the whole Cake if she found her stomach serve
her for it' unless they had been supervised by their 'School Mistress'.
'There can be no such Common Interest', it followed, unless the Harringtonian senate is 'reduced under some Government'. What is needed is not
constitutional arrangements but 'an excess in Power' to 'force the obedience
of the Other' so as to prevent 'the State of War'. From Wren's point of
view, therefore, Hobbes argued better than Harrington.[13]

Wren was able to argue in that way because he regarded the analogy of
the 'two silly girls', of which he made such fun, as the pivot of Harrington's

Corporations, the Encouragements and Limitations of Manufactures, the Licences and Prohi-
bitions of Traffique, with many more of the same Nature, by all which some Part of the
People being Gainers, and another Part Loosers [*sic*]' (*Monarchy Asserted*, 12–13).

[9] Ibid. 13.

[10] *Politicaster*, 719.

[11] Modern scholars are split over the contrast. Jonathan Scott, who seems disappointed by
Harrington's reply to Wren, believes, as Wren did, that Harrington did not understand how
seriously the public interest and private interests can contradict each other. Scott sees Harrington as a simple-minded thinker. Pocock does not. To Harrington, believes Pocock, politics
meant something more than the calculation of private interests. On the other hand, Scott considers Wren to have understood the complexity of the world of politics, whereas to Pocock,
Wren reduced politics to a mere search for the adjustment of conflicting interests. Jonathan
Scott, 'The Rapture of Motion', in Nicholas Phillipson and Quentin Skinner (eds.), *Political
Discourse in Early Modern Britain*, (Cambridge, 1993), 153; Pocock, 'Introduction', *The Commonwealth of Oceana and A System of Politics* (Cambridge, 1992), pp. xxii–xxiii.

[12] Scott takes this view, and writes that Harrington could not understand that politics is
more complex than dividing a cake. 'The Rapture of Motion', 153.

[13] *Considerations*, 23, 25, 6–7; *Monarchy Asserted*, 52, 54, 15–16.

commitment to a bicameral legislature. But was it? To define the place of that analogy within his idea, we need to return to his perspective on the history of political theory, the perspective within which he argued with Hobbes in defending ancient prudence.[14] Harrington regarded Hobbes, not himself, as a fanciful writer.

2. Reason and Experience

As we saw in Chapter 5, Harrington's history of political theory consisted of three components: two traditions and one novel doctrine. The traditions were ancient prudence and modern prudence: the novel doctrine was that of Hobbes. While the tradition of modern prudence was in his eyes defective, lacking theoretical substance, the tradition of ancient prudence was based on both 'reason and experience'.[15] This tradition was maintained by 'the ancients' and by Machiavelli.[16] But the term 'the ancients' did not, in Harrington's mind, refer exclusively to the ancient philosophers who had speculated about that prudence. It also included those who practised it: lawgivers and statesmen. Harrington uses the phrase 'politicians' to include both theorists and practitioners.[17] But it was not only politicians who had contributed to the making of this tradition. Commonwealths had done so too. They had collaborated in a variety of ways. There was the action of lawgivers: of Moses, Solon, and Lycurgus, who founded Israel, Athens, and Lacedaemon. There were the thinkers: Aristotle, 'a private man', who analysed Athens, Lacedaemon, Carthage, and other Greek commonwealths; Cicero, a statesman, who studied republican Rome and struggled to preserve it; Livy, a historian, whose history of republican

---

[14] Pocock has already emphasized that Harrington placed Oceana in English (and European) history, and has argued that Scott did not grasp Harrington's historical preoccupation. In the next section, having accepted Pocock's view, I shall emphasize that the history within which Harrington places Oceana is one not only of political events but of political theory. Scott, I shall suggest, discusses Harrington in the framework supplied by Wren. See Pocock, 'A Discourse of Sovereignty', in Phillipson and Skinner (eds.), *Political Discourse in Early Modern Britain*, 402; 'Introduction', *The Commonwealth of Ocean and A System of Politics* (Cambridge, 1992), p. xvii.

[15] *Oceana*, 180, 184 [pp. 32, 38], etc.

[16] Rahe, maintaining that Harrington did not inherit the substance of the classical ideas—the idea of *zoon politikon* among them—claims that he merely disguised himself as a follower of 'the ancients'. Rahe considers Harrington to be a writer of the modern age, because he broke with the political ideas of classical antiquity as Hobbes and Machiavelli did. Rahe, who identifies what he regards as the essential ideas of classical political thought, seems to me to confuse those ideas with Harrington's ancient prudence. See Paul A. Rahe, *Republics Ancient and Modern* (Chapel Hill, NC, 1992), 409–10.

[17] For Harrington's usage of the word 'politicians' see *Oceana*, 162, 178, 216, 264, 273, 310 [pp. 10, 29, 80, 144, 155, 205]; *The Art of Lawgiving*, 607.

Rome was the basis of modern exposition by Machiavelli.[18] Now it was Harrington's turn. He learned both from those politicians and from those commonwealths. On the basis of that knowledge he wanted to help make a new commonwealth in his country.

Thus, thought Harrington, the tradition of ancient prudence had been woven by the collaboration between reason and experience.[19] By contrast, Hobbes's idea of sovereignty by a single holder of it could not be supported by 'any reason or example', believed Harrington.[20] In the field of reason, Harrington, by employing the doctrine of the balance of the land and the analogy of the girls who cut the cake, repudiated Hobbes. At the same time he showed that Hobbes's idea could hardly be maintained by experience, since it had no examples to support it, certainly not the short-lived Rump.[21] For Harrington, Hobbes's problem was not merely to have made errors in the field of reason. Hobbes, rejecting ancient prudence and its assets, denied the idea of collaboration between reason and experience. Instead he confined himself to the field of reason, which he deliberately cut off from experience. That is why Hobbes's idea appeared to Harrington to resemble 'geometry'.[22] Before laying down his model in *Oceana*, Harrington contrasted two different attitudes 'in the fabric of a commonwealth': one was 'to follow fancy', the other to ransack 'the archives of ancient prudence'. His course was the latter; Hobbes's, he implies, the former.[23]

How, then, is Harrington's idea of an equal commonwealth supported by

---

[18] For Moses and Lycurgus, see *Oceana*, 176–7, 183, 184, 205, 207 [pp. 27–8, 37, 39, 65, 66], etc. For Solon, see *Oceana*, 183, 241, 260 [pp. 36, 113, 139]; *The Prerogative of Popular Government*, 517–18, etc. For Aristotle, see *Oceana*, 166, 177, 234, 275 [pp. 14, 29, 105, 158]; *The Prerogative of Popular Government*, 395, 465, 473–4, 518; *The Art of Lawgiving*, 628; *A Letter unto Mr Stubbe* (London, 1660), 829. For Cicero as a student of Roman politics, see *Oceana*, 187, 212, 303, 323 [pp. 41, 74, 197, 221], etc.; for his political activity, *The Prerogative of Popular Government*, 495, 509, 512–13; for Livy and Machiavelli, see *Oceana*, 178 [p. 30].

[19] Ancient prudence is sometimes called 'human prudence' by Harrington. Blair Worden points out that the movement of history was, in Harrington's belief, guided by God through human prudence. See Worden, 'James Harrington and "The Commonwealth of Oceana", 1656', in David Wootton (ed.), *Republicanism, Liberty, and Commercial Society, 1649–1776* (Stanford, Calif., 1994), 84–5. Worden emphasizes Harrington's strong concern with the Hebrew commonwealth. For the phrase 'human prudence', see also Pocock, 'Historical Introduction', *The Political Works of James Harrington*, 19–20.

[20] *Oceana*, 184 [p. 38].

[21] He claims that there had been 'nothing of this kind that I can find in story but the oligarchy of Athens, the thirty tyrants of the same, and the Roman decemvirs', ibid. 205 [p. 65].

[22] Ibid. 199 [p. 56].

[23] '[H]ow unsafe a thing it is to follow fancy in the fabric of a commonwealth, and how necessary that the archives of ancient prudence should be ransacked', ibid. 208 [p. 69].

the archives of ancient prudence? The answer is not straightforward, for the archives are not to be used uncritically. The study of them may involve the reinterpretation of history and the correction of the political thinkers (the 'politicians') of the past.

All the renowned commonwealths of ancient prudence, principally Israel, Athens, Carthage, Rome, Lacedaemon, and Venice, adopted the principle, which Harrington endorsed, of mixed government.[24] Yet Harrington does not claim that all the commonwealths of ancient prudence enjoyed lasting prosperity. Even republican Rome sank into civil war in its last phase. The only perfect models were Lacedaemon and Venice. Why had the others declined or fallen? The answer, Harrington maintains, lay not in the principle of mixed government but in the flawed application of it. So, he argues, we need to examine both the successes and the failures of commonwealths in ancient prudence. Thus from the success of the Roman republic Harrington deduces the principles of the bicameral legislature. From its failure he deduces the importance of 'rotation'.

Harrington does not always agree with the ancient politicians. They were basically right in commending the principle of mixed government, but did not think hard enough about its application. Moreover, although there had been, in Lacedaemon and Venice, perfect models of commonwealths, there had not been, before Harrington, perfect political thinkers. Even Machiavelli, 'the prince of politicians', who introduced that principle to Harrington, missed a crucial point about the strife of faction. If Machiavelli was right to regard that strife, which destroyed Rome, as inevitable, then the principle of mixed government, on which Rome was based, might seem inherently flawed.[25] But Harrington attributed the failure of Rome not to the principle but to 'some impediment or defect in the frame'.[26]

That is why Harrington's interpretation of the history of the Roman

[24] Scott comments that Harrington used the terms 'history' and 'prudence' exactly as Hobbes did ('The Rapture of Motion', 157). It is true that Hobbes thought that 'experience' might demonstrate principles which were otherwise derived from 'reason', though it cannot conclude anything of universal application. Yet there is a difference between the two writers on this matter. Whereas, for Harrington, principles of government must be substantiated by experience, Hobbes thought that they may or may not be substantiated by it. Similarly, for Harrington, if no equal commonwealths had ever been seditious in the past, it was reasonable to conclude that no equal commonwealth could ever be seditious in the future: for Hobbes, 'though a man hath always seen the day and night to follow one another hitherto; yet can he not thence conclude they shall do so, or that they have done so eternally'. See Harrington, *Oceana*, 180, 276 [pp. 30, 160]; Hobbes, *The Elements of Law*, I. 4. 10. 16.

[25] *Oceana*, 274 [p. 157]. Certainly Machiavelli's claim was not good news for 'the Lord Archon', the lawgiver of *Oceana*, who says: 'to hear the greatest artist in the modern world giving sentence against our commonwealth is that with which I am nearly concerned' (ibid.).

[26] Ibid. 180 [p. 32].

republic forms the essential part of his *Oceana*. Harrington took issue with Machiavelli's account of Roman history. Machiavelli, too, had read the archives of ancient prudence. His *Discorsi* was a study of Livy, Harrington's main source on Roman history.[27] Machiavelli was right, maintains Harrington, to raise the question 'whether means were to be found whereby the enmity that was between the senate and the people of Rome might have been removed'. Indeed 'There is not a more noble or useful question in the politics than that'.[28] But he was wrong to claim that the conflict had been incurable. Machiavelli maintained that the introduction of the tribunate had reduced the conflict to manageable proportion, and that the conflict had become politically healthy as a result. Harrington believed that the conflict had been neither necessary nor healthy. It could have been avoided, he believed, if the patricians had not been made 'a distinct and hereditary order'.

For Romulus, having in the election of his senate squared out a nobility for the support of a throne, by making that of the patrician a distinct and hereditary order, planted the commonwealth upon two contrary interests or roots which, shooting forth in time, produced two commonwealths, the one oligarchical in the nobility, and the other a mere anarchy of the people, which thenceforth caused a perpetual feud and enmity between the senate and the people, even to death.[29]

'The distinction of the patrician as an hereditary order . . . was indeed the destruction of Rome', Harrington believed.[30] Yet Machiavelli, in defending the division of Roman society into patrician and plebeian, had claimed that

---

[27] Scott maintains that Harrington was dishonest in describing Machiavelli as a retriever of ancient prudence, and that Harrington was much closer to Hobbes. My view is the other way round. Certainly, Harrington and Hobbes were concerned, even if from different angles, with the association, which concerned Machiavelli much less, of anarchy with equality. But when Harrington distinguished Hobbes from ancient prudence, his distinction related not to the content of the study of politics but to its method. Harrington and Machiavelli agreed that the study of Roman history was essential to the study of politics. Thus the two writers belonged, in Harrington's mind, to the tradition of ancient prudence. It was because of this (and not in spite of this) that Harrington was able to take issue with him by reinterpreting Roman history on the basis of Machiavelli's source, Livy. By contrast, when Harrington wanted to defend the principle of mixed government which was embodied in the phrase *senatus populusque Romanus*, he found no common footing on which to argue with Hobbes, who gave his readers the advice to 'read thy self' rather than the classics. See Scott, 'The Rapture of Motion', 158; *Oceana*, 161 [p. 9]; *The Elements of Law*, 1. 5. 14. 24; *Leviathan*, 'Introduction', p. 10 [p. 2].

[28] *Oceana*, 272 [p. 155].

[29] Ibid.

[30] Ibid. 216 [p. 80]. Harrington was particularly interested in the problem of the hereditary Roman senate because the House of Lords, in his eyes, made the same case. He thought 'the perpetual feud' existed between 'our kings and our parliaments' as well as between the senate and the people in Rome. See also *Pour Enclouer le Canon*, 729 and Sect. 6.3 above.

the same hereditary division had existed in Lacedaemon. Harrington argued that 'Machiavel . . . hath quite mistaken the orders of this commonwealth, where there was no such thing'. The political health of Lacedaemon was expressed, he maintained, not in class conflict but in its absence. Lacedaemon was 'internally at rest', since 'no man was . . . qualified but by election of the people' except for the hereditary kings 'who . . . had but single votes'. Her senate was not hereditary but elective, and therefore 'the tranquillity of Lacedaemon derived from no other cause than her equality'.[31] Moreover, in Harrington's judgement, the introduction of the tribunate in Rome was a cosmetic measure, which merely worsened the crisis, since it opened a way for the people to debate by themselves. For a bicameral legislature to work properly, he concludes, the seats of the senate must be not hereditary but elective, and senators need to be reshuffled frequently and regularly.[32] To reshuffle them in that way is, in his terminology, to make a commonwealth equal by running the legislature upon rotation. An equal opportunity of election as members of the legislature—'an equal distribution of common right'—should be given 'unto the whole people'.[33]

This notion of equality was fully embodied in Venice. He praises the ingenious constitution of Venice 'as an example of an equal commonwealth'.[34] While the senate of Lacedaemon was elective but 'for life', the senate of Venice runs upon rotation, and therefore its senators are 'always changing' in a 'pure and perpetual' stream.[35] Machiavelli attributed the internal stability of Venice to the disarmament of its subjects, but he was wrong. The secret of its 'tranquillity and peace', claims Harrington, lies in

[31] *Oceana*, 275 [p. 159].

[32] Ibid. 267–78 [pp. 149–63]. Harrington deals with Livy, II. xxi–xxxiii, and *Discorsi*, I. vi.

[33] *The Art of Lawgiving*, 696.

[34] *The Prerogative of Popular Government*, 426. His sources for Venice seem, apart from his own visit, to have been Giannotti and Contarini. For Harrington's application of Venetian institutional arrangements, see David Wootton, 'Ulysses Bound? Venice and the Idea of Liberty from Howell to Hume', in Wootton (ed.), *Republicanism, Liberty, and Commercial Society, 1649–1776* (Stanford, Calif., 1994), 345–7. Wootton suggests that Harrington learnt from Venice the rotation, the secret ballot, and the idea of the bicameral legislature. Harrington certainly seems to have learnt the first two of those features from Venice (*Oceana*, 181 [p. 34]), though he believed that the second of them, the secret ballot, had been used in Rome too. However, as Wootton acknowledges, Harrington could not single Venice out from other commonwealths of ancient prudence as the source of his bicameral legislature, for he knew that the Venetian constitution, which consisted of 'four parts: the great council, the senate, the *collegio*, and the signory', was too complicated to be squared with his own formula of a 'debating' chamber and a 'resolving' one (*The Prerogative of Popular Government*, 482–5). Perhaps he learnt the idea of the bicameral legislature from Rome, and that of 'equality' from Venice. For the possible influence of Contarini upon Harrington's notion of equality, see Appendix D below.

[35] *Oceana*, 263–5 [pp. 143–5]. See also *The Prerogative of Popular Government*, 474, 485, 494; *The Art of Lawgiving*, 612.

its rotation. The Venetian senate 'is like a rolling stone (as was said) which never did nor, while it continues upon that rotation, ever shall gather the moss of a divided or ambitious interest'. Machiavelli missed that point about Venice, he adds, since he never 'considered her orders'.[36] For students of politics, Venice is no less important than Rome. 'If I be worthy to give advice unto a man that would study the politics, let him understand Venice'.[37] In Harrington's view, 'the commonwealth of Venice, being that which of all others is the most equal in the constitution, is that wherein there never happened any strife between the senate and the people'. Indeed, 'she is of all others the most quiet, so the most equal commonwealth'.[38] It was upon that understanding of equality that he based his claim that an equal commonwealth cannot be seditious.

The idea of an equal commonwealth, Harrington believed, was his own most original contribution to ancient prudence. While equal commonwealths had existed and been registered in 'the archives', no 'politician' before him had explicitly referred to the importance of the notion of equality, or formulated the idea of an equal commonwealth—although some of them, principally lawgivers, must have tacitly recognized that idea. When Harrington debated 'the perfection of government' with Hobbes, he showed three ways of classifying commonwealths. The first classification is between single commonwealths and leagues. The second is between commonwealths for preservation and those for increase. The third is between equal and unequal commonwealths, which 'is the main point especially as to domestic peace and tranquillity'. While Harrington attributed the second classification to Machiavelli, the third one, he wrote, was 'unseen hitherto'.[39] In reply to Hobbes, Harrington based the commonwealth of Oceana on the principle of mixed government: in reply to Machiavelli he based it on the principle of equality.

Harrington saw himself as the first writer to understand the reason for 'the enmity . . . between the senate and the people of Rome', and to formulate the idea of an equal commonwealth. He was able to argue 'otherwise of this question [of that 'enmity'] than he [Machiavelli] doth', because he had 'other principles than he hath'.[40] Machiavelli missed Harrington's understanding of equality. That, in Harrington's view, was because he did not study Roman history in a sufficiently critical spirit:

---

[36] *Oceana*, 275–6 [pp. 159–60].
[37] *The Prerogative of Popular Government*, 486.
[38] *Oceana*, 180, 276 [pp. 33, 160].
[39] Ibid. 180 [p. 33]. See Appendix D below.
[40] *Oceana*, 274 [p. 158].

'with whom [=Machiavelli] that which was done by Rome, and that which is well done, is for the most part all one'.[41]

Harrington, in studying politics within the tradition of ancient prudence, did not draw his political theory of an equal commonwealth solely from its 'reason'. He deduced it from his study of Roman history; he tested it against the 'reason' to be found in Machiavelli's *Discorsi* and against the 'experiences' of Lacedaemon and Venice; and he refined his theory accordingly. The final fruit of his study was his models of commonwealth, principally his model of a commonwealth, Oceana. From Harrington's point of view, Hobbes's theory was mere 'fancy', for it had not been tested against 'reason and experience' in 'the archives of ancient prudence'.

When Harrington employs the analogy of the girls who cut the cake, it is true, he seems to be confining himself, like Hobbes, to the field of reason. But no wonder. For that analogy, it should be remembered, was quoted in his reply in *Oceana* to Hobbes's provocative phrase, '*as often as reason is against a man, so often will a man be against reason*'.[42] At the moments when Harrington wanted to confine within the domain of reason his explanation of the deficiency of Hobbes's idea of sovereignty by a single holder, he employed that analogy. Elsewhere Harrington prepared his justification for his theory in different terms, that is, in the field of reason and experience. The story of the cake was not the source of Harrington's belief in an equal commonwealth. Rather, he derived his conviction from the study of the tradition of ancient prudence, the assets of which had been accumulated by the close collaboration between reason and experience.

Now we are in a position to return to Matthew Wren, and to assess his interpretation of Harrington. It was not Hobbes but Harrington who appeared to Wren to be attempting to erect a fanciful state. Wren reached that judgement of Harrington by blurring the distinction between ancient and modern prudence, and, in doing so, by reshaping Harrington's perspective. Harrington portrayed ancient and modern prudence as two traditions in the history of political theory. Wren reduced the distinction between the two traditions to mean merely that commonwealths were older than monarchies.

To Harrington, modern prudence was a tradition of political theory which endorsed limited monarchies built upon European feudal society. Wren took modern prudence to be an endorsement of monarchy in general. Similarly, in Wren's account, ancient prudence is a term which denotes

---

[41] *Oceana*, 311 [p. 206].
[42] Ibid. 171–2 [pp. 21–3]. See Sect. 6.2 above.

arguments endorsing republics in general.[43] Thus Wren was content to clas-sify Hobbes as an exponent of modern prudence, since Hobbes preferred monarchies in general to republics in general. Harrington's triad of ancient, modern, and Hobbes was thus reduced by Wren to a bipolar system of ancient and modern.

The reason Wren was able to classify Hobbes as an exponent of modern prudence was simple. He ignored the fact that Harrington's distinction between ancient and modern was one between two historical traditions of political theory. Harrington set his commonwealth of Oceana within the tradition of political theory which derived from biblical Israel and classical antiquity. Wren, though he acknowledged Harrington's appeal to history, supposed that Harrington's purpose was only to prove that commonwealths were more ancient in origin and were therefore superior in nature. Wren thought that he could disprove Harrington by pointing to the existence of monarchies in states which had subsequently become republics, Rome being a prime example. The history of the ancient world, which, he pointed out, must properly include Assyria, Persia, Egypt, Babylonia, and China, showed that monarchy was the dominant form of government there. Harrington's claim that commonwealths were a dominant form of govern-ment in the ancient world was mistaken.[44]

Wren launched his attack upon the analogy of the two girls after breaking the unity of Harrington's history of political theory. Without that unity, Harrington's argument for the constitutional arrangements proposed in *Oceana* was disarmed. When the commonwealth of Oceana was isolated from the tradition within which he had placed it, there was no means left of defending it—except for the analogy of the cake-cutting girls. Originally, the purpose of that analogy was to reject Hobbes's claim on Hobbesian terms—in the field of 'reason', which was cut off from 'experience'. Yet Wren writes as if the analogy were Harrington's only support for his bicam-eral legislature. Wren turned Harrington into a writer who invented the analogy first and developed it into the model of a commonwealth second. The Harrington reshaped by Wren was no longer the man who extracted the idea of mixed government from an examination of the tradition of ancient prudence. As a result, it was Harrington, who had wanted to portray Hobbes as an unrealistic writer whose ideas were detached from historical experience, who came to suffer that reputation himself.

[43] 'He [=Harrington] intitles to Antient Prudence that way of Popular Government which his Book applauds, and fastens upon Modern Prudence that Monarchicall Government which it Decries' (*Monarchy Asserted*, 2).

[44] *Considerations*, 1–6, *Monarchy Asserted*, 1–6.

When he replied to Wren, Harrington tried to rescue his historical perspective to support his argument. He repeatedly affirmed that the commonwealths which had embodied ancient prudence were biblical Israel and the Graeco-Roman republics; and that the monarchies of modern prudence were the Gothic monarchies of the Christian world including the English monarchy of 'king, lords and commons'.[45] He did so because he knew the importance of his historical perspective for the defence of his *Oceana*.

Thus Harrington's account of his equal commonwealth stands upon both reason and experience. His rotating bicameral legislature is set in a historical perspective of political theory. His conviction that a legislature will never fail to discover the common interest was substantiated by his study of ancient prudence, not by the analogy of the girls cutting the cake. It is true that Harrington ignored Wren's challenge. He did not illustrate how private interests which conflicted with each other in England would be reconciled under the name of the common interest. But he did not think such an explanation necessary to his idea of an equal commonwealth.

Earlier, we saw that Harrington's notion of the common interest, which he substituted for Hobbes's notion of the common power, is nothing more than what gives the commonwealth peace and tranquillity. The common interest is considered to prevail if only the commonwealth is kept stable and not seditious. If Lacedaemon enjoyed lasting internal peace in the past, and if Venice does the same in the present, it follows that the common interest has always prevailed in those commonwealths. Oceana, which is free from the defects which were fatal to republican Rome, therefore will be internally stable.[46] And just as there is no need to specify what the common interest was in such-and-such a time in Lacedaemon (or in Venice) in order to find the secret of its longevity, so there is no need to illustrate what sort of policy should be implemented under the name of the common interest in England now—however much that question may interest Wren. Rather, if an exit from the political instability in England is to be found, the question to be tackled is why the Roman republic, unlike Lacedaemon and Venice, collapsed into civil war. To that question, of course, Harrington was confident that he had the answer, which was drawn from his reading of 'the archives of ancient prudence'.

---

[45] *The Prerogative of Popular Government*, 397; *Politicaster*, 711.

[46] '[W]hat was always so and no otherwise, and still is so and no otherwise, the same shall ever be so and no otherwise' (*Politicaster*, 722). To Hobbes, of course, this sort of reasoning cannot produce any absolute knowledge. See *Leviathan*, VII.

3. Sovereignty and Mixed Government

When an equal commonwealth is constituted, argues Harrington, the common interest will be located, and no one will rebel against the government. Thus, an equal commonwealth achieves sovereignty over a mass of independent people under the new balance of the land. Since Harrington believes that no military power existing in seventeenth-century England is capable of assuming sovereignty, his main concern is how to create sovereignty rather than how to limit or defend it. In his scheme 'the sovereign power of a commonwealth is no more bounded, that is to say, straitened, than that of a monarch, but is balanced'.[47] The notion of balance is used to denote sovereignty as well as the distribution of land.

The final cause of the popular congregation in a commonwealth is to give such a balance by their result, as may and must keep the senate from that faction and corruption whereof it is not otherwise curable, or to set it upright.[48]

Here 'balance' is used to mean the balance between the senate and the popular assembly, which allows the senate to work properly. The role of the senate, which is to locate the common interest, is called 'authority'.[49] In short, the goal of Harrington's political theory is to constitute a balanced sovereignty the basis of which would be not military power but authority.

Harrington was not the first to use the notion of balance in examining the forms of government. In England, as we saw in the earlier chapters, the word 'balance' had been often employed in the controversy over the Militia Ordinance.[50] Most notably, the writers of *His Majesty's Answer to the Nineteen Propositions*, and then Henry Ferne and Philip Hunton, used the term in their arguments. In particular, they laid stress upon the balance among the three estates; that is, the king, the lords, and the commons. Having agreed that England was a mixed monarchy, they debated the question whether the power of the king was so constrained that the constitution allowed armed resistance by parliament in an ultimate emergency.

For all the differences in the practical implications of their claims about the conflict between king and parliament, it is striking how much those writers of the earlier 1640s had in common. They were all concerned to maintain the authority of the king-in-parliament. For them, authority was a function of government which makes the judgement of government acceptable to the subjects. All of them agreed that once the authority of the

---

[47] *Oceana*, 230 [pp. 99–101].
[48] *The Art of Lawgiving*, 641. See also p. 676.
[49] See Sect. 6.2.
[50] For this, see Ch. 2 above.

king was lost, the result was irremediable disorder. Certainly, these writers do not exactly agree about the nature of authority, and their accounts of the ultimate source of allegiance differ accordingly. In the *Answer*, the exclusive power of the king allotted by the mixed constitution is expected to cause 'fear' and 'respect' among the subjects, which will secure the authority of the king. For Hunton and Ferne, whether the king violated the limitation allotted by the balance was a matter of judgement by the 'conscience'. While in Ferne's view, conscience is left to an individual's faith in God which operates separately from the constitution, Hunton thinks that when the constitution functions properly through the co-operation of the three estates, the existence of the constitution itself will bind the direction of the consciences of individuals collectively, and those individuals will accept the judgements of the government as right judgements. Nevertheless, when we set the debate of 1642–4 beside those of the Interregnum, we see that the earlier writers have in common a concern to defend authority rather than to create it.

In Harrington's theory too, balance has much to do with authority. Moreover, for Harrington authority is a function of government which unites the private judgements of individuals under the public judgement of the government. However, Harrington's balance is what causes authority rather than what keeps it. Unlike the earlier writers he does not presuppose that the government is given a divine authority by God. Nor, to his mind, could the conscience of each individual be the basis of the authority of a government. The Harringtonian authority is constituted by 'interest' instead of conscience. People will realize that judgements made by the Harringtonian government are right when they see that their private interests are included in the common interest. Admittedly the visible shape taken by his idea of balance, the idiosyncratic plan for a senate, was alien to English experience. But he could not find his balance within the English constitution.

Harrington's idea of balanced sovereignty is his reply to Hobbes's criticism of mixed government. For Hobbes, a mixed government is nothing but a disintegration of sovereignty which leads to anarchy. Only people who 'have not had the experience of that miserable estate' of civil war would endorse such a fanciful idea as mixed government. If that idea had not prevailed in England 'the people had never been divided, and fallen into this Civill Warre'.[51] Harrington's answer was that neither one man nor one council can retain the sovereign power, and that only a government

---

[51] See Sect 4.1 above.

with a division of functions can claim a balanced and absolute sovereignty.[52] Both Harrington and Hobbes consider that a government has an absolute sovereignty when there is no resistance to it. Harrington's man *will not* resist because his interests are satisfied by the government: Hobbes's man *cannot* resist because the government has the common power to suppress him. Both writers want to see judgement by the government prevail to keep peace and order. To that purpose, Hobbes expected the people, under the threat of the public sword, to renounce their private judgements about the government. Harrington, having criticized the basis of the Hobbesian public sword, allows people to exercise and express their private judgements under the name of private interests within the bicameral legislature. Harrington's belief that private judgements should be exercised in order to make the sovereignty absolute places him in diametrical opposition to Hobbes.

Harrington implies that only mixed government can establish an absolute sovereignty. In other words, he argues that the exercise of private judgements and the maintenance of absolute sovereignty, far from being contradictory, are mutually supportive. Harrington makes a positive link between the two. Philip Hunton's man will rebel against the government when his conscience tells him it is the only way to restore the constitution. Harrington's man will do so when his private interest is not satisfied by the government. Yet he will never do so as long as it is satisfied by a government equipped with the rotating bicameral legislature.

Harrington's innovation in introducing the notion of interest into the idea of mixed government led him to restore the exercise of private judgement in the matter of political obedience. He rescued private judgement from Hobbes's bitter condemnation of it. The private judgements of individuals, which Hobbes had called conscience and dismissed, resumed their place under the new name of interest in Harrington's theory. Now government became what 'secures' interest, and interest became what 'bears' government.[53] Thus Harrington tried to show Hobbes that the problem of authority could not be replaced by that of power. Something more than power is needed to solve the problem of the diversity of private judgements. It is supplied by the Polybian theory.

James Harrington's theory of government appeared after the collapse of the first republican government in England, a government which Hobbes believed to hold a monopoly of military power. The challenge Harrington posed was to constitute the authority of the government and establish the

---

[52] *The Art of Lawgiving*, 657–8.
[53] *Valerius and Publicola*, 797.

sovereignty, without presupposing, as Hobbes did, the existence of a governing military power. Harrington's answer was that a sovereignty can be, and has to be, absolute and balanced at the same time.

To conclude this chapter, we shall look at the contrast between Harrington's view of Machiavelli and his view of Hobbes. As Harrington repeatedly emphasizes, he regards Machiavelli as a theorist of ancient prudence, the prudence which Hobbes 'goes about to destroy'. Without doubt, as we have seen, that difference is the biggest one between Hobbes and Machiavelli. Yet Harrington's debt to Machiavelli may have extended beyond the awareness Machiavelli had given him of the Polybian principle of mixed government and the importance of the study of republican Rome. Machiavelli had given every attention to a question likewise central to Harrington: the control of the military power, whether by a prince or by a republic.[54] If so, we can say that Machiavelli's discussion of the subject may have given Harrington a weapon with which to attack Hobbes's theory of sovereignty. In Harrington's eyes, Hobbes made a fatal mistake in ignoring that question. That is why Harrington, talking about political power, deliberately used the phrase 'a man or an army' in the place of Hobbes's favourite term, 'a man, or an assembly'.[55] In addition, Harrington observed a sharp contrast between Machiavelli's endorsement of democracy and Hobbes's hostility towards it. Harrington shared Machiavelli's enthusiasm for political participation by the people, yet his enthusiasm has a different cause from Machiavelli's. Machiavelli thought participation important for military defence and military expansion. Harrington thought it necessary to the attainment of internal stability. In short, Harrington converted the Machiavellian principle—political participation—into his own device of mixed government in order to serve the Hobbesian concern—internal peace and order. When, in Harrington's commonwealth, the people were organized into a Harringtonian commonwealth, the basis of that organization was not to be the Machiavellian idea of the citizen militia. It was to be a set of constitutional arrangements deriving from the Polybian idea of mixed government.

[54] The question was common to Machiavelli's two major works, *Discorsi* and *Il Principe*. When Harrington claims that a mixed monarchy is unstable by nature since the military power that the king can deploy is too small to control the nobility, he alludes to Machiavelli's insight in *Il Principe*, 'that a throne supported by a nobility is not so hard to be ascended, as kept warm' (*Oceana*, 197 [p. 54]). While Harrington criticizes Machiavelli's treatment of a nobility in *Discorsi*, he accepts his view of a nobility expressed in *Il Principe*. For whereas the first concerns the principle of mixed government, the second concerns the control of the military power.

[55] *Oceana*, 163 [p. 10]; *Leviathan*, XIX. 132 [p. 97].

8

THE END OF THE ERA, 1660–1683:

Balance, Nobility, Resistance

1. The Neo-Harringtonians and the Restoration

In 1660 kingship and the House of Lords returned and the ancient constitution re-emerged. Although the Restoration regime could be described as inherently unstable, it did put an end to the anarchic situation of the last phase of Interregnum politics. Hobbes and Harrington, who shared a concern for peace and order, had tried to provide the governments of the Interregnum with new theories of sovereignty. However, ironically for both of them, the Restoration regime, which did not equip itself with any such theories, was successful in maintaining law and order. In this new world Harrington's theory of balanced sovereignty was no longer applicable. His idea of balance did survive the Restoration, but it was used for different purposes.

In the previous chapters I focused upon a new aspect of Harrington's political thought, his insistence on balanced sovereignty. I called it a new aspect because it has not been fully explored by John Pocock, who established Harrington as the hero of English republicanism. In Pocock's view, Harrington formed his doctrine of the balance of the land in order to show that an occasion for the release of personal virtue through civic participation had emerged in England. I have proposed a different view, and emphasized that the Harringtonian doctrine was a weapon to assault one of Hobbes's shortcomings, the question how to control military power.

Yet in this chapter I accept Pocock's view that, in the Restoration period, Harrington's idea was adapted and summoned to the defence of the English constitution.[1] According to Pocock, Harrington's language was decisively influential on the following generation, but only after his original idea had been strikingly modified. The phrase 'neo-Harringtonians' is Pocock's

---

[1] See J. G. A. Pocock, *The Machiavellian Moment* (Princeton, 1975), chs. xii–xiii; 'Historical Introduction', *The Political Works of James Harrington*, 128–35.

invention, and I use it here. The neo-Harringtonians are, like Harrington himself, much concerned with the relationship between independence of others and the holding of land. Yet unlike Harrington they regard the English constitution as stable and healthy. They try to maintain, or restore, the Gothic nobility, to which Harrington attributed the conflicts and tumults that had occurred under the English constitution. When they do so, they forget Harrington's concern for balanced sovereignty. In Pocock's view, this neo-Harringtonian thinking, born in the Restoration period, supplied some of the basic materials of the political controversies of the eighteenth century.

Here, largely following the path laid out by Pocock, I shall study several writers who inherited Harrington's argument concerning the relationship between independence and the landownership after the Restoration. What we shall find is that Harrington's idea of balanced sovereignty disappeared in the process by which those writers adopted the notion of balance; and that ancient prudence, which Harrington had opposed to modern prudence, was merged with it. The materials to be examined are one pamphlet and one speech in the 1670s, and the productions of two writers in the 1680s, Henry Neville and Algernon Sidney.[2] Except for Sidney, these materials have already been discussed by Pocock himself. I risk some repetition of Pocock's argument, because I want to show the uniqueness of Harrington's idea of balanced and absolute sovereignty by contrasting it with the ideas of his successors.

According to Pocock, the Harringtonian language was restated twice in 1675: in a speech delivered in the House of Lords by the first Earl of Shaftesbury on 20 October 1675 and subsequently published; and in a pamphlet entitled *A Letter from a Person of Quality to his Friend in the Country*, published in November of that year.[3] These documents, argues Pocock, should be termed 'neo-Harringtonian' rather than 'Harringtonian', for while they are profoundly indebted to Harrington, they also depart radically from his original intention. Harrington considered the politics of modern prudence to be unstable by nature, and attributed its conflicts to the hereditary nobility. By contrast, the neo-Harringtonians welcomed the political role of the peerage and expected the peers to keep parliament independent of the influence exercised by the Court through patronage. The hereditary

---

[2] For this period, see also Blair Worden, 'Republicanism and the Restoration', in David Wootton (ed.), *Republicanism, Liberty, and Commercial Society*, 1649–1776, (Stanford, Calif., 1994), 139–93.

[3] *State Tracts: being a collection of several treatises relating to the Government. Privately printed in the reign of K. Charles II* (London, 1689), 57–61, 41–56.

nobility had now become the core of the constitution and the source of political health and stability.

Shaftesbury, exploiting a conflict between the two Houses of Parliament, the case of Shirley versus Fagg, emphasizes the role of the nobility in the constitution. He makes the Harringtonian statement that 'there is no *Prince* that ever Govern'd without *Nobility* or an *Army*'.[4] *A Letter from a Person of Quality*, which criticizes 'a Military Government', concurs with Shaftesbury.[5] The power of the House of Lords ought to be maintained, 'For the Power of *Peerage* and a *standing-Army*, are like two Buckets, the proportion that one goes down, the other exactly goes up'.[6] When Harrington claimed that monarchy had to be supported either by an army or by a nobility, he meant that monarchy must be either stable and absolute by conquest or rest on the unstable basis of modern prudence. Yet Shaftesbury and his associates did not hesitate to approve the Gothic polity, which Harrington had renounced.

Henry Neville likewise approved the Gothic polity in his work *Plato Redivivus* (1681).[7] At first sight, admittedly, Neville's argument is quite similar to that of Harrington, whose close friend he had been. Neville accepts not only Harrington's doctrine of the balance of the land but the idea of the separation of powers between 'proposing' and 'resolving'.[8] Yet, as Pocock suggests, Neville accepts the English constitution.[9] Thanks to the happy co-ordination of the lords and the commons, Neville claims, 'our government imitates the best and most perfect commonwealth that ever were'. The House of Lords, filled with a vigorous nobility, is the

---

[4] Ibid. 59.

[5] The pamphlet particularly addresses objections to the bill entitled 'An Act to prevent the dangers which may arise from Persons dis-affected to the Government'. Under this Act, all members of both Houses of Parliament as well as all Officers of Church and State would be required to take an Oath, which includes the statements that '*I* A.B. *do declare, that is not Lawful, upon any pretence whatsoever, to take up Arms against the King*'. According to this pamphlet, this bill might deprive 'either of the Houses of *Parliament*, or any of their Members, of their ancient freedom of Debates, or Votes, or other their Privileges whatsoever' (*State Tracts*, 45–6).

[6] Ibid. 55.

[7] Henry Neville, *Plato Redivivus* in *Two English Republican Tracts*, ed. Caroline Robbins (Cambridge, 1969). Neville was one of the 'Harringtonians' in the parliaments of 1659 who tried to put Harrington's programme into practice. In the Restoration period, Harrington, due to mental illness, could no longer write political treatises. Neville, his disciple, published *Plato Redivivus* after Harrington's death. For Neville's political career during the Interregnum, see Robbins's introduction in *Two Republican Tracts*, 6–12.

[8] *Plato Redivivus*, 87, 92, 85.

[9] Blair Worden suggests, however, that Neville's deference to the regime was a strategic device, which concealed a more radical purpose. See Worden, 'Republicanism and the Restoration', 144–52.

equivalent of a senate in a well-ordered commonwealth. The 'great nobility' are the people's 'protectors'.[10]

Algernon Sidney, who wrote *Discourses Concerning Government* between 1681 and 1683, also praised the English constitution as a Gothic monarchy.[11] In Gothic monarchies, monarchy had been restrained by 'their general assemblies, under the names of diets, cortez, parliaments, senates, and the like'. A general assembly had the entire legislative power: 'the power of making, abrogating, changing, correcting, and interpreting laws'. Moreover, it was entitled to depose the king and to regulate the succession of the crown.[12] The vitality of those powerful assemblies lay in the estates which composed the assemblies. 'All the kingdoms peopled from the north', Sidney tells us, 'observed the same rules. In all of them the powers were divided between the kings, the nobility, clergy, and commons.'[13] The English constitution is one of those Gothic monarchies. Sidney claims that William I accepted the conditions proposed by 'the nobility, clergy, and commons'.[14]

Those claims may simply characterize Sidney, as Pocock suggests, as an English equivalent to the 'monarchomachi', the spokesmen for constitutional monarchy and resistance in France in the later sixteenth century. Pocock does not see Sidney as a neo-Harringtonian.[15] Certainly neo-Harringtonianism is not forward in his mind, as it is in those of other writers of the Restoration period whom we have been discussing in this chapter. Even so, there is a neo-Harringtonian streak in him. When he denounces the courtier-nobility created by the monarchy, saying that they cannot 'perform the duties required from the antient nobility of England', it is because he believes 'they have neither the interest nor the estates required for so great a work'. They merely 'have estates at a rack-rent', and therefore have 'no dependents', that is, 'no command of men' to curb 'the insolent'.[16] By contrast, the ancient noblemen had 'the greatest interests in nations,

[10] *Plato Redivivus*, 130, 87.
[11] For Sidney, see also Blair Worden, 'The Commonwealth Kidney of Algernon Sidney', *Journal of British Studies*, 24 (1985), 1–40; Jonathan Scott, *Algernon Sidney and the English Republic* (Cambridge, 1988); *Algernon Sidney and the Restoration Crisis* (Cambridge, 1992). For the question when Sidney wrote *Discourses*, see Worden, 'The Commonwealth Kidney of Algernon Sidney', 38–40.
[12] *Discourses Concerning Government*, ed. T. Hollis (London, 1763), 378 (III. 27).
[13] Ibid. 232 (II. 30).
[14] Ibid. 327 (III. 17).
[15] Pocock has recently made it clear that he does not consider Sidney to be a 'neo-Harringtonian'. See his review article, 'England's Cato: The Virtues and Fortunes of Algernon Sidney', *Historical Journal*, 37 (1994), 931, 935.
[16] *Discourses*, 420 (III. 37).

and were the supporters of their liberty', and 'by birth and estate enjoyed greater advantages than kings could confer upon them for rewards of betraying their country'.[17] Sidney believes that the private interests of a nobility correspond to the public interest as long as they are the owners of a nation's lands.[18] While Harrington's premise is that landownership, if large enough to feed a man, makes him independent, Sidney argues that land, if vast enough, makes him virtuous as well as independent.

Sidney's nobility, as Blair Worden argues, had not only a political role but a moral one too.[19] The nobility is responsible for the moral education of the nation. Harrington had not thought in such terms. He wanted to see a balanced sovereignty erected on the basis of mixed government because he believed that otherwise conflicts among equals must be perpetual. Sidney was not troubled by that prospect. That is partly because he saw no necessary conflict between the interest of the nobility and the public interest. But it is also because he supposed that the peace of society should be supported by what he calls 'antient integrity' or 'principles of common honesty', concepts to which no equivalents can be found in the writings of Harrington. If these principles are 'once extinguished', Sidney warns us, 'mankind must necessarily fall into the condition Hobbes rightly calls "bellum omnium contra omnes"'.[20] That is why the education of the people becomes the crucial task of the magistrates, who are expected to come from the nobility (for 'this is not every man's work').[21] They are to

[17] Ibid. 388 (III. 28), 419 (III. 37).

[18] In the *Discourses*, the private 'interests', 'passions', and 'concernments' of a king or of a corrupted nobility are often set against 'the interest of the public', etc. Thus: 'There is another ground of perpetual fluctuation in absolute monarchies; . . . that they cannot be restrained by law . . . in some measure relating to the inclinations of the monarch, that is, the impulse of ministers, favorites, wives, or whores, who frequently govern all things according to their own passions or interests' (p. 109 (II. 11)); 'the absolute monarch, who governs for himself, and chiefly seeks his own preservation' (p. 146 (II. 19)); 'for private passions and concernments he departed from the interest of the publick' (p. 201 (II. 25)); 'A prince that sets up an interest in himself' (p. 210 (II. 27)); 'they [=kings] who . . . acknowledge no rule but their own will, set up an interest in themselves against that of their people' (p. 242 (II. 30)); 'no man must be the judge of his own case, . . . in which his own passions, private interest . . . will always lead him out of the way of justice' (p. 425 (III. 38)); 'Whether therefore such matters are ordinary or extraordinary, the decision is and ought to be placed where there is most wisdom and stability, and where passion and private interest does least prevail to the obstruction of justice' (p. 445 (III. 43)). However, in the next passage, both 'the public interests' and 'the concernments of private men' are set against the 'passions' of a king. 'The public interests, and the concernments of private men in their lands, goods, liberties, and lives, . . . cannot be preserved by one who is transported by his own passions or follies, a slave to his lusts and vices' (pp. 368–9 (III. 26)). The landed nobility would be classified as belonging to this sort of 'private men'.

[19] Worden, 'The Commonwealth Kidney of Algernon Sidney', 24.

[20] *Discourses*, 342–4 (III. 19).

[21] Ibid. 38–9 (I. 16).

maintain the 'principles of common honesty' among the people. They are to 'encourage virtue and justice; teach men what they ought to do, suffer, or expect from others; fix them upon principles of honesty'.[22] Noblemen excel commoners in 'purity of manners'[23] and as the preservers of pure manners. Liberty should be respected; a high esteem should be given to military valour; and virtue, honesty, and justice should be encouraged.[24] Thus will the nobility lead the people towards moral as well as political fulfilment.

Harrington detested the House of Lords. He regarded its membership, because hereditary, as 'unequal', as the Roman senate had been. But in Shaftesbury's view, the judicature held by the Lords is the essence of the constitution: 'your *Judicature* is the Life and Soul of the Dignity of the *Peerage* of *England*'. 'My Principle is also, *That the Lords House, and the Judicature and Rights belonging to it, are an Essential part of the Government*, and Established by the same Law.'[25]

On this point, too, Neville betrayed his master. Admittedly, unlike the other neo-Harringtonians, he proposed a clear series of reforms of the English constitution, and suggested that certain prerogatives of the crown should be handed over to parliament. However, he did not dare to propose an elective senate in place of the House of Lords:[26] 'when this new constitution shall be admitted', Neville believes, 'the lords cannot have any interest or temptation to differ with the commons in anything wherein the public good is concerned.'[27] Unlike his master Harrington, Neville did not insist upon rotation. He argued that the Lords could fulfil its function properly even though its membership remained hereditary.[28]

The main concern the neo-Harringtonians had in common was to limit the prerogative and to defend liberties. Shaftesbury emphasized the role of the judicature in the constitution. *A Letter from a Person of Quality* feared

---

[22] *Discourses*, 343 (III. 19).   [23] Ibid. 150 (II. 19).

[24] Ibid. 201 (II. 25), 344 (III. 19), 386 (III. 28).

[25] *State Tracts*, 58, 60 (Shaftesbury's italic).

[26] *Plato Redivivus*, 185–7. Parliament is to appoint four executive councils, whose consent the king must secure for the exercise of executive powers: one for the making of war and peace; one for disposing and ordering of the militia; one for nominating and appointing of officers, civil, military, and ecclesiastical; and one for spending of the public revenues of the crown.

[27] Ibid. 193.

[28] Neville's attitude towards the English constitution had changed from his position in 1659, when he opposed *The Humble Petition and Advice* in Richard Cromwell's Parliament: 'Let us not return to the Government of the Long Parliament. It was an oligarchy, detested by all men that love a commonwealth . . . We that are for a Commonwealth, are for a single person, senate, and popular assembly; I mean not King, Lords, and Commons. I hope that will never be admitted here. . . . The Petition and Advice settled power in a prince to have kingly authority over a people. . . . I shall move that . . . [we] declare the Protector to be Chief Magistrate' (*Diary of Thomas Burton*, ed. J. T. Rutt (4 vols., London, 1828), iii. 134).

that the bill it opposed might deprive 'either of the Houses of *Parliament*, or any of their Members, of their ancient freedom of Debates, or Votes, or other their Privileges whatsoever'.[29] Neville wanted to guarantee the execution of 'all our statutes from the highest to the lowest, from Magna Charta to that for burying in woollen'.[30] The king's power should be regulated, argues Sidney, as it has been regulated in the Gothic monarchies, 'within the limits of the law, by the virtue and power of a great and brave nobility'.[31]

By what means, then, ought the king's power to be regulated? Neville, who believed that his reform package could be implemented without rebellion, held the most moderate of the positions taken by the neo-Harringtonians. 'There cannot, nor ought to be, any change but by his majesty's free consent.' That reform would be 'his [=the king's] own interest, preservation, quiet and true greatness', for his people's prosperity ought to be his own.[32] Other neo-Harringtonians, by contrast, allowed the subjects to defend their rights by armed resistance *in extremis*. 'How there can be a distinction then left between absolute and bounded Monarchies', cried *A Letter from a Person of Quality*, 'if *Monarchs* have only the fear of God, and no fear of humane Resistance to restrain them'.[33] Sidney took a more aggressive line. When legal remedies do not work, the people are allowed to use 'extraordinary' means to remove evildoers. Resistance is just and honourable if it attempts to restore the initial principle of the constitution, the liberty of the people. The people have a right, even a duty, to rise against the king who subverts the constitution.[34]

Neville did not argue for resistance. But he did echo the concerns and proposals of men who had resisted the king in 1642. His proposals that the nomination of the Privy Councillors and other officers should be approved by both Houses, and that the militia should be controlled by them, followed *The Nineteen Propositions* of that year.[35] Other neo-Harringtonians also thought in the terms of the early 1640s. In the threat of absolutism in the 1670s they saw a revival of the ambitions of Archbishop Laud.[36] More

---

[29] *State Tracts*, 46.   [30] *Plato Redivivus*, 185.
[31] *Discourses*, 419 (III. 37).   [32] *Plato Redivivus*, 177–8.
[33] *State Tracts*, 48.
[34] *Discourses*, 120 (II. 14), 180–1 (II. 24), 186 (II. 24), 205 (II. 25), 413 (III. 36), 434 (III. 40).
[35] Cf. *The Nineteen Propositions*, *Historical Collections*, ed. John Rushworth, part III, vol. i (London, 1691), 722–4.
[36] See *State Tracts*, 55, 60; Sidney, *Discourses*, 8 (I. 2). Johann Sommerville suggests that those who opposed Laud's policies before the civil wars in the 1640s might have been provoked to some extent by the subtle theological difference between Arminianism and orthodox Calvinism, but that their principal motive was the fear that Laudian policy would lead to unlimited absolutism and infringe the rights of the subjects. J. P. Sommerville, *Politics and Ideology in England, 1604–1640* (London, 1986), 222.

significantly for our purpose, they discussed the constitution, as the parliamentarians of the early 1640s had done, within the Fortescuian framework
of prerogative and liberties. Their concern was to prevent, not anarchy,
but tyranny. When Sidney claimed that the king cannot change any law, it
was to Fortescue, the spokesman for the liberty of the subject to whom the
parliamentarians of the 1640s had looked back, that he turned for support.[37]
In the neo-Harringtonians' hands, Harrington's language was absorbed
into the old parliamentarian cause.

2. The Absorption of Ancient within Modern Prudence

In the reign of Charles II Harrington's idea of balanced sovereignty vanished. The neo-Harringtonians were far from taking up his innovative
theory of sovereignty. Harrington had proposed two concepts of balance:
balance in the distribution of the land and balance among the functional
divisions within the government. In his theory, the former was the premise
of the latter. The two had a tight logical connection and were inseparable.
The idea of the balance of the land articulated the problem to be tackled:
the idea of balance within constitutional arrangements presented the solution to the problem. Harrington's notions of necessity and fear highlighted
the equality of power among independent individuals, which inevitably led
to anarchy, Harrington's version of a 'state of war' among equals. His
notion of interest offered a remedy and established the idea of balanced
sovereignty.

The neo-Harringtonians cut the link between the two kinds of balance.
They show little interest in the idea of the balance among the functional
divisions within the government, and consequently do not adopt the idea
of balanced sovereignty. Instead they inherit the idea of the balance of the
land alone. When they cut that link, they change the implication of the
idea of the balance of the land, as John Pocock pointed out.[38] When Shaftesbury asserted that a monarchy has to be supported by either an army or a
nobility, his preference was evidently for a nobility; that is, in Harrington's
terms, for 'mixed monarchy'. But in Harrington's judgement, mixed monarchy upon the Gothic balance was inherently unstable. That was because,
in mixed monarchy, the nobility had no 'grand signor' above their heads

---

[37] *Discourses*, 310 (III. 14), 315 (III. 15). Like Charles Herle's co-ordination theory, Sidney's theory claims that parliament, which makes and interprets law, is entitled to override
the king's veto.

[38] Pocock, 'Historical Introduction', *The Political Works of James Harrington*, 128–52.

and there was no necessity or fear to solve their conflicts. For the neo-Harringtonians, however, the notions of necessity and fear, which had been used to secure obedience in Harrington's system, were of no interest. Harrington was greatly concerned with the question who obeys whom among independent landowners, a question which leads to the further question how to institute a civil society. Yet the neo-Harringtonians, to whom the Gothic balance appears a healthy basis for stable government, are little concerned with those questions.

In the neo-Harringtonians' argument, the focus returns to the contest between the subject and the king. Their insistence on the rights of landowners and on the leadership expected from them is deployed to support the subjects' claim against the king. They base a new interpretation of the English constitution upon their new interpretation of Harrington's balance of the land. The word 'balance' is now used for the protection of the subjects' rights rather than for the consolidation of the government. The focus of the argument of the writers is no longer upon the prevention or ending of anarchy.

Here the era of the *Answer*, Ferne, Hunton, and Harrington has gone. The framework of classical mixed government survives the Restoration but serves the old parliamentarian cause. The argument for mixed government in this period seems to have returned to the positions of Henry Parker and Charles Herle. However, there is a crucial difference. The neo-Harringtonians, unlike Parker, Herle, and the old parliamentarians, are able to exploit the doctrine of the balance of the land and to modify their understanding of the English constitution accordingly. They are able to present the hereditary nobility as the champion of the constitution.

Thus the neo-Harringtonians assimilated the Polybian idea of mixed government into the Fortescuian one. The distinction between the two had been crucial in the years after 1640, since theorists using the former model tried to prevent war, while those who used the latter encouraged armed resistance to the king. After the Restoration, however, the contrast is obscured by the neo-Harringtonians. Admittedly, they recall the Fortescuian frame of reference, the balance between the prerogative and the subjects' rights. But at the same time they exhibit the influence of the Polybian idea in emphasizing the role of the lords rather than of the commons. Although the main focus of argument may have moved, in particular in Sidney, from the difference among the governmental bodies to that among the social estates—from the difference between the role of the House of Lords and that of the House of Commons to that between the role of the lords and that of the commons—the neo-Harringtonians' special insistence on the nobility can be considered to be the residue of the principal characteristic of the Polybian idea. Where Harrington's concern was the senate, which was one of the components within his government, the neo-Harringtonians focused their attention upon the hereditary nobility, which was one of the three estates in England.

When Parker and Herle referred to the three estates, the king, the lords, and the commons, they did so because, seeking to restrain the prerogative, they wanted to emphasize that the king was no more than one of the three components of the constitution. But when the neo-Harringtonians refer to the three estates, they do so because they want to emphasize the role of the nobility, as distinct from those of the other two. Their Polybian streak differentiates the lords from the commons in terms of the defence of the subjects' rights, and the role of the lords (if not the House of Lords) is highlighted. Because of this Polybian colour, they depart from Parker and Herle. Of course, the case of Neville, who favoured the House of Commons, does not suit this pattern. But Neville did not disapprove of the House of Lords. He tried to adapt it to the defence of the subjects' rights.

Thus ancient prudence was first brought into England by the *Answer* on the brink of the civil wars, radically explored and adopted by Harrington in the 1650s, and then absorbed into modern prudence, which Harrington had opposed, after the Restoration.

3. Conclusion: Conscience, Fear, Interest

The years of the English civil wars (1640–60) were a new era of English political thought. In that period the government of the king and the two Houses first fell into serious trouble and then disappeared. There emerged writers who examined, in the most acute way, the problem of preventing anarchy. Among them, we have discussed the writers of the Polybian idea of mixed government between 1642 and 1644: Thomas Hobbes, who wrote *The Elements of Law* and *De Cive* between 1640 and 1647 and *Leviathan* in the early 1650s; and James Harrington, who wrote between 1653 and 1660. In the early 1640s the English exponents of the Polybian theory, and Hobbes in developing his theory of sovereignty, had the same end, peace and unity. Even so, Hobbes's treatment of 'private judgement' was opposite to that to be found in the theories of mixed government. Philip Hunton and Henry Ferne looked to 'conscience' to restore peace after the breakdown of the constitution: Hobbes denounced 'conscience' as the cause of anarchy, and deployed 'fear' instead.

When the Rump Parliament collapsed, Harrington challenged Hobbes's endorsement of it. He turned instead to the Polybian idea of mixed government. Yet he also believed, with Hobbes, that absolute sovereignty was needed to restore internal peace. In bringing those two ideas together, he remoulded the idea of mixed government as it had been developed in the 1640s. He replaced conscience with 'interest' and presented the theory of balanced and absolute sovereignty.[39] This was a direct response to Hobbes's denunciation of the Graeco-Roman tradition of political theory. Harrington argued that a government cannot have authority unless individuals are allowed private judgement concerning political obedience. The functions of the government have to be divided and differentiated in order to create sovereignty and to secure the obedience of the people.

The prime concern of Harrington's idea of mixed government, as of Polybius', was how to secure internal stability, not how to prevent tyrannical rule or invasion from outside. Polybius pointed out that the weakness of the Athenian constitution had been revealed once external dangers had been removed. Harrington implied that the Rump Parliament was inherently incapable of controlling its army. The Rump, which had defeated the external threats to its survival by 1651, collapsed thereafter like the pure democracy of Athens before it. The first republican government suffered fatal conflicts between the army and parliament after the battle of Worcester, which ended the threat of royalist invasion for the foreseeable future.[40]

Some modern commentators deny that Harrington adopted the Polybian idea, on the simple ground that the key part of Harrington's government consists of no more than two elements, the senate and the popular assembly.[41] They believe that mixed government has to consist of three elements, monarchical, aristocratic, and democratic. These critics fuse the Polybian idea (to be found in the *Answer*) with the traditional Fortescuian understanding of the three estates (to be found in Henry Parker).[42] It is true that Polybius articulated the neat triad of monarchy, aristocracy, and democracy. However, the number 'three' is not important to Polybius. All he showed was why the three simple forms of government are unstable, and why the Roman government achieved stability nevertheless. He offered no theoretical explanation why the combination of the three elements is

---

[39] In my treatment of the relationship between conscience and interest, I have been inspired by Sheldon Wolin's phrase, 'the substitution of interest for conscience'. S. S. Wolin, *Politics and Vision* (Boston, 1960), 331. For the word 'interest' in 17th-cent. English political thought, see also David Wootton, *Divine Right and Democracy* (London, 1986), 70–7.

[40] Blair Worden, *The Rump Parliament 1648–1653* (Cambridge, 1974), pts. iv–v.

[41] J. R. Goodale, 'J. G. A. Pocock's neo-Harringtonians', *History of Political Thought*, 1 (1980), 237–59; K. Toth, 'Interpretation in Political Theory: The Case of Harrington', *Review of Politics*, 37 (1975), 317–39.

[42] For an instance of this, see M. Mendle, *Dangerous Positions* (Alabama, 1985), ch. i.

better than other patterns of combination. He did not describe how the three elements help one another and work together in abstract terms. What he bequeathed was the argument that the Roman government had kept its internal stability even in peacetime because the functions of the government had been divided among more than one governmental body.

Moreover, the phrase *senatus populusque Romanus* does not imply a mixture of the three elements. Rather it underpins Harrington's idea of mixed government. That is why Harrington employs it when he rebukes Hobbes for his criticism of mixed government. Like Polybius, Harrington claims that the supreme power cannot be located in the Roman republic.[43]

The identity of the Polybian mixed government lies, not in the principle that a government is formed by the three elements, but in the principle that a government, within its decision-making process, has functional divisions and differentiations among its components. This perception gives us a better understanding of the importance of *His Majesty's Answer to the Nineteen Propositions*. Articulating functional divisions in the English constitution, the *Answer* offered a theory of consolidation, a theory for peace. From Falkland and Colepeper to Harrington, the English exponents of Polybian mixed government maintained its traditional formula: a balance within the government which secures domestic peace.

However, after Harrington the theorists of mixed government became less concerned with domestic peace than their predecessors. Following the Restoration the Polybian idea is assimilated into the Fortescuian idea of mixed government. Now the Polybian idea is exploited to defend the role of the nobility in the English constitution. The new writers do not believe that the balance is the basis of the authority of the king, as the *Answer to the Nineteen Propositions* maintained. Hobbes warned in 1640 that the idea of mixed government would encourage resistance. Yet in 1642–4 the theorists of Polybian mixed government shared Hobbes's concern for peace and order. It was in the reign of Charles II that theorists of the new generation used the idea of mixed government in the way against which Hobbes had warned.

This change is clearest in the *Discourses* of Algernon Sidney. Sidney discusses mixed government in exactly the manner against which *The Elements of Law* had warned. Sidney, who hates 'slavery' under absolute monarchy, believes in mixed government because he wants to avoid that condition. Just as Hobbes feared men would, Sidney endorses acts of armed resistance, saying they are 'the most just and honourable actions that have been per-

---

[43] See also Sect. 6.2 above.

formed for the preservation of them [=people's liberties]'. 'Civil war, in Machiavel's account, is a disease; but tyranny is the death of the state.'[44] Hobbes's straw-man in the 1640s, who inspires rebellion with the idea of mixed government, obtains substance in the 1680s.

Charles II dissolved the Oxford Parliament in March 1681. Shaftesbury's parliamentary strategy against the king could no longer be pursued, and he was convinced that Charles would call no parliaments. He now gave serious consideration to armed resistance, to be undertaken without parliamentary approval. In the summer of 1682, when he still had influence in London, Shaftesbury formed a plot to overthrow the government. Yet after the king had regained control of the capital, Shaftesbury abandoned the plan and fled to Holland in despair.[45] During the following period of fierce loyalist reaction, the so-called Rye House Plot was used to destroy the Whig leaders. Lord Russell and Algernon Sidney were executed, and Essex killed himself (or was murdered) before his trial. Admittedly, the evidence for the conspiracy was far from concrete. Yet the claim that those men had plotted rebellion against the king—rebellion without endorsement from parliament—was probably correct. In such a rebellion, neo-Harringtonian ideas would have found practical expression.

In the eighteenth century, traces of Harrington's theory of balanced sovereignty are hard to find. It is absent from the ideas of mixed government held by Montesquieu and James Madison. When Montesquieu praises the English mixed monarchy, his concern is not how to secure obedience but how to keep the French monarchy moderate. Madison, in *The Federalist No. 10*, sees mixed government as the means to spare the minority from the tyranny of the majority. Yet in the middle of the seventeenth century, when the English nation was profoundly divided, neither Harrington nor Hobbes could expect any solid majority to be formed.

The two decades of the civil wars were a unique era of English political theory. Montesquieu thought of those civil disturbances as benign winds guiding a vessel into the harbour of liberty.[46] To the passengers amidst the storm of the mid-seventeenth century, the prospect was less serene. Most

---

[44] *Discourses*, 12 (I. 5), 413 (III. 36), 434 (III. 40).

[45] Richard Ashcraft, *Revolutionary Politics and Locke's Two Treatises of Government* (Princeton, 1986), 313–59.

[46] Montesquieu believed that political disturbances had always contributed to the development of liberty in English history; 'Ce sont ici les historiens d'Angleterre, où l'on voit la liberté sortir sans cesse des feux de la discorde et de la sédition' (Lettres Persanes, CXXXVI, *Œuvres Complètes de Montesquieu*, ed. Roger Caillois (Paris, 1949–51), i. 336); 'L'Angleterre est agitée par des vents qui ne sont pas faits pour submerger, mais pour conduire au port' (*Mes Pensées*, 816, ibid. i. 1402). I am indebted to Dr Yoshie Kawade for help with these references.

political thinkers, instead of contending with the gales, contended against each other over the direction of the ship. Harrington, Hobbes, and the new English theorists of mixed government saw shipwreck ahead. While others perpetuated the quarrels of the civil wars, they argued against the wars and offered deliverance from them.

APPENDIX A
Religion and Sovereignty in Hobbes and Harrington

I. FAITH AND CONSCIENCE

Hobbes and Harrington both advocated absolute sovereignty in civil matters. Neither of them argued for persecution in religion. On the contrary, both men believed that absolute sovereignty and religious toleration could stand together. In that, they went against the orthodoxies of their time.

In Hobbes's theory of sovereignty, 'conscience' was often denounced as a cause of anarchy. Yet that does not necessarily mean that he forbade the subjects to have conscience. It is not possible, or even necessary, Hobbes recognized, to force the subjects to give up their conscience. The business of the sovereign is only 'the actions' and not 'the heart' of a man.[1] Even though a man is forbidden to exercise conscience as 'private judgement' of political activity, he may be allowed to exercise it as 'faith'.

As is emphasized by John Pocock, Hobbes's argument is tied to the medieval trinity of reason, experience and faith.[2] Through reason, a knowledge of logical certainty based upon the definition of words is to be obtained. Experience offers a knowledge of temporal consequence, and through faith men acquire a knowledge the certainty of which derives 'not from the thing it selfe, or from the principles of naturall Reason, but from the Authority, and good opinion wee have, of him that hath sayd it'.[3] Reason, experience, and faith correspond to philosophy, history, and religion respectively. Men only need reason to understand God's command, and to establish the sovereign. In the field of reason, the sovereign has to define the meaning and usage of words, and to unify the criteria against which truth and falsehood will be judged. In the domain of faith, too, the sovereign has to monopolize all sorts of judgement, if the question of obedience to the sovereign is at issue. Yet unlike in the case of reason, the sovereign does not necessarily have to authorize everything in the case of faith, because there may be some items which have nothing to do with obedience.[4] On the other hand, the exercise of conscience involves a matter of faith as well as of reason. Here, therefore, there remains the possibility of liberty of conscience, which need not be controlled by the sovereign.

---

[1] '[N]o human law is intended to oblige the conscience of a man, but the actions only . . . no man (but God alone) knoweth the heart or conscience of a man, unless it break out into action, either of the tongue, or other part of the body (*The Elements of Law*, II. 6. 3. 146).

[2] J. G. A. Pocock, 'Time, History and Eschatology in the Thought of Thomas Hobbes', *Politics, Language, and Time* (New York, 1971), 154.

[3] *Leviathan*, V. 31–2 [p. 18]; VI. 36–7 [p. 22]; VII. 48–9 [pp. 31–2].

[4] Pocock, 'Time, History and Eschatology in the Thought of Thomas Hobbes', 191.

In fact, the degree to which the sovereign should control doctrine cannot be decided by the requirements of the sovereign's absoluteness. The degree of the control is a matter for the sovereign's discretion. In order to maintain peace and order, it is true, the renunciation of (the right of following) private judgements concerning political action is necessary. Yet this necessity is fully intelligible from the knowledge gained in the domain of reason. Since the domain of reason is independent of that of faith, the scope of Hobbes's theory of sovereignty is not confined to Christian commonwealths, but open to any commonwealths of any religion. Admittedly, no religious doctrine which urges the religious authority to intervene in the secular authority can be allowed. But apart from this, the question how to control religious doctrine is left to the discretion of the sovereign.

What interests us is that Hobbes said more than his theory of sovereignty required him to say. Through the three political writings, *The Elements of Law*, *De Cive*, and *Leviathan*, Hobbes laid down in detail how the sovereign should handle the matter of faith. The question is, in principle, left to the sovereign to answer as he likes. Yet nevertheless, for the case of a Christian commonwealth, Hobbes in each of the three writings took the trouble to offer an answer as a commendable example.

His answers are not quite the same in the three writings. In *De Cive* Hobbes's account of Christianity is declared to be compatible with the doctrine of the Church of England. First, Hobbes demands, the interpretation of the Bible should be unified and controlled under the authority of the sovereign. Secondly, the interpretation should be made through the legitimately ordained clergymen (*per Ecclesiasticos rite ordinatos*). The sovereign himself is expected to appreciate the interpretation made by his church, and to help the interpretation penetrate the whole country by forcible measures. Why should he not interpret the Bible for himself, and set forth the true interpretation, as he has to do so in the field of philosophy? The answer is, because matters directly concerning faith, such as the duty of the saviour, punishment and reward in the world to come, sacraments, forms of ceremonies, cannot be understood by reason. No matter how impeccably the meaning and usage of words may be defined, the correct interpretation of the Bible by the sovereign cannot be guaranteed. Only Jesus Christ himself—and his successors who have inherited his infallibility—are able to understand the words of God without making errors. Only the apostolic Church, it follows, is entitled to interpret the Bible. Here, Hobbes approved the significance of the Church of England, which stands upon the holy apostolic tradition.[5] Hobbes's theory of sovereignty based on reason may not, of course, leave a free hand to the Church of England. Its doctrine and practices may have to be squared with his theory. Yet in the answer to the question of faith which he recommends, Hobbes tried to show that his theory is compatible with the mainstream Anglican doctrine.[6]

---

[5] *De Cive*, XVII. 28. 278–9 [E: pp. 248–9]; R. Tuck, *Hobbes* (Oxford, 1989), 83–5.

[6] Johann Sommerville, however, suggests that Hobbes's Anglicanism in *De Cive* is only 'skin-deep'. See his *Thomas Hobbes: Political Ideas in Historical Context* (London, 1992), 127.

In *De Cive* the notion of liberty of conscience is not referred to, and no denominations other than the Anglican are allowed. In *Leviathan*, however, his argument changes radically.[7] He welcomes the collapse of episcopacy and endorses Independency. First, he leaves the Bible in the hands of the sovereign, who is a secular ruler in the domain of reason, and who has nothing to do with the apostolic tradition derived from Christ. Thus Hobbes refuted the significance of an apostolically ordained Church. Provided only that he has been baptized, the sovereign is considered to be the supreme pastor even without ordination by 'the Imposition by Hands'.[8] This claim has serious consequences for the question of church organization. Once the one apostolic Church is deprived of its claim to authority, the sovereign does not need to maintain a single unified Church.[9] He can still force the subjects to accept any doctrine he endorses, and may need to. But that is not the same as to force them to follow the one form of religious service under the one Church under his authority. It could be, then, that the sovereign would choose a doctrine under which all are free to worship the Christian God with a minister, and under a form, that they choose. In Hobbes's view, that is what happened in the primitive Church and what should happen now. In the age of the Apostles, the people converted 'out of Reverence, not by Obligation: Their Consciences were free, and their Words and Actions subject to none but the Civill Power'.[10] In that period, claims Hobbes, there existed a liberty of conscience. Unfortunately, that liberty had been suppressed for centuries by the threefold 'knots', namely, the Presbytery, the Episcopacy, and the Roman Papal system. But with the Reformation, history moved into reverse, and England was cut off from the Papacy. In the 1640s, the Episcopacy was abolished. By the 1650s, all three knots have been dissolved.

> And so we are reduced to the Independency of the Primitive Christians to follow Paul, or Cephas, or Apollos, every man as he liketh best: Which, if it be without contention, and without measuring the Doctrine of Christ, by our affection to the Person of his Minister, (the fault which the Apostle reprehended in the Corinthians,) is perhaps the best: First, because there ought to be no Power over the Consciences of men, but of the Word it selfe, working Faith in every one, not alwayes according to the purpose of them that Plant and Water, but of God himself, that giveth the Increase: and secondly, because it is unreasonable in them, who teach there is such danger in every little Errour, to require of a man endued with Reason of his own, to follow the Reason of any other man, or of the most voices of many other men; Which is little better, then to venture his Salvation at crosse and pile.[11]

The tenet of this famous argument for Independency and toleration (which he identified with each other, as Harrington did) differs much from his treatment of

---

[7] This radical change was to contribute to his expulsion from Paris. For the relationship of *Leviathan* to Hobbes's involvement in the politics in the exiled court of Charles II, see R. Tuck, *Philosophy and Government* (Cambridge, 1993), 320–6.

[8] *Leviathan*, XLII. 377 [p. 299].

[9] Tuck, *Hobbes*, 86–8.

[10] *Leviathan*, XLVII. 479 [p. 384].

[11] Ibid. XLVII. 479–80 [p. 385].

religion in *De Cive*. In *Leviathan*, the word 'conscience' clearly has two faces: liberty of conscience as private judgement concerning obedience is denounced; liberty of conscience as Christian faith is to be defended so long as it is separated from the question of obedience.[12]

Between *De Cive* and *Leviathan*, then, Hobbes's account of a Christian commonwealth underwent a big swing, while his position on civil matters remained largely static. But the change does not show inconsistency. Hobbes leaves a large part of religious policy to the sovereign's discretion. The swing shows the width of that discretion. The different approaches to religious policy in Hobbes's writings are no more than examples of the positions which the sovereign may adopt. In the case of *Leviathan*, Hobbes did not say that all sovereigns must adopt a policy of toleration in order to keep peace and order. He expected that a sovereign of a Christian commonwealth would rule without toleration. He also thought that a pagan sovereign would be intolerant towards Christians. Even so, those sovereigns would still be 'Lawfull Soveraign[s]', against whom any form of resistance would be prohibited. Yet Christians in such commonwealths should still feel secure, Hobbes thought. That is because, while '*Faith* and *Obedience* are both Necessary to Salvation', 'faith' in this sense means belief that '*Jesus is the Christ*' and no more. No matter how intolerant the sovereign may be, he will never deny that minimum belief if he is a Christian. If the sovereign is an infidel, and forces his Christian subjects to deny that belief, the subjects 'have the licence that Naaman had', and are allowed to disguise their belief to avoid further persecution.[13]

If a policy of intolerance can live alongside the Hobbesian sovereignty in that way, what, then, of the policy of tolerance? The latter policy looks much harder for the absolute sovereign to adopt. Once liberty of conscience is set free, even if only upon the strict condition that it does not provoke political actions, will it not encourage the subjects to disobey the secular power? Why did Hobbes not calculate the worst possibility, that liberty of conscience may lead to civil liberty?

Unlike the Hobbes of *De Cive*, the Hobbes of *Leviathan* was not troubled by that possibility. He laid down a novel interpretation of Christianity at length. He made a brave attempt to carry out an interpretation of the Bible, as far as possible, by reason, and marched forward even into the territory which in *De Cive* had been protected as belonging to the domain of faith. The borderline between reason and faith was now radically redrawn in favour of reason. Once a standard interpretation, which is protected by reasonable demonstration, was established, Hobbes hoped, there would be no room for the seditious intervention of 'Enthusiasme, or supernaturall Inspiration'.[14]

The weapon he deployed was his peculiar materialist claim that nothing incorporeal can be considered to exist. On the basis of that materialism, he went so

[12] As far as the argument for secular sovereignty—the domain of reason—is concerned, the balance between covenant and conquest was tilted towards the latter in *Leviathan*, as we saw in Ch. 4. I have been unable to find any theoretical link between this shift towards 'conquest' and the change in Hobbes's religious argument.

[13] *Leviathan*, XLIII. 413–14 [pp. 330–1].   [14] Ibid. XXXII. 259 [p. 198].

far as to deny the immortality of the soul.[15] He claimed that a human soul is mortal; that if righteous people are reincarnated in the place called heaven, that place cannot exist anywhere other than on earth; that if the damned people have to suffer eternal torment, that means no more than that they are banned from reincarnation, since there cannot be a place called hell; that once Saul succeeded to the crown of Israel, God's direct rule was terminated; and that Jesus will definitely come again to reconstruct the kingdom of God on earth, but that no one can have any idea when.[16]

This view of Christianity is designed to make the sovereign unassailable even in the eyes of religious fanatics, who may happen to believe that obedience to God conflicts with obedience to the sovereign. Under that new doctrine of Hobbes's, no one need fear punishment after death, since the soul simply perishes; what should be feared is punishment not by God but by the sovereign.[17] No Christian can find any solid basis for arguing with the sovereign, when the existence of any incorporeal items other than the existence of God, such as a human soul, a holy ghost, and hell, are denied. That novel argument sweeps away the theoretical basis both of Catholicism and of Presbyterianism, while also disarming the 'enthusiasm' of the sects. Hobbes concedes that his argument 'will appear to most men a novelty'. Yet 'the Principles of it are true and proper; and the Ratiocination is solid' and is 'New and well proved Truth'. He insists that 'it may be profitably printed, and more profitably taught in the Universities'.[18]

Thus a policy of toleration can be accommodated by Hobbesian sovereignty. If a policy either of tolerance or of intolerance can coexist with the maintenance of sovereignty, which of them is better suited to that end? We shall be better equipped to answer that question when we have visited Harrington's account of religion.

---

[15] David Johnston, 'Hobbes's Mortalism', *History of Political Thought*, 10 (1989), 647–63.

[16] *Leviathan*, XXXV. 284 [p. 219]; XXXVIII. 306–22 [pp. 238–48]; XL. 328–9 [pp. 254–5]; XLI. 332–4 [pp. 261–3], etc.

[17] Richard Tuck claims that when Hobbes laid down this new understanding of Christianity, he intended not only to give the sovereign a monopoly of sanctions, but to relieve men of the fear of an afterlife. See his 'The Civil Religion of Thomas Hobbes', in Nicholas Phillipson and Quentin Skinner (eds.), *Political Discourse in Early Modern Britain* (Cambridge, 1993), 131–2.

[18] *Leviathan*, XXXVIII. 311 [p. 241]; 'A Review, and Conclusion', 489–91 [pp. 394–5]. However, for most Christians, the question would not be whether the universities can successfully indoctrinate the nation, but whether Hobbesian Christianity can properly be called Christianity. In his doctrine, which is dominated by his extreme materialism, what does it mean for a man to believe that Jesus is Christ? To that most difficult question, perhaps the best answer we have now is the one given by Pocock. According to Pocock, the fact that the Third and the Fourth Parts of *Leviathan* are written in the past tense shows that Hobbes's account of Christianity belongs to the domain of history as well as to that of faith. That history is a sacred history for Christians; and for them, to believe that Jesus is Christ means to believe in that sacred history, namely, to believe that God ruled the Christian commonwealth by himself in the past, and that Christ will come again in the future. Pocock, 'Time, History and Eschatology in the Thought of Thomas Hobbes'.

2. CONSCIENCE AND THE NATIONAL RELIGION

If Harrington was a critic of the First and the Second Parts of *Leviathan*, he was an admirer of the Third and the Fourth Parts. He largely accepted Hobbes's account of Christianity, and argued for liberty of conscience.

In Hobbes's terminology, the notion of conscience belonged to two domains: the domain of political obedience and that of private faith. Hobbes argued that the two domains can be clearly separated. Harrington's advantage was that, writing after Hobbes, he could inherit that dualism, which it had cost Hobbes great efforts to vindicate. In the sphere of political obedience, conscience, which had been denounced by Hobbes, was revived in the form of 'interest' in Harrington's system. Conscience as private faith, which was vigorously kept alive even in Hobbes's system, was treated by Harrington in the same manner. Harrington, adopting the notion of 'interest', employs a much simpler terminology than Hobbes's: interest belongs to the domain of obedience, and conscience concerns only private faith.[19]

This distinction of interest and conscience is particularly important for his secular institution, the legislature of the commonwealth. Harrington expected the legislature to identify the common interest. But he did not believe that all variations of private concern can be accommodated by the common interest. Private religious concerns cannot be integrated into the common interest: they are distinguished from private interests and are called private conscience. When what cannot be handled by the legislature is excluded as conscience, the common interest will be found, and everyone will be satisfied.

A man has a private conscience, claims Harrington, and a commonwealth is the national conscience. He emphasizes that liberty of conscience can live in harmony with the national religion. Those opinions may sound similar to his account of interest. However, the relationship of private conscience to public conscience is far from parallel with that of private interest to public interest. Unlike private interest, private conscience is not expected to be identified with public conscience.[20]

Liberty of conscience, thinks Harrington, means that different denominations and religions are allowed to live in peace in a commonwealth. For instance, Elijah was able to sacrifice in a place outside the temple of the national religion in Israel. John the Baptist and Jesus, too, taught the people outside the national temple, and 'the Christian religion grew up according unto the orders of the commonwealth of Israel'. When Paul was questioned in Israel, the Sadducees and the Pharisees lived together.[21] And in Athens, Paul witnessed three religions—the Epicurean, the Stoic, and the Christian—living together: 'it must needs follow that in the common-

[19] There can be found one usage of 'conscience' to mean obedience or 'allegiance', but it is an exceptional case: 'the whole dispute will come upon matter of conscience, and this, whether it be urged by the right of kings, the obligation of former laws, or of the oath of allegiance, is absolved by the balance' (*Oceana*, 203 [p. 62]).

[20] Ibid. 185–6, 204 [pp. 39–40, 63]; *Pian Piano* (London, 1657), 386; *Brief Directions* (1658), 595; *The Art of Lawgiving* (London, 1659), 658, 681.

[21] *Oceana*, 186 [p. 40].

wealth of Athens, there was liberty of conscience'.[22] When this liberty is guaranteed, a man is free to worship God as he likes, and 'no violence for this cause' is offered to any man.[23] That idea of liberty of conscience is basically the same as the one commended in *Leviathan*. Like the Hobbes of *Leviathan*, Harrington endorses a policy of toleration.

In the eyes of their contemporaries, Hobbes and Harrington followed a common line in religion.[24] Henry Ferne, the Anglican divine, whom we have met as an exponent of mixed government in the early 1640s, placed them in the same religious camp.[25] When Harrington, in reply, vindicates the legitimacy of 'gathered congregations', he cites 1 Corinthians, as Hobbes had done before him.

> Nor doth Paul blame the congregations of Apollos and Cephas (1 Corinthians, 1) in that they were gathered, but in that they put too much upon them that gathered them.[26]

Harrington repeats the necessity of the national religion, but holds that worship according to the national religion should not be obligatory. With the exception of the Roman Catholic, the Jewish, and idolatrous religions, liberty of conscience is guaranteed institutionally. The council for religion is to be set up to substantiate this liberty, and other parliamentary measures will be added for this purpose. Regardless of denominations, equal political rights will be guaranteed.[27]

When he approves a policy of toleration, Harrington presupposes that the question of political obedience is a solely secular matter, and that no clergymen should be allowed to exercise their authority independent of the secular authority. In vindicating those presuppositions, Harrington depends wholly on the argument of Hobbes.

> It is true I have opposed the politics of Mr Hobbes, to show him what he taught me, with as much disdain as he opposed those of the greatest authors, . . . Nevertheless in most other things I firmly believe that Mr Hobbes is, and will in future ages be accounted, the best writer at this day in the world.[28]

---

[22] *A Discourse upon this saying . . .* (London, 1659), 743.

[23] *The Prerogative of Popular Government* (London, 1658), 513.

[24] Pocock, 'Historical Introduction', 78.

[25] '[W]hat is said [by Harrington] in relation to the church, or religion in the point of government, ordination, excommunication, had better beseemed Leviathan and is below the parts of this gentleman, to retain and sit down with those little things and poor mistakes which the ignorance or wilfulness of many in these days hath broached in way of quarrel against the Church of England' (*Pian Piano*, 370–1),

[26] *Pian Piano*, 386. For Hobbes's usage of 1 Corinthians, see the quotation from *Leviathan* in the previous section.

[27] 'That no religion being contrary unto or destructive of Christianity, nor the public exercise of any religion being grounded upon or incorporated into a foreign interest, be protected by or tolerated in this state. That all other religions, with the public exercise of the same, be both tolerated and protected by the council of religion' (*The Art of Lawgiving*, 681). See also *Oceana*, 216–17 [pp. 81–2].

[28] *The Prerogative of Popular Government*, 423.

Certainly, Harrington did not dare to follow Hobbes's interpretation of the Bible into mortalism. But he did largely accept Hobbes's version of Christian history. Hobbes claimed that ancient Israel was the kingdom of God, and that God's direct rule was terminated when Saul succeeded to the crown. It follows that even the kingdom of David, Jesus's ancestor, was not the kingdom of God. The office of the clergy in a Christian commonwealth is no more than to preach the restoration of the theocracy by Jesus in the future. It has nothing to do with the power of the sovereign. Consequently, the clergy are to be appointed by the secular ruler in exactly the same manner as the secular magistracy of the commonwealth. The doctrine that the spiritual authority is conveyed by '*chirothesia*'—by laying hands on the shoulder of the ordained—is wholly discredited. Having accepted these claims of Hobbes, Harrington differs from him only when it comes to the question how the secular authority should be organized.[29]

When Hobbes denounced the significance of *chirothesia*, and referred to '*chirotonia*' (holding up hands in votes of the congregation) as an alternative method of ordination, his aim was to deny the special authority of the apostolic Church, and to claim that clergymen had been ordained by the secular authority. Harrington took the argument further: when he referred to *chirotonia*, he emphasized that the secular authority was a popular congregation—'*ecclesia*'—rather than one man.[30]

[29] See Pocock, 'Historical Introduction', 78–9. On the question of the ordination of clergy, Harrington argues with Henry Hammond, who attacked Hobbes: 'Now, except any man can show that Matthias ever received the imposition of hands, these several things are already demonstrated. First, that the *chirotonia* is not only the more ancient way of ordination in the commonwealth of Israel, but in the church of Christ. . . . And fifthly, that ordination and election in this example are not two, but one and the same thing. The last of these propositions having been affirmed by Mr Hobbes, Dr Hammond tells him plainly that his assertion "is far from all truth". Let us therefore consider the Doctor's reasons, . . .' *The Prerogative of Popular Government*, 544–5.

[30] '[I]n this chapter I am showing that the *chirotonia* is election by the many, so in the next I shall show that the *chirothesia* is election by one, or by the few' (*The Prerogative of Popular Government*, 518); 'The word *ecclesia* was also anciently and properly used for the civil congregations or assemblies of the people in Athens, Lacedaemon and Ephesus, where it is so called in Scripture (Acts, 19: 23)' (*Oceana*, 175 [p. 26]). The equivalent passage of *Leviathan*, XLII is *The Prerogative of Popular Government*, 499–566, in which Harrington analysed the primitive Church. According to Pocock, the difficulty Harrington faced was that the Church was born in the age when all republics were corrupt under the rule of the Roman Empire (Pocock, 'Historical Introduction', 81). It is tempting to say that a Harringtonian commonwealth handles both secular matters and religious matters in the same manner. He uses the word 'corruption' to criticize defective ordinations as well as defective legislature. (Cf. Mark Goldie, 'The Civil Religion of James Harrington', in Anthony Pagden (ed.), *The Languages of Political Theory in Early-Modern Europe* (Cambridge, 1987), 212–13.) However, Harrington did not apply the idea of mixed government—the bicameral principle—to religion. When he used the word '*ecclesia*', he did not mean the bicameral legislature (the senate and the popular assembly) but the popular assembly, the 'resolving' chamber, only. Secular matters are handled by the combination of the two chambers, and religious matters by the popular congregation. See Harrington's usage of '*ecclesia*' in the following: 'Why then had not those cities their senates and their *ecclesiae*, or congregations of the people, as well as that of Ephesus

How, then, does the national religion advance liberty of conscience? Harrington's aim was not to publish the standard interpretation of the Bible, but to offer the basic knowledge which is required for a correct interpretation of the Bible. Admittedly, the national religion has much to do with the 'true religion', but it does not claim to be the true religion itself. There are 'degrees of knowledge', and a correct interpretation of the Bible is required to attain the true religion. But the Bible cannot be interpreted correctly until the ancient languages are studied and learned satisfactorily. The national religion is nothing more than an instrument which studies and spreads that knowledge. The commonwealth is to fulfil its responsibility to God not by offering the people the knowledge of what the true religion is but by keeping the way to that knowledge open to all.[31]

Harrington's vital concern is, therefore, how to institute that instrument. He expects the two universities—Oxford and Cambridge—to educate clergymen so that they can read the Bible in the original languages. The clergy will be sent to all parishes, and anyone in the commonwealth who wishes to read the original Bible will be able to seek assistance from the parish pastor.[32] Harrington firmly believed that the King James translation was misleading. It concealed the fact that *ecclesia* meant a congregation and the fact that *chirotonia* meant an election by the holding up of hands in a congregation.[33] He thought the doctrine of *chirothesia*, which is

---

and those whereof Pliny gives account to Trajan?' (*The Prerogative of Popular Government*, 515); 'Such was the genius of the Roman commonwealth, where by the way you may also observe the manner of her debate and result: *auctoritate patrum et jussu populi*; by the advice of the senate and the *chirotonia* of the people' (ibid. 507) .Like secular magistrates, it is true, religious magistrates are appointed by the resolving chamber (see ibid. 519). Yet whereas the laws which the secular magistracy execute have a binding legal force upon the people, the national religion which the clergy preaches is not obligatory.

[31] 'For there be degrees of knowledge in divine things; true religion is not to be attained unto without searching the Scriptures; the Scriptures cannot be searched by us unless we have them to search; and if we have nothing else or (which is all one) understand nothing else but a translation, we may be (as in the place alleged we have been) beguiled or misled by the translation, while we should be searching the true sense of the Scripture, which cannot be attained unto in a natural way (and a commonwealth is not to presume upon that which is supernatural) but by the knowledge of the original and of antiquity, acquired by our own studies or those of some other, for even faith cometh by hearing. Wherefore a commonwealth, not making provision of men from time to time knowing in the original languages wherein the Scriptures were written, and versed in those antiquities . . . can never be secure that she shall not lose the Scripture and by consequence her religion, which to preserve she must institute some method of this knowledge, and some use of such as have acquired it, which amounteth unto a national religion (*Oceana*, 217–18 [pp. 82–3]. The point is repeated at ibid. 306–7 [pp. 200–1].

[32] Ibid. 216–17 [pp. 80–2].

[33] For '*ecclesia*', ibid. 175 [p. 26]. As to '*chirotonia*', the passage in question is Acts 14: 23: 'where they should have rendered the place "and when they had ordained elders by the holding up of hands in every congregation" they render it "when they had ordained them elders in every church"' (*Pian Piano*, 384). See also *Oceana*, 217 [p. 82]. Harrington carried out a comparison of several European translations both by Protestants and by Catholics, and concluded that it was only in the King James version that the passage describing an election by the holding up of hands was dropped. See *The Prerogative of Popular Government*, 558–9.

pernicious to the secular authority, had been mainly advanced as a result of the mis-leading English translation. But once the knowledge of ancient languages prevailed, he believed, the error of that dangerous doctrine will be easily revealed to the people. In this sense, the role of the Harringtonian national religion is a basically defensive one. It does not positively advance any particular doctrine, but protects the people from encroachment by erroneous doctrines. The pivotal institution is not so much the church as the university, which builds up a protective wall for the secular authority by education—and not by censorship or persecution.[34]

When Harrington allots a key role to the universities, his account of religion again looks close to Hobbes's. Yet he is theologically less radical than Hobbes. Certainly, like Hobbes, he denied any supernatural role to the Holy Ghost in the process of the imposition of hands. But he did not deploy any materialist argument to sub-stantiate his claim. He did not trouble to discuss such matters as the immortality of the soul, or the existence of heaven and hell.[35] When Hobbes approved a policy of toleration, he coupled it with a novel doctrine of Christianity, which precluded resis-tance against the secular authority. When Harrington approved such a policy, he coupled it with a detailed scheme for the religious education of the people.

3. TOLERATION AND SOVEREIGNTY

Both the Hobbes of *Leviathan* and Harrington argued for religious toleration. In their view, toleration does not necessarily threaten peace and order, which is the primary aim of sovereignty. If toleration does not have serious negative effects upon the maintenance of absolute sovereignty, does it have any positive effects upon it? In other words, between toleration and non-toleration, which is the more conducive to sovereignty?

Hobbes's sovereign has a free choice of religious policy. He may choose persecu-tion or toleration as he likes. Yet which is preferable in Hobbes's system? When he approved 'the Independency of the Primitive Christians', which, like Harrington, he identified with toleration, and which he said was 'perhaps the best', what did he mean?[36]

---

[34] 'The education that answers unto religion in our government is that of the universities. . . . We cut down trees to build houses, but I would have somebody show me by what reason or experience the cutting down of an university should tend unto the setting up of a common-wealth' (*Oceana*, 305 [pp. 198–9]); 'in searching the Scriptures by the proper use of our uni-versities, we have been heretofore blessed with greater victories and trophies against the purple hosts and golden standards of the Romish hierarchy, than any nation' (ibid. 307 [p. 200]).

[35] At the end of *Oceana*, there is a passage (p. 332 [p. 232]) in which Harrington claims that 'the commonwealth of Oceana' is 'the kingdom of Christ'.

[36] Hans-Dieter Metzger argues differently: *Thomas Hobbes und die Englische Revolution 1640–1660* (Stuttgart and Bad Cannstatt, 1991), 179–82, 201, 227–8. Hobbes, Metzger claims, saw Independency not as a goal but as an anarchic but necessary stage towards the uni-fication of ecclesiastical authority under a 'Moses-like sovereign'. Behind Metzger's claim lies his thesis of what he calls 'the double revolution'. Hobbes, says Metzger, observed the historic coincidence of two circular cyclical changes, one of secular, the other of ecclesiastical organ-

One might argue that persecution, as a means of keeping the subjects quiet, would be counter-productive. But Hobbes does not make that case. Under an intolerant sovereign, Hobbesian subjects do not need to disobey the sovereign, since they know that to attain salvation they only have to hold the minimum belief that 'Jesus is Christ'. Even under a cruel pagan sovereign, who forces the subjects to deny that minimum belief, they will feel free to disguise their belief to avoid persecution, if only they are reasonable enough to accept Hobbes's doctrine of Christianity. Subjects under toleration, it is certain for Hobbes, would not disturb the social order, because they are expected to understand Hobbes's doctrine. If so, it ought to be equally certain that subjects under persecution would accept his doctrine and remain silent. The reason the Hobbes of *Leviathan* preferred toleration does not directly concern the maintenance of obedience.

Rather, in Hobbes's view, it is simply impossible to enforce dogma. Such attempts are unreasonable and should be avoided. That is, of course, partly because inquisition is pointless so long as individuals can conceal their true minds. But it is mainly because Hobbes believes that thinking is beyond the control even of the individual himself.[37] When a 'miracle' is reported to have been found, for instance, it is certainly the sovereign who decides whether that report is true or false. But it is an individual who decides whether to believe it to be a miracle, 'because thought is free'.[38] If the sovereign still enforces some belief on his subjects, he does so contrary to reason, and his attempt is not, therefore, preferable in the way that it is when he violates the laws of nature, the dictates of right reason. On the other hand, as the sovereign is not obliged to observe the laws of nature, nothing can oblige the sovereign to be tolerant, and the subjects cannot claim liberty of conscience against him; they are not entitled to blame the sovereign who behaves contrary to reason. Perhaps it was in this sense—that toleration is approved by reason but not obligatory—that Hobbes meant that toleration is 'the best'.[39]

---

ization. For the dissolution of the Stuart monarchy brought a return to the (secular) state of nature, and the supremacy of Independency a return to what Metzger calls the 'religious state of nature'. But (i) the idea of cyclical changes of government, which may be hinted at in *Behemoth*, cannot be found in *Leviathan*; (ii) Hobbes never alludes to a religious state of nature, or associates Independency with anarchy.

[37] Alan Ryan, 'Hobbes, Toleration, and the Inner Life', in David Miller and Larry Siedentop (eds.), *The Nature of Political Theory* (Oxford, 1983), 207–8. See also Noel Malcolm, 'Hobbes and Spinoza', in J. H. Burns (ed.), *The Cambridge History of Political Thought, 1450–1700*, 543.

[38] *Leviathan*, XXXVII, 306 [pp. 237–8].

[39] However, the relationship of a sovereign in general to the laws of nature is not exactly parallel with that of a Christian sovereign to the policy of toleration. According to Hobbes's account of religion in *Leviathan*, such misleading ideas as the infallibility of the apostolically ordained Church—ordained, that is, by imposition of hands—and the present existence of the kingdom of Christ are derived from unreasonable interpretations of the Bible. Those misleading ideas underlined the pernicious challenges by the Roman Catholics and the Presbyterians to the secular authority. Hobbes claims that sovereigns who allow such unreasonable interpretations in the universities are to be blamed (*Leviathan*, XLVII. 478 [p. 384]). If so, it could be inferred that sovereigns who pursue an intolerant policy are to be blamed as well,

In the case of Harrington, on the other hand, toleration has more serious implications for the maintenance of sovereignty. A Harringtonian sovereign in the state of an equal distribution of lands, who has no instrument of coercion in the first place, is incapable of enforcing any belief on the subjects. Once the subjects rise up against an intolerant sovereign, he cannot suppress them with military power, whereas a Hobbesian sovereign could easily do that. A policy of non-tolerance only ends up by endangering the domestic peace.

> If the public, refusing the liberty of conscience unto a party, would but be the cause of tumult, how much more a party refusing it unto the public?[40]

The worst Harrington fears is that a dominant party may usurp the government, and enforce its religion on the people under the pretext of the national religion. In that event, the commonwealth will collapse in utter confusion. To prevent any such usurpation, Harrington designed his tolerant national religion. Thus the existence of the national religion itself protects liberty of conscience in Harrington's system.

On the question how to prevent people's 'discontents', Harrington wrote:

> The discontents, whether of the few or the many, derive from that which is, or by them is thought to be, some bar unto their interest, and those interests which are the causes of sedition are three: the desire of liberty, the desire of power, and the desire of riches; nor be there any more, . . . Those also under the name of religion make not a fourth, but come unto one of the three.[41]

Religion cannot constitute the fourth category of those interests, insists Harrington. In fact, however, he was much concerned with the question of religion in his search for peace and order. To deal with the question of religion, he discussed toleration and the national religion at length. In doing so, perhaps he thought that he was tackling the question of liberty—liberty of conscience—rather than the question of religion. When 'the desire of liberty' of conscience is met by toleration, 'discontents' will be prevented.

Even so, a policy of toleration cannot, of course, accommodate every kind of desire of liberty. There remains the question of liberty which is distinguishable from liberty of conscience. This is the question of 'civil liberty'.[42] Whereas liberty of conscience lives outside the Harringtonian bicameral legislature, civil liberty exists only within it. Civil liberty means that individuals freely seek their interests, but in Harrington's judgement they can do so in peace only if they are helped by the bicameral legislature. It is there that the questions of 'riches' and 'power' will

because that policy is unreasonable and may encourage unreasonable policy and may thereby encourage unreasonable interpretations of the Bible.

[40] *The Art of Lawgiving*, 678.
[41] *The Prerogative of Popular Government*, 424.
[42] *A Discourse upon this saying*, 744; *A Discourse Showing That the Spirit of Parliaments, With a Council in the Intervals, Is not to be trusted for a Settlement . . .* (London, 1659), 750–1; *Aphorisms Political*, 764.

be solved. The Harringtonian sovereignty, which cannot be maintained by the public sword, is established only when all sorts of 'discontents' towards the government are averted. Liberty of conscience and civil liberty, it follows, have to be guaranteed both outside and inside the legislature at once.[43] Oliver Cromwell made a mistake when he treated those two liberties unevenly.[44]

Hobbes argued for absolute sovereignty and toleration, and Harrington echoed his claim. Yet for the Hobbesian sovereign, who is expected to hold the sword, toleration is a matter of choice: for the Harringtonian sovereign, it is a matter of necessity.

---

[43] 'Where there is no liberty of conscience, there can be no civil liberty; and where there is no civil liberty, there can be no security unto liberty of conscience' (*The Art of Lawgiving*, 703).

[44] 'It was the only excuse that the late tyrant pretended for his usurpation, that he could see no other means to secure the liberty of conscience' (*A Discourse upon this saying*, 742).

APPENDIX B

An Agrarian Law and the Immortality of Oceana

When, in Harrington's argument, the lands are distributed equally among most of its people, there results a state of equality where no conqueror can emerge, 'for equality of estates causeth equality of power'.[1] If this is so, will not an effort to fix a balance of the land merely preserve anarchy? Harrington does not believe so. He claims that an agrarian law, which will prevent the balance of the land from changing, is necessary and important. Without it, he warns, the nobility might restore their lands and 'overbalance' the people again.[2] When the nobility overbalances the people, we have 'the Gothic balance'. But the state of equality is, in Harrington's account, no less unstable than the Gothic balance. As far as stability is concerned, there seems nothing to be gained from preventing the state of equality from slipping into the Gothic balance. What is an agrarian law really meant for? Our search for the answer to that question will show us what makes *Oceana* unique in Harrington's political writing.

An agrarian law itself cannot provide peace or order. If it has any function, it must be because, like 'rotation', it provides a precondition of the smooth working of the bicameral legislature. To understand Harrington's warning against the return of the Gothic balance, we should recall that the old monarchy under the Gothic balance 'was indeed no more than an unequal commonwealth', where the bicameral legislature could not work properly.[3] The purpose of an equal agrarian law is to stop an equal commonwealth from becoming an unequal one. When Harrington says that the agrarian law prevents the nobility from overbalancing the people, he means that the law prevents the nobility from creating a faction which may threaten the peace of the commonwealth.

As we noted earlier, Harrington insisted on 'rotation' to secure equality in the legislature.[4] The aim of an equal agrarian law is to support the rotation: that is, to maintain the number of citizens eligible for the office of the senate to such a degree that the rotation will work efficiently.[5] The system of rotation limits the tenure of office by the senators, and imposes upon ex-senators a certain period of compulsory

---

[1] *Oceana*, 170 [p. 20].

[2] Ibid. 181 [pp. 33–4]. Since an agrarian law, in general, is a law which fixes the balance of the land, there can be different agrarian laws according to different forms of government. Strictly speaking, a law to fix the equal balance of the land in a commonwealth, a law which in this appendix I normally call 'an agrarian law', should be given Harrington's full term, 'an equal agrarian law'.

[3] *Pour Enclouer le Canon*, 729.

[4] See Sect. 6.3 above.

[5] *Oceana*, 181 [p. 34].

vacation before they can be re-elected. The members of the senate should be reshuffled as efficiently as possible to prevent the senate from becoming factious. For the same purpose, senators ought to be elected from among as large a number of people as possible. When the senators are recruited only from a limited number of people, the members of the senate cannot be efficiently refreshed even by strict rotation. From this point of view, the office of senator ought to be open to everyone. On the other hand, however, the senate is expected to form a natural aristocracy, as we saw earlier.[6] To be a member of the Harringtonian debating chamber is not an easy job. It should be confined to those who have leisure to study politics, that is, to substantial landowners. Eligibility ought to be restricted to men with a certain minimum of real property, which is thought to reflect the level of political intelligence.

Harrington has to find a compromise between those two conflicting demands. In his judgement, if the number of the senators is three hundred, the size of the social group from which they will be drawn must exceed five thousand if corruption is to be prevented. So there must be more than five thousand substantial landowners. For this purpose, an agrarian law, an institution which prevents the concentration of land tenure, is needed. It must set a limit to the size of any inherited estate. In Oceana that limit is two thousand pounds.[7] A landowner with a large estate is required to divide it equally among his sons. The proper operation of the principle of rotation is thus provided for.

If that is the purpose of the agrarian law, how effective is it? In the Harringtonian world, where men are basically allowed to seek what they want, how can that law bind their desire for lands? The introduction of that law causes great difficulty in his system. Indeed it creates the polarization of the citizen over this issue.[8]

Harrington himself concedes that the agrarian law may not be smoothly accepted. He devotes pages of *Oceana* to an examination of the agrarian law, which he conducts in the form of an imaginary exchange in 'the Council of Legislators' between an opponent of that law and 'the Lord Archon'. He recognizes two sorts of objectors to the law: the one is that the upper limit is too low; the other that it is too high. This difference reflects the difference of social class between the two sets of objectors. The first objection is held by rich proprietors, that is, the nobility; the second, small proprietors. Yet Harrington insists that everyone will be willing to obey his agrarian law. To prove his point he provides two explanations, one to meet objections made by the rich, one objections made by the poor.

As for the nobility, there can be two sorts of problem. There is the case where an estate already exceeds the limit, and another where it is on the way to doing so. In

---

[6] See Sect. 6.2 above.

[7] 'As to instance yet farther in that which is proposed by the present order to this nation, the standard whereof is at two thousand pounds a year: the whole territory of Oceana, being divided by this proportion, amounteth unto five thousand lots. So the lands of Oceana, being thus distributed, and bound unto this distribution, can never fall unto fewer than five thousand proprietors' (*Oceana*, 236 [p. 108]). See also *The Art of Lawgiving* (London, 1659), 687–8.

[8] See Sect. 6.3 above.

the first case, Harrington does not resort to confiscation, which would directly con-tradict the private interests of great landlords.[9] Instead, he forbids primogeniture in excess of the limit. Large estates will gradually be divided into smaller ones over the generations.[10] Admittedly, while that measure is much less aggressive than con-fiscation, it still conflicts with the commonly accepted customs of the English nobi-lity, and will surely provoke opposition from them. Harrington, acknowledging that certainty, argues boldly that it is the interest of the great landowners to give up primogeniture and to have their lands inherited equally among their sons:

> They would enjoy their estates; who touches them? They would dispose of what they have according unto the interest of their families; it is that which we desire. . . . therefore this must be the interest of the family; or the family knoweth not her own interest. If a man shall dispute otherwise, he must draw his argu-ments from custom and from greatness, which was the interest of the monarchy, not of the family.[11]

This being the interest of the great landowners, believes Harrington, they will soon come to understand it to be so.

The second case is that of a proprietor whose estate is currently worth less than two thousand pounds a year but, through his acquisitive activity, is on the way to exceeding that value. Here Harrington recognizes that the acquisitive proprietor, unlike the rich nobleman who practises primogeniture, is acting in accordance with his private interest. Harrington's answer is to redirect that interest. The acquisitive proprietor is to be encouraged to pursue it abroad, rather than within the common-wealth: to go overseas in a war for conquest:

> such an agrarian maketh a commonwealth for increase: the trade of a common-wealth for increase is arms; arms are not born by merchants, but by noblemen and gentlemen. The nobility therefore having these arms in their hands by which provinces are to be acquired, new provinces yield new estates; so, whereas the merchant hath his returns in silk or canvas, the soldier will have his return in land.[12]

Harrington's advocacy of military expansion is related to his concern for the effec-tiveness of the agrarian law.[13] Expansion is essential if the agrarian law is to be squared with the Harringtonian commonwealth, which has no coercive power to prevent individuals from seeking their private interests. Under that law the acquisi-tive energy of private interests is canalized into the expansion of the commonwealth.

How should the discontents of the poor be handled, then? Unlike Harrington, the author of this measure, they would not be much interested in the preservation of the natural aristocracy. To make things worse, those who do not have much land

---

[9] *The Prerogative of Popular Government*, 406; *The Art of Lawgiving*, 631.
[10] *Oceana*, 231.
[11] Ibid. 237 [pp. 108–9].
[12] *The Prerogative of Popular Government*, 471.
[13] Pocock, 'Historical Introduction', *The Political Works of James Harrington*, 71.

are the majority of the people, and under Harrington's proposed electoral arrangements they would have massive influence upon the decisions of the resolving chamber. What happens if they demand a drastic law for the equal redistribution of the land in their favour—for 'levelling'? The popular assembly will clash with the senate, and the confrontation may be expected to lead to a civil war.

Having raised that grave possibility, however, Harrington denies it. A civil war, if the people resort to it, will be counter-productive for them, since 'if they make a war, they obstruct industry' and consequently 'obstruct their own livelihood'.[14] They will refrain from making a war, in Harrington's view, not from a calm calculation of their private interests, but from a sort of natural instinct.

> That which in beasts is instinct, whereof they can give no account, is in itself that wisdom of God whereby he provideth for them; so is it with the people; they are not levellers, nor know they why, and yet it is because to be levellers were to destroy themselves.[15]

Of the features of Harrington's vigorous defence of his agrarian law, none is more revealing than his handling of 'interest'. In the passages above, he abandons the vital principle which he opposed to Matthew Wren: 'if a man know not what is his own interest, who should know it?'[16] When he claims that his arrangement 'must be the interest of the [rich noble] family; or the family knoweth not her own interest', and that the poor hates upheavals by 'levelling', it is no longer the rich or the poor, but Harrington himself, who knows what their true interests are. Harrington, who designs the commonwealth, knows better than the people themselves what they want. If Harrington is better able than the people to make a law which handles their interests, why cannot Wren's prince do a better job than the Harringtonian bicameral legislature?

For Harrington, it seems, this contradiction was hard to avoid. In the defence of the agrarian law, Harrington was led to discuss what would satisfy the private interests of the people who live in the commonwealth he designed. In the vindication of the Harringtonian bicameral legislature, however, there was an iron rule: a man has to be given the freedom to judge where his true interest lies, for without that freedom he cannot be convinced that his private interest is accommodated by the common interest.[17]

Usually Harrington made every effort to confine his words about interest to the level of the abstract. The content of the common interest was to be left not to Harrington but to the people in the bicameral legislature. In his reply to Wren, too, he did not specify what sort of policy should be implemented under the name of the common interest in England.[18] When it comes to the agrarian law, however, Harrington does have to consider the content of interest, for he could not ignore

[14] *Oceana*, 293 [p. 182].
[15] *The Prerogative of Popular Government*, 429.
[16] *Politicaster*, 719. For the exchange between Wren and Harrington, see Sect. 7.1 above.
[17] See Sect. 6.3 above.
[18] See Sect. 7.2 above.

the fact that lands may be the object of the interest of individuals, not merely the basis on which a man uses his sword to assert his will.

Everyone wants to get, to retain, or to increase, his land. The rich want to retain what they already have, and the poor want to see a radical redistribution of lands. In this way Harrington begins to speculate where the people inside the legislative chambers locate their private interests. Once he goes beyond the boundary which he originally set, and moves his argument into that direction, he has to deal with the interests of factions rather than those of individuals. Now different interests have taken concrete shape. Harrington has to concede, it follows, that the people will be divided into 'Gainers' and 'Loosers [*sic*]' by the introduction of the agrarian law, whatever the level at which he may set the upper limit.[19] As a result, he is led to contemplate the situation in which the commonwealth becomes polarized between 'the interest of the few' and 'the interest of the many'. Yet the clearest lesson Harrington learnt from the failure of Rome was to prevent the polarization of the people at all costs. Once 'two distinct interests' have formed, the Harringtonian bicameral legislature will be unable to reconcile them. When the bicameral legislature fails, Harrington himself has to override it by his own arguments. That was why he insisted that he knew better what the true interests of the people were than they themselves did. In doing so, Harrington contradicted himself.

Thus in the introduction of an agrarian law, Harrington has presented himself with a series of serious problems. Why then, knowing as he does that the introduction of an agrarian law will provoke opposition and great trouble, does he go to such trouble to provide for its introduction? Is it worth his while to take such risks? If he really hoped to put his model of a commonwealth into practice, would he not have been wise to omit the agrarian law from it?

In fact, in the models he produced in the works written after *Oceana* he often omits the agrarian law. Here *Oceana* is an exception rather than a rule. Whereas the other principal features of his model, the bicameral legislature and rotation, appear in all of the models of commonwealth published by Harrington between 1656 and 1660, the agrarian law appears only in *Oceana* (1656) and in book III of *The Art of Lawgiving* (1659), the work which summarized *Oceana*. In the several small pamphlets which he rushed to publish between May and October in 1659— when the Rump Parliament was briefly restored, and when Harrington had almost his last hope of putting his ideas into practice—he did not mention the agrarian law. Moreover, even in *The Art of Lawgiving* he compromises on the introduction of that law: the law now regulates inheritance only, not acquisition by other means; an additional clause is added which guarantees that the law will be enacted from 'the generation to come' and thus will not concern 'any man living'; and it is emphasized that the next generation is to be free to repeal the law.[20] Furthermore,

[19] Of course, Wren was not discussing that particular issue when he used those words. Cf. *Monarchy Asserted* (Oxford, 1659), 13.

[20] *The Art of Lawgiving*, 664–5.

when he reduced his plan for a new commonwealth into six points at the outset of book III, the agrarian law was not among them.[21]

Unlike the bicameral system and rotation, which mediate between private interests and the common interest, the agrarian law is only a secondary institution in Harrington's mind. It is not at the core of his constitutional arrangements. It is not the proposal which tackles the problem of the present anarchy. Instead it is designed to perpetuate the stability which he expects the bicameral legislature and rotation to achieve. The agrarian law works only in the longer term. The bicameral legislature and rotation are institutions for the present: the agrarian law is for the future.[22]

This explains why Harrington stuck to that law particularly in *Oceana*, where he seems to have been obsessed by the notion of immortality. The purpose of *Oceana* was to establish a commonwealth which would be not only stable but eternally stable, 'an immortal commonwealth'. His concern was not confined to the near future. It looked far ahead. The task of the agrarian law in *Oceana* is to help guarantee this immortality.

Among Harrington's political writings, *Oceana* is unique in style and tone. He uses, in a playful spirit, a sequence of imaginary proper names, almost as in a fairytale. The uniqueness of the work among Harrington's writings is not confined to its literary character. The notion of an immortal commonwealth appears only in *Oceana*—and in *The Prerogative of Popular Government* (1658), which vindicates the arguments of *Oceana*.[23] It does not appear in his subsequent writings. The feature is particularly evident in the last part of *Oceana*. There, a well-ordered commonwealth is considered to be 'the kingdom of Christ', where liberty of conscience is guaranteed.[24] He believes that a ceaseless flow of the citizens passing through his governmental bodies arranged by the rotation will symbolize the eternal life of the commonwealth. The rotation of the members of the legislature and the executive is compared to the revolution of the heavenly bodies and the circulation of blood. While individuals are not immortal, 'the people . . . never dies'.[25] As we noted earlier in this section, the agrarian law is intended to secure the efficiency of the rotation. Thus the agrarian law and the rotation are the 'proper centre' of the 'spherical motions' of the citizens.[26]

Yet in *Oceana*, the significance of the agrarian law goes beyond its relationship to the rotation. The equal balance of the land is called 'the balance of justice', because

[21] Ibid. 662–3.

[22] How far into that future does Harrington look? If he had expected a radical change in the balance of the land to occur within a few years, the problem would have been a matter, if not for the present, then at least for the immediate future. But Harrington did not believe that the process would be speedy. He thought it might be half a century before the number eligible for the senate would drop below five thousand. *The Art of Lawgiving*, 664–5.

[23] *Oceana*, 209, 229, 321–2, 341 [pp. 71, 99, 218–20, 244]; *The Prerogative of Popular Government*, 431.

[24] *Oceana*, 332 [pp. 231–2].

[25] Ibid. 229 [p. 99]. See also p. 287 [p. 174].

[26] Ibid. 230–1, 333–4 [pp. 100–1, 234].

the people of Oceana under that balance are free from the oppression of the Gothic balance. The agrarian law defends this balance of justice. In Harrington's view, the people of Oceana must not be allowed to remain content with their own liberation. '[S]he is not made for herself only, but given as a magistrate of God unto mankind.' As 'a minister of God upon earth', this commonwealth ought to export its agrarian law abroad, and crusade for the liberation of the people of the world from the yoke of the Gothic empires.[27]

When Harrington praises the eternal stability of an immortal commonwealth, and celebrates the kingdom of Christ with the Song of Solomon, his Oceana makes a striking contrast with Hobbes's Leviathan, a mortal God.[28] Hobbes needed a stable government, but he was not interested in creating eternal stability. Historians have discerned a millenarian streak in Harrington's political thought.[29] This streak, we should observe, is largely peculiar to the last part of *Oceana*. It is rarely evident in his other writings. It is no coincidence that the insistence on the agrarian law, and the prominence of millenarianism, figure both in *Oceana* and *The Prerogative of Popular Government* but are generally absent from his other works.[30]

---

[27] *Oceana*, 322–3 [pp. 220–1].   [28] Ibid. 333 [p. 233].

[29] Pocock, 'Historical Introduction', 72–6. Cf. J. C. Davis, *Utopia and the Ideal Society* (Cambridge, 1981), ch. vi, and his 'Pocock's Harrington: Grace, Nature and Art in the Classical Republicanism of James Harrington', *Historical Journal*, 24 (1981), 687–97.

[30] David Armitage believes that the argument in *Oceana* for a commonwealth for expansion contains a reply to the speech which Oliver Cromwell delivered at the opening of parliament on 17 Sept. 1656 (see his 'The Cromwellian Protectorate and the Languages of Empire', *Historical Journal*, 35 (1992), 531–55). According to Armitage, *Oceana* reflects the hostility to the Protectorate ignited by the disastrous failure of the expedition to the West Indies in the previous year. Thus Harrington criticized Cromwell's expansionism as immoral and tyrannical, and presented an alternative vision. The crucial passage in *Oceana*, Armitage claims is, '*nos magis patronatum [= patrocinium] orbis terrarum suscepimus, quam imperium* [we have rather undertaken the patronage than the empire of the world]' (323 [p. 221]). Harrington is here quoting Cicero's *De Officiis*, ii. 27. Cicero argued that military expansion should be undertaken for the happiness of the provinces, not merely in the interest of Rome. Harrington presents a similar view in religious language. The expansion of Oceana, he says, will offer 'a holy asylum' or 'sanctuary' to the peoples oppressed by the 'Gothic empires' (*Oceana*, 323, 329 [pp. 221, 229]). Similarly, Cicero uses the words *portus* and *refugium* in *De Officiis*, ii. 26. Yet the contrast between 'patronage' and 'empire' for Harrington is not very important. If it had been, he would not have cried that 'this empire, this patronage of the world, is the kingdom of Christ' (*Oceana*, 332 [p. 232]). In the passages which immediately follow his invocation of Cicero, the question Harrington raises is not which principle—patronage or empire—the commonwealth should adopt in expanding. His concern is with the fact of expansion, not its method: 'If you, not regarding this example—like some other nations that are upon the point to smart for it—shall, having attained unto your own liberty, bear the sword of your common magistracy in vain, sit still and fold your arms, or which is worse, let out the blood of your people unto tyrants, to be shed in the defence of their yokes like water, and so not only *turn the grace of God into wantonness*, but his *justice into wormwood*, you are not now making a commonwealth, *but heaping coals of fire upon your own heads*' (*Oceana*, 323 [p. 221]; Harrington's italic).

Armitage claims that Harrington saw expansion by empire as a Machiavellian politics of necessity, and discerned that evil principle in Cromwell's speech. Yet when Harrington

As we saw in the previous chapters, one essential aspect of *Oceana* is the theory of balanced sovereignty, of which the aim is stability. The millenarian streak of *Oceana* exists alongside that theory. *Oceana* seeks stability and immortality at the same time. The combination makes for a complex structure of argument. This book has been about stability, not immortality. It has dwelled on the Harrington who, in search of stability, challenged Hobbes and provided a new route to it.

criticized Machiavelli, he focused not on Machiavelli's insistence on the politics of necessity but on his failure to notice the distinction between an equal commonwealth and an unequal one. Moreover, even for Harrington, expansion is not a matter of choice but a matter of necessity, for 'an agrarian maketh a commonwealth for increase'. If the agrarian law is to be effective, the acquisitive energy of private interests has to be channelled abroad. I cannot find any solid reason to infer that Harrington's discussion of expansionism was written with Cromwell's speech in mind.

Armitage is right to point out that expansionism is peculiar to *Oceana* among Harrington's writings. But it is there tightly connected to the problem of the effectiveness of the agrarian law. In *Oceana*, there is a unique set of ideas which brings together expansionism, millenarianism, and the agrarian law. What underlies them is not so much anti-Cromwellian sentiment as a preoccupation with immortality.

APPENDIX C

'Mutual Fear' and 'Commonwealth by Institution' in Hobbes

This appendix, which supplements my discussion of Hobbes's attitude towards the sovereign-making contract, examines how he found a logical exit from the circularity of argument in *The Elements of Law* and *De Cive*.[1] He seems to have thought that 'mutual fear' might generate a binding force even before the common power was formed, and that that fear might substantiate the sovereign-making contract.

As we have seen, while the Hobbes of his earlier writings—*The Elements of Law* and *De Cive*—claimed that a covenant has a binding force on its own, the Hobbes of *Leviathan* denied that claim.[2] Apparently, his earlier attitude is more convenient if he wants to get out of the state of nature by 'a commonwealth by institution'. However, his contempt for 'words' in *Leviathan* looks more compatible with his picture of *bellum omnium in omnes* than his appreciation of the binding force of 'a covenant' itself in *De Cive*. Were *pactum per se* to be universally reliable, his idea of absolute sovereignty would become less plausible since the power of punishment would not be absolutely necessary. Men would be able to lead their lives in peace and order according to a certain set of covenants and without resort to the common power. On the other hand, if covenants cannot claim any binding force by themselves— that is, unless they are substantiated by the fear of punishment—the institution of a commonwealth will hardly be possible in any circumstances.[3] It will be impossible to establish the common power in the state of nature, from which there can be no exit. In short, if 'a word' were perfectly reliable, 'the public sword' would not be needed. And if 'a word' were powerless, 'the public sword' could not be formed in the first place.

Yet it is still possible to overcome this predicament, since, for a commonwealth to be set up, only a specific sort of contract—a sovereign-making contract—needs to be considered to be valid in the state of nature. Not every sort of covenant needs that sanction. What is required is to distinguish a sovereign-making contract from others. In addition, even if a sovereign-making contract has to have a 100 per cent binding force to institute a commonwealth, only a part of that binding force needs to be generated by the contract itself. The rest of it can be supplied by 'fear'.

The Hobbes of the earlier works seems to have taken that position, by making two

---

[1] See Sects. 3.4 and 4.2 above.
[2] See Sect. 4.2 above.
[3] *The Elements of Law*, I. 15. 10. 78; *De Cive*, II. 11. 102–3 [E: pp. 94–5); *Leviathan*, XIV. 96 [p. 68].

moves. First, he admitted that all contracts (including a sovereign-making contract) generate a binding force to a limited extent. We have already seen that he made this first move by committing himself to the idea that 'covenants oblige us'. Secondly, he singled out a sovereign-making contract from other contracts by specifying a certain peculiar type of fear which would support a sovereign-making contract only, and which at the same time would not guarantee any other contracts in the state of nature. It was a mutual fear that he used for this purpose.

While the fear of punishment, which must be caused by the common power, is available only in the civil society, a mutual fear exists in the state of nature. Hobbes seems to have thought that a mutual fear substantiates the sovereign-making contract—at the very moment of the institution—and that a fear of punishment substantiates the civil laws (and also the sovereign-making contract after the institution). In comparison with any other sorts of contract in the state of nature, sovereign-making contracts are unique solely because they are made in order to eliminate a mutual fear. This fear justifies sovereign-making contracts only, and not other sorts of contract in the state of nature.

Certainly, a mutual fear may be weaker than the fear of punishment caused by the common power, and, unlike the fear of punishment, may not be able to guarantee the sovereign-making contract on its own. But all contracts are given a binding force to some extent in Hobbes's earlier works. Thus the binding force generated by the sovereign-making contract itself and that generated by a mutual fear can work together to attain the full binding force needed to set up a commonwealth. In this way, the sovereign power can be established in the state of nature without our presupposing the existence of the common power. Here the circularity of his argument can be broken.

Of the three writings, it is in *De Cive* that Hobbes most enthusiastically explains the notion of a mutual fear, and that he lays least emphasis on the notion of the common power. Just as he did in explaining the notion of covenant (*pactum*), Hobbes inserted a note to explain the notion of a mutual fear in the second edition of *De Cive*.[4]

Admittedly, in *Leviathan* too, 'Feare of Death' in the condition of nature is counted as one of the passions which make men desire peace.[5] Yet desire has to be strictly distinguished, at least in his argument, from a sense of obligation. The Hobbes of *Leviathan* strictly observes that distinction. What makes a covenant effective must be the latter and not the former. However, a mutual fear in *De Cive* seems to mean more than that:

> We must therefore resolve, that the Originall of all great, and lasting Societies, consisted not in the mutuall good will men had towards each other, but in the mutuall fear they had of each other. (*De Cive*, I. 2. 92 [E: p. 44])

---

[4] *De Cive*, I. 2, 'Annotation', pp. 92–3 [E: p. 45].

[5] 'The Passions that encline men to Peace, are Feare of Death; Desire of such things as are necessary to commodious living; and a Hope by their Industry to obtain them' (*Leviathan*, XIII. 90 [p. 63]).

Interestingly enough, in *The Elements of Law* and *De Cive* a mutual fear is some-times not clearly distinguished from a fear of punishment. Hobbes says that men 'will neither give mutuall help, nor desire peace, except they be constrained to it by some common feare'.[6] What is 'some common fear'? It might involve a fear of pun-ishment by the common power, since that fear is described as being able to coerce (*coercere*) people to help each other. But on the other hand that fear has to be a mutual fear which exists in the state of nature, since that which makes people desire peace is, according to Hobbes's original formula, a mutual fear in the state of nature.[7] Hobbes seems inclined to claim that a mutual fear in the state of nature not only induces but somehow forces men to form a commonwealth and to keep the covenant. For the phrase 'mutual fear' he may have deliberately fused 'a mutual fear' in the state of nature with a 'common fear' of punishment substantiated by the common power.[8] By contrast, in chapter 13 of *Leviathan* he uses the words 'continuall feare' in place of mutual fear. The Hobbes of *Leviathan* appears to avoid the ambiguity of that phrase.[9]

Perhaps *De Cive*, in which Hobbes wrote most enthusiastically about a mutual fear and least so about the common power, was the work in which he made his lar-gest effort to construct a logical exit from the state of nature through a common-wealth by institution. The apparatus he employed was the combination of covenant and mutual fear. Of course, it is questionable whether that formulation was convincing. His usage of the notion of a mutual fear sometimes appears in-consistent and loose. What should be noted here is the keen concern shown in *De Cive* to save the notion of commonwealth by institution from the circularity of the argument, and his commitment to maintain the subtle balance between word and sword.

The Hobbes of *Leviathan* seems to have given up that attempt. There the effectiveness of covenant by itself is denied. The ambitious phrase 'mutual fear' is scrapped.[10] The constellation of his key notions is clarified. Particularly, the function of a mutual fear is never confused with that of the fear of punishment. However, when his argument becomes less ambiguous about the relationship between cove-nant and fear, the consequences, as we saw above, are serious.[11]

---

[6] *De Cive*, v. 4. 132 [E: p. 87].

[7] 'The cause of mutuall fear consists partly in the naturall equality of men, partly in their mutuall will of hurting' (*De Cive*, I. 3. 93 [E: p. 45]); 'And so it happens that through feare of each other we think it fit to rid our selves of this condition, and to get some fellowes' (*De Cive*, I. 13. 97 [E: p. 50]).

[8] See the following usage: 'it is impossible, not only that their consent to aid each other against an enemy, but also that the peace should last between themselves, without some mutual and common fear to rule them' (*The Elements of Law*, I. 19. 4. 101–2).

[9] *Leviathan*, XIII. 89 [p. 62].

[10] I have not noticed Hobbes using the phrase 'mutual fear' through the whole book of *Leviathan*.

[11] See Sect. 4.3 above.

APPENDIX D

'Equality' in Harrington and Contarini

According to Harrington, his idea of an 'equal commonwealth' was his most original contribution to ancient prudence.[1] Unlike the distinction between single commonwealths and leagues, or that between commonwealths for preservation and those for increase, that between equal and unequal commonwealths was 'unseen hitherto'.[2] Yet before Harrington, Gasparo Contarini, whose *The Commonwealth and Government of Venice* appeared in English in 1599 and was widely known in England, had been as warm as Harrington in favouring equality within a commonwealth. In this appendix, the possible influence of Contarini upon Harrington's notion of equality will be suggested. Harrington quotes Contarini's book only twice (in Italian), but so warm a devotee of Venetian constitutional machinery as Harrington is likely to have had a close knowledge of that standard work on the subject.

In Harrington's scheme, the notion of equality was embodied in the principle of 'rotation'. An equal opportunity of election as members of the legislature—'an equal distribution of common right'—should be given, argued Harrington, 'unto the whole people who are possessed of the might'.[3] Contarini had a similar view:

> nothing is more proper to a commonwealth, then that the common authority and power should belong to many: for it is iust that the citizens, by whom the state of the Cittie is maintained, being otherwise among themselues equall, should not in this distribution of honors bee made vnequall.[4]

Moreover, where Harrington emphasized the notion of equality in relation to the prevention of factions and to the making a commonwealth 'perfect', Contarini pointed to the link between equality and perfection:

> there cannot happen to a commonwealth a more daungerous or pestilent contagion, then the ouerweighing of one parte or faction aboue the other: . . . if you will haue your commonwealth perfect and enduring, let not one parte bee mightier then the other, but let them all (in as much as may bee) haue equall share in the publique authoritie. . . . not onely in the senate, but also in all other offices there shoulde not bee any more of one kindred or allyance, then the preseruation of equalitie required.[5]

---

[1] See Sect. 7.2 above.
[2] *Oceana*, 180 [p. 33].   [3] *The Art of Lawgiving*, 696.
[4] Gasparo Contarini, *The Commonwealth and Government of Venice* tr. Lewis Lewkenor (London 1599), 33.
[5] Ibid. 67. See also p. 78.

Admittedly, whereas Harrington's main concern was to prevent the emergence of factions by reshuffling the senators as frequently as possible, Contarini commends the Venetian rule that 'there cannot in all be aboue three [senators] of a kindred', which prevents any particular family from dominating the senate.[6] When Harrington mentions the Venetian practice that 'In the sixty of the senate, there cannot be above three of any one kindred or family', it is true, he neither refers to Contarini nor uses the word 'equality'.[7] The passages of Contarini which are quoted in *Oceana* are not about equality.[8] However, Contarini does share Harrington's conviction that the equal distribution of public office prevents factions and that the perfection of the Venetian government is expressed in its internal stability.[9]

[6] *The Commonwealth and Government of Venice*, 67.
[7] *The Prerogative of Popular Government*, 483.
[8] *Oceana*, 213, 283 [pp. 76, 170].
[9] If Harrington was indebted to Contarini for the notion of equality, why did he not say so? Perhaps the answer is that, while the two writers agreed that the Venetian commonwealth was equal, they were split over the character of the Roman republic. Unlike Harrington, Contarini did not claim that Rome had been 'unequal'. He did concede that Rome had been seditious, but he attributed that quality to defects in the Roman judicial procedure, which allowed 'any citizen whatsoever' to accuse others, whereas 'in Venice no priuate man may performe such office' (*The Commonwealth and Government of Venice*, 88).

Contarini, it is true, anticipated Harrington's claim that Venice was equal, but no one before him claimed that Rome was unequal and that inequality was the cause of her downfall. Perhaps that is why he felt entitled to claim that the distinction between equal commonwealths and unequal ones had been 'unseen hitherto'.

INDEX